HOW TO DO THINGS WITH PORNOGRAPHY

How to Do Things ~~~~~~~~~~

~~~~~~~~~~ with Pornography

NANCY BAUER

~~~~~~~~~~~~~~~~~~~~~~~~~~~~~~~~~

▌▌▌ Harvard University Press

Cambridge, Massachusetts

London, England

2015

First Printing

Library of Congress Cataloging-in-Publication Data

Bauer, Nancy
How to do things with pornography / Nancy Bauer.
pages cm
Includes bibliographical references and index.
ISBN 978-0-674-05520-9
1. Pornography—Philosophy. 2. Sex—Philosophy. 3. Feminism—
Philosophy. I. Title.
HQ471.B294 2015
306.7701—dc23   2014042518

For MAXWELL ANTHONY BAUER COOPER,
who has been very patient

Contents

Preface

For twenty-five years, that is, since I started as a doctoral student, I have been preoccupied with the question of how to understand feminist philosophy as something other than a contradiction in terms. If philosophy is supposed to be about investigating the most fundamental aspects of the world in an assiduously open-minded way, then how can it start from and stay responsive to a political commitment? My first book began by confronting this question head-on.[1] I argued that feminist philosophers must take the apparent contradiction seriously and not just because sidestepping it might give our many skeptical colleagues—colleagues who may have deep feminist commitments but grave doubts about mixing their politics with their philosophical theorizing—a reason to marginalize our work. The book suggests that Simone de Beauvoir's *The Second Sex* provides a powerful example of how to resolve the apparent contradiction. Beauvoir, I argue, succeeds in finding a way to hold her own experience as a woman in the same space as her philosophical inquiry. More specifically, she uses that experience as a way of keeping the inquiry grounded—that is, making sure that she is writing about the real world and not a mere philosophical construct—while at the same time allowing the inquiry to transform her understanding of her experience. *The Second Sex*, I claimed—and I still believe—is the best example we have of a piece of writing whose philosophical achievements and power to change the real world are a function of one another.

As I was preparing the Beauvoir book to go to press, Sally Haslanger, newly arrived in the Department of Linguistics and Philosophy at MIT, invited me to speak at a departmental symposium called "Pornography, Subordination, and Silence: Feminist Applications of Speech-Act Theory." Sally knew that I not only had been a feminist philosopher from the get-go but also had worked as a graduate student with Stanley Cavell and so was very much an admirer of the philosophy of J. L. Austin, known to most philosophers as the signature "speech-act theorist." I am embarrassed to confess—and, luckily, Sally did not know—that at the time I was completely unaware of the applications that Rae Langton, Jennifer Hornsby, and others had been making of Austin's *How to Do Things with Words* to their analysis of the effects of pornography on women. I was eager to bring myself up to speed and hopeful that in this feminist appropriation of Austin I would find another model for doing feminist philosophy.

Well before I began reading this material, I had found the all-but-ubiquitous inheritance in analytic philosophy of Austin as a mere "speech-act theorist" puzzling and depressing. Even so, as I read Langton's and Hornsby's work, I was stunned by the magnitude of the differences between my understanding of what Austin was up to and theirs. I began to think seriously about these differences and about how Austin's contributions to philosophy as I understood them might be appropriated in the service of thinking about feminist issues.[2]

In their particulars, Langton's views and Hornsby's differ in important ways.[3] But both philosophers—along, in the intervening decade or so, with a number of others—have been keen to appeal to Austin and other philosophers of language to defend a central claim of Catharine MacKinnon's, which is that pornography, understood as that body of materials that depicts women in particular degrading ways, doesn't just inspire men who consume it to harm women (and is thus just a form of "speech," in the legal sense of the term, albeit perhaps a very powerful form) but in and of itself *constitutes* a form of harm.[4]

MacKinnon herself occasionally makes mention of Austin's work.[5] But though throughout her writings she exhibits an admirable familiarity with many texts in historical and contemporary philosophy, she resolutely and explicitly is skeptical of philosophy's powers—especially as they are manifest in the contemporary academy—to change things in the world, at least for women.[6] Indeed, in a preface she composed for a recent volume of philosophical papers on speech and harm, MacKinnon is decidedly lukewarm about the real-world value of philosophy, particularly in its analytic incarnation:

> [O]ne cannot help wondering why some schools of philosophy have become a place where what something actually does is not considered pertinent to the exploration of what it could or might do. Life is not a game of logic, an argument's plausibility is not unaffected by the social reality to which it refers, and power's denial of abuse is not a function of not having read a philosophical proof that such abuse is possible.[7]

Though, as will become clear later in this book, I do not accept MacKinnon's blanket views about what pornography is and does, I share her doubts about whether philosophy *as it stands*—that is, in its current professional incarnation—is capable of transforming the world. Indeed, I find MacKinnon's theoretical writing quite powerful: it challenges me to grapple with her views and to clarify my own. In this way MacKinnon's writing differs, at least for me, from that of those feminist philosophers who admire her greatly but seem to think that her words require a philosophical clarification or defense or otherwise cannot stand on their own: for the most part, writing that attempts to prop up MacKinnon's claims leaves me unmoved. I simply do not believe that people—even philosophers—who reject MacKinnon out of hand do so because they think that her views are not supported by careful enough argumentation. They reject her because they think what she says does not aptly describe how things actually are in the world and is, therefore, indefensible. And philosophers who reject feminist philosophy, including the body of work that has been produced on pornography and MacKinnon over the last couple of decades, are essentially following suit: they turn up their noses not because the arguments presented in feminist philosophical writings are weaker as a group than any other set of philosophical arguments but because they are uneasy about mixing philosophy, understood as at heart a politically neutral method of inquiry, with the political concerns that are ultimately driving their authors.[8]

This book—which falls somewhere between a monograph and a collection of essays—is an attempt on my part to write about pornography and related issues that matter in the real world in a way that challenges the methodological status quo in feminist philosophy, especially in its analytic incarnation. I try to talk about real-life phenomena in real-life terms and to avoid abstract theorizing while at the same time producing prose the ambitions of which, at least, are recognizably philosophical. The chapters can be read separately, but they work together to make a case for what I hope constitutes at least the beginnings of an alternative way of thinking about how philosophy, and particularly feminist philosophy, can do things. The book's aspirations sort themselves out as follows:

- Chapters 1 and 2, "Pornutopia" and "Lady Power," are reprints of articles I have published in a literary magazine and a newspaper, respectively.[9] They treat many of the same subjects that I write about in later chapters, including pornography, sexual objectification, hookup culture, and the nature of philosophical authority. They model, I hope, a nonacademic way of discussing these matters that is nonetheless philosophical in its bearings.
- Chapter 3, "What Philosophy Can't Teach Us about Sexual Objectification," takes aim at the practice among certain philosophers of imagining that analyzing our terminology will tell us something important and substantive about the phenomena those terms name. I claim that the arguments in the literature about what constitutes "objectification" do not in fact help us when it comes to making vivid to skeptics what's so bad about sexual objectification.
- Chapter 4, "Beauvoir on the Allure of Self-Objectification," is reprinted here with minor corrections from *Feminist*

Metaphysics, an anthology of writings on the subject edited by
Charlotte Witt. This essay is in effect an academic version of
"Lady Power"; it attempts to persuade philosophers to reflect
on various paradoxes that confront many ambitious contemporary young women.[10]

- Chapter 5, "How to Do Things with Pornography," the very
  first draft of which was the MIT presentation that launched
  my interest in this project, is reprinted here, with substantive
  changes, from a Festschrift volume for Stanley Cavell, edited
  by Alice Crary and Sanford Shieh.[11] Here I provide an over-
  view of my concerns about the antiporn philosophical literature that has been produced in the wake of Rae Langton's
  1993 paper "Speech Acts and Unspeakable Acts."[12]

- In Chapter 6, "What Is to Be Done with Austin?," I lay out a
  reading of Austin on which it is a grave mistake to see him as a
  mere "speech-act theorist" who meant to confine himself to
  the secondary business of linguistic "pragmatics" while leaving
  the more primary work of syntax and semantics to other philosophers of language. I argue that for Austin our being able to
  do things with our words is the source of their being able to
  mean anything at all. And I show that this suggests that
  understanding what it is to use language is fundamentally an
  ethical matter.

- Chapter 7, "On Philosophical Authority," is a meditation on
  the idea, espoused by many authors of antiporn philosophical
  arguments, that pornography can have the power to subordinate and/or silence women only if it is "authoritative." I suggest that not enough attention has been given to the question
  of what this species of (nonexplicit) cultural authority comes
  to, especially since it is presumably the antiporn philosopher's
  goal to exploit the authority of *reason* to counter the authority
  of pornography. In other words, I ask what authorizes the philosopher's speech acts.

- Chapter 8, "Getting Things Right," is an expansion of a
  paper I wrote for a conference that took place at Harvard in
  the fall of 2011 on the topic of philosophical progress. I discuss
  two dominant ways of understanding what counts as good

philosophy, which I call the "Great Man" paradigm and "scientism," and I argue that both are bad for women. I also suggest that there is a link between how we write philosophically and the possibility that feminist thinking will find a true home in the profession.

- Chapter 9, "Reel Girls and Real Girls: What Becomes of Women on Film?," is a reading (in Cavell's sense of the word, or so I at least hope) of the film *Lars and the Real Girl*, which is about a lonely young man who buys a life-size and lifelike sex doll that (I claim) humanizes him. The surprising transmogrification of both the actors and the doll demonstrates, I argue (à la Cavell), the extent to which film occasions, and perhaps even competes with, philosophy in its powers to spur reflection on what it means to be human.

The reader will find that there is some overlap in the published material; this is a function of my wanting to preserve the integrity of each piece.

I have tried to keep a polemical tone out of these essays, but I know that I haven't been entirely successful on that front. Some readers will no doubt be irritated; others will be disappointed that I am not spending more time defending a "positive" proposal. I'm not sure I have one of those. If I do, it's that we philosophers ask ourselves at every turn what we are doing with our words—and why.

HOW TO DO THINGS WITH PORNOGRAPHY

1

Pornutopia

CRITIQUES OF PORNOGRAPHY, though now by and large relegated to academic journals, have not changed since the 1980s, when they routinely made front-page news. The average antiporn argument still turns on the idea that there is a vast underground pornosphere, the horrifying details of which are not public knowledge. A locus classicus of this genre is the 1986 report of the Meese Commission on Pornography, which contains a bullet list of the titles of what it says are 2,325 distinct pornographic magazines. Here is a sampling from the Gs:

901. Girls Who Crave Big Cocks
902. Girls Who Eat Cum
903. Girls Who Eat Dark Meat
904. Girls Who Eat Girls
905. Girls Who Eat Hot Cum

This goes on for some fifty pages.

The members of the Meese Commission then give us a taste of the contents of the materials they have catalogued. Here, for example, is the first part of a plot summary for the book *Tying Up Rebecca*:

Chapter One introduces 13-year-old gymnast Becky Mingus and her middle-aged coach Vern Lawless—who hasn't had sex in seven years. In the locker room a 15-year-old cheerleader named Patty begins to masturbate, but mistakenly sticks her fingers in Becky's vagina. Patty then goes into the boys' locker room, discards her towel, rubs her breasts, and exposes her genitals. A boy forces Patty to her knees; Patty tongues his anus; he shoves her face in the drain; Becky masturbates; the boy performs cunnilingus; Patty performs fellatio; the boy has vaginal intercourse with Patty.

Chapter Two. At home, Vern's wife wants to make their marriage better, and has bought a skimpy bra and crotchless panties from a girl in the lingerie store who had submitted to Vern's wife's uncontrollable sucking on her breasts and fingering her vagina. Lawless is aroused and masturbates when he sees his wife lying on the rug in the lingerie, but he loses his erection when he spots a picture of Becky. Vern explains his problem, and his wife says she understands and goes to the bathroom to masturbate.

Chapter Three. Becky's father, Henry, sits at home remembering a teenage encounter with a girl and masturbates. He accidentally ejaculates on Becky's face just as she comes in the room. Her face dripping with semen, Becky sees her father's erection and runs to her room crying. The next day, Louise decides to tell Henry, Becky's father, about Vern's lust for Becky. They go to a room upstairs that is equipped with leather clothing, ropes, chains, metal sheaths. Henry unbuttons her blouse, pulls up her skirt, pulls down her panties. His erect penis splits his pants. He performs cunnilingus and analingus. She performs fellatio.

Tying Up Rebecca is the only novel the report discusses in detail. One imagines that the commissioners' agenda in letting it stand as *the* example of pornographic writing was to license their condemning in the strongest terms the eroticization of, at least, adultery, pederasty, incest, and rape. But of course the plot summary itself *reenacts* this eroticization. The commissioner-author forgoes the possibility of arid description and resorts instead to conventional pornographic lingo ("tongues his anus," "uncontrollable sucking on her breasts," "dripping with semen"). And the sense that the summary was written in pornographic breathless haste is reinforced by the writer's sloppiness: the ambiguity about the recipient of the Chapter One boy's oral favors; the failure to identify "Louise" as Vern's wife; the unintuitive uses of the concepts of "mistake" and "accident."

I suppose it's conceivable that the members of the Meese Commission were too busy crusading to see that to describe a piece of porn is to produce a piece of porn—that in this subgenre of writing, at least, intentions count for nothing. There are people who enjoy accusing Andrea Dworkin, the iconic antiporn feminist, of being asleep at the same wheel. But, as implausibly extreme as her views were, Dworkin was no Meese Commissioner. She understood that readers of her 1981 book *Pornography*, which is basically one graphic *Tying Up Rebecca*–ish plot summary after the next, are at least as likely to hold their genitalia as they are their noses. Dworkin's strategy was to persuade us that the sensibilities of contemporary men—all men, not just habitual users of porn—are founded on pornography's eroticization of the subordination and abuse of women. Her goal in documenting instances of porn was to get us to experience the discomfort of becoming aroused by what she hoped she had convinced us is fundamentally soul-crushing, and not just for women.

What Dworkin demanded of us was a species of deep self-hatred, the kind you might live with if you weighed 300 pounds and were desperate to lose weight but just couldn't stop yourself from succumbing to the temptation to eat a pint of Ben & Jerry's. Dworkin hoped to elicit in ordinary prurient adults the kind of self-loathing our present culture hopes to elicit in pederasts. In other words, Dworkin was asking us, we who cannot just throw off our pornographic investments, to inhabit a state of shame. This demand differs from that of the moralistic Meesian, who in his bad-faith posturing would have us pretend that pornography and decent people by definition have nothing to do with each other, that only certain fringy folks get aroused by anything other than the touch of another human being (preferably, one's spouse), and that everyone but the real sickos has the wherewithal simply to swear off smut. Dworkin wanted all of us to recognize and despise the sickos within ourselves.

☙ THIS DESIDERATUM, that we hate ourselves for having sexual feelings, is itself soul-crushing. And the idea that porn is the root determinant of men's sexuality, and that men's sexuality is itself invariably

and dangerously misogynistic, was hyperbolic and empirically untest-
able. Which may be why the culture so resoundingly rejected it.

And yet there is a nub of truth in Dworkin's understanding of
how porn works. The objectification of other people is arousing.
Not always, not under every circumstance, not for every person in
every situation. But everyone is sometimes sexually aroused by the
objectification of a person or people whose humanity is, at that
moment, beside the point. This experience is not unique to porn
consumers: every normal adult is familiar with that twinge of desire
that a stranger, real or depicted, can instantly evoke.

My fellow feminist philosophers have produced an enormous literature on what's wrong with sexual objectification. Their abiding faith
in reason's ability to quash desire has resulted in a certain consensus
on how to condemn these urges. The standard tactic is to define objectification as "treating a person like an object." You give an analysis of
what an "object" is (something that can be owned and therefore used
or transformed or destroyed), and sometimes what "treating" comes
to (not just conceiving of a person as a thing, but reducing her to that
status). Then you argue that people are not like objects in certain
important ways (because people are autonomous, for example) and
that to treat people in these ways is to violate their humanity.

There's nothing particularly controversial in this analysis. That's
precisely the problem with it. No one argues that people are the
same as things and so can always be treated in the same way. We
don't need a philosopher's help to grasp that to the extent that pornography objectifies people, and to the extent that this objectification is dehumanizing, it's morally problematic.

No philosophical analysis of pornographic objectification will
enlighten us unless it proceeds not from the outside, from the
external standpoint of academic moralism, but from the inside, from
a description of pornography's powers to arouse. Such a description
reveals that, within the pornographic mise-en-scène, there is no
space for the concept of objectification. The world as pornography
depicts it is a utopia in which the conflict between reason and sexual
desire is eliminated, in which to use another person solely as a means
to satisfy one's own desire is the ultimate way to respect that person's humanity and even humanity in general.

In the real world, the unbridled expression of sexual desire is fundamentally incompatible with civilization, and in every culture there are harsh punishments for those whose lust gets the better of them. Most of us, the lucky ones, can discipline ourselves, more or less, not to act on our sexual urges when we don't think we should. We sublimate, harnessing our sexual vitality in the service of advancing civility and civilization.

In pornographic representation, civilization, though it sometimes gamely tries to assert itself, always ultimately surrenders to lust. But sexual desire is shown to be a gentlemanly victor: rather than destroy civilization, it repatriates it. Civilization pledges to uphold the laws of the pornutopia, in which the ordinary perils of sexual communion simply don't exist. Everyone has sex whenever the urge strikes, and civilization hums along as usual: people go to work and school, the mail gets delivered, commerce thrives. The good citizens of the porn world, inexorably ravenous, are also perfectly sexually compatible with one another. Everyone is desired by everyone he or she desires. Serendipitously, as it always turns out, to gratify yourself sexually by imposing your desires on another person is automatically to gratify that person as well.

Here, we see Kant turned on his head. Rather than encouraging us to live as though in a kingdom in which our common capacity for rationality enjoins us to regard all people, ourselves included, as ends-in-themselves, the porn world encourages us to treat ourselves and others as pure means. And what's supposed to license this vision is the idea that desire, not reason, is fundamentally the same from person to person, as though our personal idiosyncrasies were merely generic and reason could have no role to play in a true, and truly moral, sexual utopia.

In the pornutopia, autonomy takes the form of exploring and acting on your sexual desires when and in whatever way you like; to respect your own and other people's humanity, all you have to do is indulge your own sexual spontaneity. No one in the pornutopia has a reason to lose interest in or fear or get bored by sex; no one suffers in a way that can't be cured by it; no one is homeless or dispossessed or morally or spiritually abused or lost. When Daddy fucks Becky, she doesn't experience it as rape. She comes.

*   *   *

ॐ TWENTY YEARS AFTER the porn wars raged at their height, the triumph of pornography is everywhere evident. Its imagery is just a couple of clicks away for anyone with an internet connection or a cable-TV remote.

According to the old battle lines, the pornographization of everyday life constitutes a victory for the proponents of free speech and a defeat for conservative moralists and radical feminists. But we are past the point, if we ever were there, at which a bipolar politics of pornography, for or against, could be of use to us. It does not help us understand the massive proliferation of porn since the mid-'80s if we insist on analyzing it in terms of free speech protections or advancements in artistic expression or, on the other side, as incitements to violence against women or a sign of moral lassitude.

We lack the words to articulate the role of pornography in our lives. What we need now is not a new politics of porn but, rather, a candid phenomenology of it, an honest reckoning with its powers to produce intense pleasure and to color our ordinary sense of what the world is and ought to be like. Such a reckoning will have to involve a refocusing of our attention, from the male consumers who took center stage in the porn wars to the women for whom the pornutopia provides a new standard both of beauty and of sexual fulfillment.

I have in front of me as I write a back-cover advertisement for the September 11, 2006, issue of the *New Yorker*. Actually, there are two identical back covers, twinned with a two-page front cover. The topmost front cover features a tightrope walker holding a long balancing rod, his head almost bumping into the Y in Yorker, against a white background; the second front cover positions the same man, in an identical position, over lower Manhattan, directly above the empty footprints of the Twin Towers. We are to recognize here the spirit of Philippe Petit, the tightrope artist who in 1974 changed the tide of negative public opinion against the expensive and aesthetically questionable World Trade Center, then still under construction, when he surreptitiously strung his wire between the buildings and, as thousands of early-morning commuters stared up in astonishment, literally danced his way across.

While the "Soaring Spirit" on the white page looks as though he is dancing on air, on cover two he seems to be in helpless free fall, not a single other soul in sight, the concrete and steel survivors of lower Manhattan standing not as monuments to human achievement but as stolid witnesses of our self-delusion. The front covers ask us to reflect on the powers and limitations of the human spirit in the making and losing of civilization. A solitary man, apparently a thoughtful man of focus and courage and joie de vivre, is attempting to maintain his balance in a life-or-death situation, one in which it is no longer clear whether a genuine civilization will be there to cradle him if he should fall.

On each of the back covers, two women are suspended against a black background. The one on the right is dressed in a very shiny red latex bodysuit covering everything but her face. Two little devil's horns spring from her head. She is heavily made-up—wet crimson lips, kohl eye shadow, penciled parentheses for eyebrows. Her mouth is open, as though in the middle of a word, maybe a roar. Facing us, she cocks one of her hips ever so slightly toward her counterpart. This woman is dressed in an impossibly tight full-length white Lycra gown, its armpits cut down to her waist, ending in a puddle of fabric. Her nipples are erect. Arching her back, she stands sideways, her rear end just a couple of inches from the devil woman's out-thrust hip, her head resting on the devil woman's shoulder, her pelvis pushing forward, and her two-foot feathery wings clasped to the devil woman's chest. The angel woman, ethereally made-up, has long, blond, wavy hair, the ends of which fall exactly at the devil woman's pubis. The devil woman's sinuous red "tail" wraps around the angel woman, so that its pointy tip aims directly at the C in the big Campari logo at the bottom of the ad. One of the angel's hands holds a bottle of Campari; the other, a rocks glass. Her eyes are shut, her lips are slightly parted, as she surrenders, not obviously without fear, to the grip of ecstasy.

The back covers ask us to pledge our allegiance to what they represent to be a much more desirable and robust world than the precarious one of the front covers. Here, there is no room even for the idea of a human spirit, no question about whether there are any souls to be found—let alone to be saved. Two female sexual archetypes feed on the pleasures of instant sexual reciprocity, pleasures that, our own helpless consumption suggests, stand to multiply magically and endlessly. We are asked to take even more pleasure in being savvy enough to get the joke—to entertain the idea, just for the fun of it, that there could possibly be an important difference between the angelic and devilish. The choice between heaven and hell turns out, in this fantasy civilization, to be a product not of any kind of reasoned struggle, moral or otherwise, but a matter of mere preference—blonde or brunette? submissive or dominant? straight or on the rocks? It doesn't matter. Everyone lives more and more happily ever after.

New Yorker front covers as a rule include a half-inch gutter running down the left margin. In this issue, the gutters of both front covers, like the backgrounds of both back covers, are black, which means that, when you lay the open magazine down to save your place, the back cover appears to creep onto the front. How is it that we manage not to see what is going on in the juxtaposition of these images, that we are able to ignore the clash between civilization and the pornutopia, as these two visions of the world compete for space in a magazine that prides itself on its sophistication and encourages us to congratulate ourselves for our own?

Contemporary pornography is noteworthy for cataloguing the incredibly huge range of things that get our blood flowing. The Meese Commission's interminable list of fetish magazines hardly makes a start on the project. Look on the internet and you will find websites devoted to people who are sexually excited by the sound of balloons popping (and those who find these people disgusting because they think that what's sexy about balloons is blowing them up to just before the popping point); instructions on how to make love with a dolphin (including an exhortation to go back to the sea the next day to reassure the dolphin that you still respect her, or him); advice on how to tie your leg up so that other people will think it's amputated and stare at you, or how to find a doctor who will actually amputate a limb or digit for you (possibilities which that some amputee-obsessed people find sexy and others experience as lifesaving in roughly the way, they say, that transgendered people experience coming out).[1]

Part of the process of becoming civilized—of becoming a genuinely human being—is learning to keep the finer details of your sexual longing to yourself and your consenting intimates. Freud occasionally voiced the view that we are inclined to move too far in that direction: we overestimate the extent to which civilization is incompatible with sexual expression. (I am thinking here of what he says in

Civilization and Its Discontents about the persecution of homosexuals.) Freud didn't have a T1 connection and so could not possibly have imagined just how polymorphously perverse we human beings are, but I don't think that the vast array of pornography on the web would have fazed him. It might even have pleased him, for pornography allows us to explore and even come to grips with our sexual desire in all its quirks and moral instability. It enables the discovery that the twists and turns of one's erotic longing are not sui generis, that no one is a true sexual freak. Insofar as it substitutes for the psychoanalyst's couch, it can increase our real-world sexual self-awareness.

That ought to be a good thing. The Meese Commission incriminated itself when it found no room in its 1,960-page report even to wonder about what the wide diversity of interests represented in the thousands of one-off fetish magazines it rooted out in urban convenience stores and sex parlors might say about the nature of human sexuality. But it is not clear what will happen to pornography's power to enlighten us about ourselves, what the cost of it might come to be, as the everyday world gets more and more pornographized and as we accustom ourselves to the mindless enjoyment of all the twinges of arousal that ordinary culture increasingly represents as our birthright.

❧ MORE THAN FIFTY YEARS AGO, Simone de Beauvoir observed in *The Second Sex* that, for women, the line between full personhood and complete self-objectification is whisper thin.[2] A genuinely human being, Beauvoir argued, is one who experiences herself as both a subject and an object—and at the same time. A subject, she said, is a being who has the wherewithal to express her sense of what matters in the world, to dare to have a say in it. But part of being a subject, Beauvoir thought, is allowing yourself to be the object of other people's judgment, rational or irrational: to risk being ridiculed or condemned or ignored or, worse, to find yourself convinced that the harsh judgments of others are true—or, maybe worst of all, to be confused about these judgments, to discover that, after all, you don't know who you are.

For Beauvoir herself, the path to humanity took the form of writing about her own experience as that of a representative human being. She was daring to test whether, to invoke Emerson's famous formulation, what she knew in her own heart was true for all people. But the second half of her groundbreaking book is all about how difficult true self-expression is for women. The world sets things up so that we are wildly tempted to expose ourselves to public judgment, yes. But the vehicle of this exposure is not supposed to be self-expression. It's supposed to be self-objectification.

Women are rewarded—we are still rewarded—for suppressing our own nascent desires and intuitions and turning ourselves into objects that please the sensibilities of men. It's because it threatens the man-pleasing enterprise that feminism long ago hit a wall as a political movement. The very idea that we are now in some sort of postfeminist era hints at our extraordinary "separate but equal" schizophrenia: we believe that we have achieved full social parity with men, and we take this supposed achievement to license a hyperbolic reinvestment in feminine narcissism. Everywhere we turn we find images daring women of all sexual temperaments to revel in and express their fuckability, as though a woman's transforming herself into the ultimate object of desire should or could satisfy her need for other people to attend to the depth and breadth of her true self, even her true sexual self.

"Look—but don't touch." That's the incoherent rule that used to govern displays of feminine self-objectification. It enjoined women to take their pleasure in arousing desire in men and then withholding the satisfaction of this desire. Some pleasure. Some rule. But the new rule, having emerged from the pornographic subterranean and now ubiquitously shoved in our faces—"Don't just look—touch!"—has proved to be even more bizarre. It makes sense in the pornutopia, where everyone arouses everyone else's desire, and physical contact between and among human beings inevitably leads to orgasm all the way around.

Its oddness in the real world emerges in my female students' explanation for spending their weekend evenings giving unreciprocated blow jobs to drunken frat boys: they tell me they enjoy the sense of power it gives them. You doll yourself up and get some guy helplessly aroused, at which point you could just walk away. But you don't. Instead, you take pleasure in arousing the would-be fellatee's desire—and then not withholding the satisfaction of it. The source of the first phase of this pleasure is easy to identify, since it is identical to the pleasure afforded women under the old order of female narcissism. It's the pleasure of reveling in someone else's discomfort and frustration—in a word, of sadism. Women who play by the rules—that is, women who wish to survive in a man's world, rather than undertake the daunting work of attempting to transform it—have always been tempted to substitute the pleasures of sadism for the pleasures (and pains) of Beauvoirian subjectivity. But we still have the question of what pleasure there could be, as a young woman affects to walk away from her prey, in turning around and allaying the discomfort and frustration she worked so hard to produce.

I don't want to condescend to my students, and I don't want to speak for them. But I wish I could understand, at least, why they have so little interest in being serviced in return. An astonishingly large number of girls, as they have reverted to calling themselves, have told me that they feel more comfortable confronting a strange man's exposed hard-on than exposing their own, always shaven, vulvas. (We now live in a world where no part of a woman's body is too private to be subject to public standards of beauty.) Here, we are beyond the point of self-objectification. You forgo your own pleasure, be it sadistic or orgasmic, for the sake of another person's; you perhaps experience discomfort and frustration as you carry out this sacrifice; and then you find yourself not just pretending to enjoy, but actually reveling in, your own self-effacement.

My students' experience in their sexual interactions with men confirms the logic of the pornutopia: to please someone else sexually is to please yourself, and there's no reason to wonder whether what's making you happy is something that you really desire, or whether you're really fulfilled at all. One wonders: could the pleasure of providing some guy with an unreciprocated blow job be the pleasure of masochism? Of martyrdom, even? Or if it is an internalization of the logic of the pornutopia, what precisely has driven it, and what sustains it in the face of the realities of real-world sexuality? I find that when I ask my students what sense they can make of their experience, they, like all of us, are at a loss for words.

2

Lady Power

$\mathcal{I}$F YOU WANT to get a bead on the state of feminism these days, look no further than the ubiquitous pop star Lady Gaga.[1] Last summer, after identifying herself as a representative for "sexual, strong women who speak their mind," the 23-year-old Gaga seemed to embrace the old canard that a feminist is by definition a man-hater when she told a Norwegian journalist, "I'm not a feminist. I hail men! I love men!"[2] But by December she was praising the journalist Ann Powers, in a profile in *The Los Angeles Times*, for being "a little bit of a feminist, like I am." She continued, "When I say to you, there is nobody like me, and there never was, that is a statement I want every woman to feel and make about themselves."[3] Apparently, even though she loves men—she hails them!—she is a little bit of a feminist because she exemplifies what it looks like for a woman to say, and to believe, that there's nobody like her.

There is nobody like Lady Gaga in part because she keeps us guessing about who she, as a woman, really is. She has been praised for using her music and videos to raise this question and to confound the usual exploitative answers provided by "the media." Powers compares Gaga to the artist Cindy Sherman: both draw our attention to the extent to which being a woman is a matter of artifice, of artful self-presentation. Gaga's gonzo wigs, her outrageous costumes, and her fondness for dousing herself in what looks like blood are supposed to complicate what are otherwise conventionally sexualized performances.

In her "Telephone" video, which has in its various forms received upwards of 60 million YouTube hits since it was first posted in

March, Gaga plays a model-skinny and often skimpily dressed inmate of a highly sexualized women's prison who, a few minutes into the film, is bailed out by Beyoncé. The two take off in the same truck Uma Thurman drove in *Kill Bill*—à la Thelma and Louise by way of Quentin Tarantino—and stop at a diner, where they poison, first, a man who stares lewdly at women and, then, all the other patrons (plus—go figure—a dog). Throughout, Gaga sings to her lover about how she's too busy dancing in a club and drinking champagne with her girlfriends to talk to or text him on her telephone.

Is this an expression of Lady Gaga's strength as a woman or an exercise in self-objectification? It's hard to decide. The man who drools at women's body parts is punished, but then again so is everyone else in the place. And if this man can be said to drool, then we need a new word for what the camera is doing to Gaga's and Beyoncé's bodies for upwards of 10 minutes. Twenty years ago, Thelma and Louise set out on their road trip to have fun and found out, as they steadily turned in lipstick and earrings for bandannas and cowboy hats, that the men in their world were hopelessly unable to distinguish between what a woman finds fun and what she finds hateful, literally death-dealing. The rejection by Gaga and Beyoncé of the world in which they are—to use a favorite word of Gaga's—"freaks" takes the form of their exploiting their hyperbolic feminization to mow down everyone in their way, or even not in their way.

The tension in Gaga's self-presentation, far from being idiosyncratic or self-contradictory, epitomizes the situation of a certain class of comfortably affluent young women today. There's a reason they love Gaga. On the one hand, they have been raised to understand themselves according to the old American dream, one that used to be beyond women's grasp: the world is basically your oyster, and if you just believe in yourself, stay faithful to who you are, and work hard and cannily enough, you'll get the pearl. On the other hand, there is more pressure on them than ever to care about being sexually attractive according to the reigning norms. The genius of Gaga is to make it seem obvious—more so than even Madonna once did—that feminine sexuality is the perfect shucking knife. And Gaga is explicit in her insistence that, since feminine sexuality is a social construct, anyone, even a man who's willing to buck gender norms, can wield it.

Gaga wants us to understand her self-presentation as a kind of deconstruction of femininity, not to mention celebrity. As she told Ann Powers, "Me embodying the position that I'm analyzing is the very thing that makes it so powerful." Of course, the more successful the embodiment, the less obvious the analytic part is. And since Gaga herself literally embodies the norms that she claims to be putting pressure on (she's pretty, she's thin, she's well-proportioned), the message, even when it comes through, is not exactly stable. It's easy to construe Gaga as suggesting that frank self-objectification is a form of real power.

If there's anything that feminism has bequeathed to young women of means, it's that power is their birthright. Visit an American college campus on a Monday morning, and you'll find any number of amazingly ambitious and talented young women wielding their brain power, determined not to let anything—including a relationship with some needy, dependent man—get in their way. Come back on a party night, and you'll find many of these same girls (they stopped calling themselves "women" years ago) wielding their sexual power, dressed as provocatively as they dare, matching the guys drink for drink—and then hookup for hookup.

Lady Gaga idealizes this way of being in the world. But real young women, who, as has been well documented, are pressured to make themselves into boy toys at younger and younger ages, feel torn. They tell themselves a Gaga-esque story about what they're doing. When they're on their knees in front of a worked-up guy they just met at a party, they genuinely do feel powerful—sadistic, even. After all, though they don't stand up and walk away, they in principle could. But the morning after, students routinely tell me, they are vulnerable to what I've come to call the "hookup hangover." They'll see the guy in the quad and cringe. Or they'll find themselves wishing in vain for more—if not for a prince (or a vampire, maybe) to sweep them off their feet, at least for the guy actually to have programmed their number into his cell phone the night before. When the text doesn't come, it's off to the next party.

What's going on here? Women of my generation—I have a Gaga-savvy daughter home for the summer from her first year of college—have been scratching our heads. When we hear our daughters tell us that in between taking AP Statistics and fronting your own band you may be expected to perform a few oral sexual feats, we can't believe it. Some critics of "hookup culture" have suggested, more or less moralistically, that the problem is that all this casual sex is going to mess with girls' heads. But whatever you think of casual sex, it's not new. What's mind-boggling is how girls are able to understand engaging in it, especially when it's unidirectional, as a form of power.

Jean-Paul Sartre, taking a cue from Hegel's master-slave dialectic, proposed in *Being and Nothingness* that what moves human beings to do things that don't quite square with one another is that we are metaphysical amalgams. Like everything else in the world, we have a nature: we're bodily, we can't control what happens around us, and we are constantly the objects of other people's judgments. Sartre called this part of ourselves "being-in-itself." But at the same time we're subjects, or what he, following Hegel, called "being-for-itself": we make choices about what we do with our bodies and appetites, experience ourselves as the center of our worlds, and judge the passing show and other people's roles in it. For Sartre, the rub is that it's impossible for us to put these two halves of ourselves together. At any given moment, a person is either an object or a subject.

The Cartesian dualism that drives Sartre's understanding of human beings as metaphysically divided from themselves is decidedly out of fashion these days. Most contemporary philosophers of all stripes reject the idea that we possess selves that are made of more than one type of metaphysical stuff. But we shouldn't forget that the claim at the heart of Sartre's picture is thoroughly phenomenological: it's not so much that people *are* split as that they *experience themselves* as such. Notoriously, Sartre was convinced that we are inclined to deal with the schism by acting in "bad faith." On occasion we find ourselves pretending that we're pure subjects, with no fixed nature, no past, no constraints, no limits. And at other times we fool ourselves into believing that we're pure objects, the helpless victims of others' assessments, our own questionable proclivities, our material circumstances, our biology. Sartre's view gives us a way to understand how a girl might construe her sexually servicing a random guy or shaking her thong-clad booty at a video camera as an act of unadulterated self-expression and personal power. But this interpretation comes at the cost of an epistemic superiority complex, according to which young women are hiding from themselves the ugly truth about what they're "really" doing.

Leave it to Simone de Beauvoir to take her lifelong partner Sartre to task on this very point. If you have it in your head that *The Second Sex* is just warmed-over Sartre, look again. When it comes to her incredibly detailed descriptions of women's lives, Beauvoir repeatedly stresses that our chances for happiness often turn on our capacity for canny self-objectification. Women are—still—heavily rewarded for pleasing men. When we make ourselves into what men want, we are more likely to get what we want, or at least thought we wanted. Unlike Sartre, Beauvoir believed in the possibility of human beings' encountering each other simultaneously as subjects and as objects. In fact, she thought that truly successful erotic encounters positively demand that we be "in-itself-for-itself" with one another, mutually recognizing ourselves and our partners as both subjects and objects. The problem is that we are inclined to deal with the discomfort of our metaphysical ambiguity by splitting the difference: men, we imagine, will relentlessly play the role of subjects; women, of objects. Thus our age-old investment in norms of femininity and masculinity. The few times that Beauvoir uses the term *bad faith* she's almost always lamenting our cleaving to gender roles as a way of dealing with what metaphysically ails us, rather than, à la Sartre, scolding women for doing the best they can in an unjust world.

The goal of *The Second Sex* is to get women, and men, to crave freedom—social, political, and psychological—more than the precarious kind of happiness that an unjust world intermittently begrudges to the people who play by its rules. Beauvoir warned that you can't just will yourself to be free, that is, to abjure relentlessly the temptations to want only what the world wants you to want. For her the job of the philosopher, at least as much as the fiction writer, is to re-describe how things are in a way that competes with the status quo story and leaves us craving social justice and the truly wide berth for self-expression that only it can provide.

Lady Gaga and her shotgun companions should not be seen as barreling down the road of bad faith. But neither are they living in a world in which their acts of self-expression or self-empowerment are distinguishable, even in theory, from acts of self-objectification. It remains to be seen whether philosophers will be able to pick up the gauntlet that's still lying on the ground more than half a century after Beauvoir tossed it down: whether we can sketch a vision of a just world seductive enough to compete with the allures of the present one.

∾ *"Lady Power" appeared in the* New York Times *philosophy blog* The Stone *in June 2010. My editor, Peter Catapano, invited me to write a second post in response to readers' comments on the piece. This post, which follows, was published on June 30, 2010.*

Authority and Arrogance: A Response

What subjects are fit to be addressed in public by a philosopher? Many of the responses to essays in *The Stone* raise this issue. Actually, commentators have been pressing at least two versions of the question. What sorts of things are worth looking at philosophically? And about what, if anything, do philosophers have any special authority?

In the case of my contribution, "Lady Power," the first question takes the form of commentators' doubting (to use the weakest possible verb) that a pop star merits philosophical attention, or even virtual space in *The Times*. Mike A. was the first of many people to criticize me for what was taken to be my claim that Lady Gaga herself is espousing a philosophical position that we ought to take seriously. "I'm sure it's fun for LG to be getting all this attention," Mike A. writes. "It certainly bolsters the illusion that this overblown hullabaloo means something." Terence Erndt is so outraged that the profession of philosophy would accommodate my reflecting on Lady Gaga, nay, my going so far as to write a book called *How to Do Things with Pornography*, that he called for the discipline itself to "vanish in the stampede toward majors in technology and business."

I can understand why people might balk at the claim that, at the tender age of 24, a pop star should be seen as having a coherent philosophy that we should both take seriously and hold her to. But I didn't make that claim. By quoting Gaga a couple of times, I did imply that her self-understanding in relation to feminism seems to be unstable, with respect to both what she takes feminism to be and the extent to which she identifies with it. (In the *Rolling Stone* interview that appeared a few days after my post did, Gaga goes beyond what she had previously said and now calls herself a feminist, full stop.[4])

And, after I quoted her as saying that she takes herself to be embodying the position she's analyzing, I noted that the logic of this strategy entails that "the more successful the embodiment, the less obvious the analytic part is."

Indeed, these were my main points about Lady Gaga: that her identification as a feminist is complicated and shifting and that what she regards as a commentary on feminine sexuality is not easily distinguishable from frank self-objectification, no matter what she intends. You can endorse (or reject) these claims whether you think that Gaga is a money-grabbing, talentless self-promoter or the second coming of Madonna or a cutting-edge artist and social commentator nonpareil. I made the claims not because I wanted to philosophize about Lady Gaga but because I take her various remarks about feminism and her self-presentation to epitomize something that I did want to think about in philosophical terms: the conditions under which young women today have to grapple with their own self-expression, behavior, and self-understanding, especially when it comes to the tricky concept of "power." I was inviting readers to reflect on the question of exactly what Lady Power—as manifested in both Lady Gaga's self-presentation and the so-called hookup culture—comes to and whether we can even hope for a stable answer to this question in a world in which women are still heavily rewarded for making themselves into what they think men want.

In a comment recommended by many readers, Rosie accuses me of going further than this, of ignorantly "continu[ing] to conflate being sexy with being promiscuous." The word *continuing*, I take it, is meant to evoke the specter of certain prominent second-wave feminists—Catharine MacKinnon leaps to mind—who indeed hold the view that, in a misogynistic world, a woman's investment in being sexy is inevitably a form of self-objectification. Would that things were this straightforward; at least it would be obvious that they needed to change, and how. But the situation is decidedly more complicated than MacKinnon and her ilk insist. To say that a woman's wanting to be sexy can't possibly amount to more than a desire for self-objectification or wanton promiscuity is to fail to take women's experience of themselves and their intentions seriously. This kind of move should be antithetical to feminists.

Or so, following Simone de Beauvoir, I have been arguing for a long time. Twenty years after I began to read *The Second Sex*, I remain convinced that the philosophical lens through which Beauvoir analyzes the complexities of sex difference is as acute and powerful as ever, despite the dramatic social changes and shifts in intellectual fashion that have taken place in the 60 years since the book's appearance. "Lady Power" was meant in part to invite readers who were intrigued by my description of the Zeitgeist to pick up Beauvoir's magnum opus and take another look.

This brings me to the second question I posed above. What gives a philosopher the authority to describe the world in one way or another? In my case, what gives me the right to make pronouncements about how things are at the moment for certain young women in the terms that I do? After all, as Jim Greene correctly notes, I am not a social scientist and do not adduce empirical evidence for my central claims, other than my informal correspondence and conversation with young women over the last decade. This failure to appeal to "hard" evidence is perhaps the feature of philosophy that most irritates its detractors. Even within the profession of philosophy there's now a movement urging philosophers to learn how to test certain of our claims empirically.

But the claims I was making about "lady power" are not strictly speaking empirical. What I was doing was pointing to certain phenomena and suggesting a way to conceptualize and understand them.

No one disputes that these phenomena—Lady Gaga, her performances, her way of understanding herself, her self-presentation, "hookup culture," young women's desire to be confident and powerful, and so on—exist. They're as plain as the nose on Gaga's face. (A nose, by the way, that does not seem to me to distract from Gaga's attractiveness in conventional cultural terms, despite guffawing on the part of some commentators—including, incredibly, a writer for the *Chronicle of Higher Education*—in the face of my casual judgment that Gaga is "pretty."[5])

What *is* in dispute is how to understand the facts, what to make of them. This is where the question of the philosophy professor's authority presses hardest. A philosopher's authority to weigh in on the subjects that interest her is not one that she earns in a more or less once-and-for-all way. It's an authority that must continually be appropriated and then granted—or not—by one's interlocutors. Philosophers typically try to illuminate with a combination of argument and (re)conceptualization. But the most careful and perspicuous argumentation, as indispensable as care and perspicuity are, will not convince someone who is disinclined to accept a philosopher's way of framing a problem or phenomenon. And, as the philosopher Stanley Cavell has stressed repeatedly, nothing guarantees that the arrogation of philosophical authority, no matter how well intended, will not turn out to be an act of mere arrogance. In this way, in fact, philosophical expression and young women's sexualized attempts at self-expression have something in common: neither can be fully controlled by an author's intentions, and nothing guarantees that they will come off in the way their authors hope they will.

Philosophers like to think that argument—"the pure light of reason"—will eventually lead everyone to accept *the* correct way to think about whatever they are writing about. But if we are honest, we will admit that the chances that all sensible readers will embrace the terms in which a philosopher proposes to illuminate some dark corner of the world are no higher than the chances that someone who is awed by Lady Gaga's sui generis self-comportment could say or do anything to convert people who find the mere mention of her name beneath contempt. For some, this fact will mean that philosophy is fundamentally no better than the sniping that characterizes much Internet discourse. For others, it will constitute a challenge to acknowledge with due humility the arrogance that doing philosophy inevitably courts.

❧ 3

What Philosophy Can't Teach Us about Sexual Objectification

$\mathscr{I}$N 1959, A Cleveland, Ohio, cinema owner named Nico Jacobellis was arrested on obscenity charges for having screened the English version of Louis Malle's 1958 film *The Lovers*. He was subsequently tried, convicted, and fined $2,500. On appeal, the case went all the way to the Supreme Court, which in 1964 overturned Jacobellis's conviction on the grounds that the Malle film was in fact not obscene. In his statement of concurrence, Justice Potter Stewart noted that though the majority view was correct, the Court had nonetheless failed to answer the central question raised by *Jacobellis v. Ohio*, namely: what makes something count as an instance of "obscenity" or as "hard-core pornography"? Indeed, Justice Stewart acknowledged his personal incapacity to provide a list of criteria for something's being an instance of these phenomena. And yet, he insisted, in one of the most notorious lines ever uttered by a High Court judge, "I know it when I see it."[1]

One thing that makes Justice Stewart's line so memorable is the irony of a Supreme Court justice's setting himself up as a connoisseur of illegal erotic materials. But there's an even greater irony in Stewart's falling back entirely on his own private, unarticulated (and evidently, for him, inarticulable) judgment about what does and does not count as an instance of pornography: he thereby emptied *Jacobellis* of any potential to serve as a robust legal precedent.

The Court in effect set out to rectify its failure to specify the marks and features of hard-core pornography in the 1973 case *Miller v. California*, in which it established three criteria that would render something by definition obscene. By the lights of this case, a book or film or photograph or presentation is obscene if and only if:

1. "the average person, applying contemporary community standards," would find that the work as a whole appeals to "the prurient interest";
2. the work depicts sexual conduct "in a patently offensive way"; and
3. the work as a whole "lacks serious literary, artistic, political, or scientific value."[2]

Alas: the extra verbiage here notwithstanding, these criteria are hardly an advance on Justice Stewart's "I know it when I see it." For they consist not of observable marks and features of obscenity but of subjective *judgments* about community standards; offensiveness; and literary, artistic, political, and scientific value. In effect, they say, if a person is average and if she or (more likely, in 1973) he thinks that something is sexual in an offensive way without having any other redeeming value, then that thing is obscene. In other words, the only advance in this case is to suggest that Justice Stewart may not be alone in his capacity to judge the obscene—that the Court welcomes an army of Justice Stewarts. In both the *Jacobellis* and *Miller* cases, then, the Court managed to sidestep the tough problem that it was prevailed upon to solve, namely, articulating the criteria for what counts as smut. Instead, the Court in both cases commended to the citizenry the blunt, unjustified, inarticulate judgment of the nonprofessional—Justice Stewart in *Jacobellis* and his Platonic Form, "the average person," in *Miller*.

There is reason, of course, to question the Court's motives and wisdom in trying to regulate our exposure to the obscene in the first place. But insofar as the Court is committed to achieving this goal, it seems to owe us more than an appeal to what are after all bound to be wildly varying judgments among the citizenry about what does and doesn't count as smut. If we are going to regulate access to the obscene, then we need a set of more or less objective criteria to do so fairly and effectively. That said, it is hardly surprising that the Court declined to provide us with such a set. I submit that this declining was not simply a function of the fact that what counts as "hard-core pornography" or "obscenity" is inherently controversial or varies unpredictably with the waxing and waning of other developments in the social world. Rather, I want to claim that when human beings make judgments about what counts as what, it's *often* the case, no matter what phenomenon is at stake, that, if for whatever reason we are called upon to adduce explicitly the criteria that we are using, we have great difficulty doing so, even when we are absolutely convinced that we know what we are talking about. There are exceptions, as when an expert is helping a nonexpert identify something that requires technical knowledge. But when it comes to words that we use in nontechnical contexts, we are unlikely to make headway and very likely, in fact, to be way off the mark.

Take a mundane case. We all know a wastebasket when we see one. But just try to specify what criteria something has to possess (or not posses) in order to count as a wastebasket, and you'll soon find yourself in trouble. Limiting your list-making attempts to the marks and features of just the central cases won't help you. Yes, that thing you bought from Staples that was marked *WASTEBASKET* on its label is made of a tolerably sturdy material, is hollow on the inside, is wide and tall enough to hold ordinary household or office trash, and so on; and with some thought you can refine this start on a list of a wastebasket's central defining features. But what about that plastic bag from CVS that you've stretched over an old cardboard carton? I take it we can agree that this contraption would make a tolerable wastebasket. If a guest of yours needed to get rid of a used tissue she would not balk if you gestured at the thing. And yet this makeshift object shares only a few of its marks and features with the Staples product. That both are used as a wastebasket is true, but this fact won't help us. For insisting on the "is used as a wastebasket" criterion would cause problems for the unused thing still sitting on the shelf at Staples. Indeed, I submit, no list of possible criteria for what counts as a wastebasket, no matter how complicated or disjunctive, is going to strike us as exhaustive or decisive.

The problem at which I'm hand-waving here is of course one that many philosophers of all stripes have grappled with. I myself am partial to the ones who do this grappling within the phenomeno-logical tradition—from Husserl to Wittgenstein to Austin to Cavell to Beauvoir.[3] Such thinkers are determined to give skepticism about the possibility of exhaustively specifying criteria for what counts as a particular phenomenon its due, while refusing to lose sight of, or discount, our ordinary powers of making our way about the world using our concepts. In other words, they all understand that the criteria-specifying enterprise, while it has its place, has to come to an end somewhere and that recognizing this fact is fundamental to the enterprise of philosophizing. For these thinkers and their ilk, holding on to our faith in our criteria is tolerably easy when it comes to thinking about what counts as a wastebasket, or a game, or a goldfinch, or a genre. Identifying what counts as an instance of these and other such things rarely keeps us awake at night. Even in bor-derline cases or shifting social circumstances, we often are attuned with one another when it comes to the question of *what's at stake* in raising questions about whether a particular phenomenon should be counted as an instance with respect to a particular category. Suppose you and I are talking about the film *The Matrix*; I claim that it's a horror film, and you balk. Still, we will agree that there is a substan-tive question between us about how to interpret *The Matrix* or about what counts as a horror film or both.

The vast majority of our interchanges, however, proceed with no such balking or demurral because, to put the point in the way Cavell might, we human beings are more or less attuned to each other in our sensibilities at least when it comes to the mundane. When I ask you to pass me the jug of beer that's next to you on the table, you may deny me; but you're unlikely to press me for my criteria for using *jug* or *beer*—and that's the case even if you yourself would have used the terms *pitcher* and *ale*. A certain sort of metaphysician may spend a career worrying about what counts as a wastebasket or Lake Huron or a dream. But, to say the least, these are worries the ulti-mate pertinence of which to our everyday lives is not obvious. For the most part, when it comes to those lives, we know these and many other things when we see them.

And yet the problem gets much harder when it comes to phenomena whose names are tied up with very particular ways of perceiving and understanding the world—political ways, for example. Take the phenomena that people understand themselves to be referring to when they use, in full voice, a term such as *communist sympathizer* or *bitch* (when referring to a woman) or *treating a person like an animal* or *transgendered* or, again, *smut*. What these expressions have in common is that each is connected up with a particular normative way, or ways, of perceiving and understanding the world. Unless you endorse a certain normative outlook, you won't be able to use these terms without ironic scare quotes around the words. For example, a person who doesn't believe that a "communist" is an evil person threatening to destroy everything valuable in the world will find that, for her, the extension of the term *communist sympathizer* is the null set. And a person who thinks that someone with XY chromosomes who was born with a penis is by definition a man will be unable to use the term *transgendered* in full voice. Generally speaking, whether you think that a term that gets its sense only within a particular worldview or views picks out any phenomenon at all depends on the broad outlines of your own view of the world, your own set of investments and concerns.

I submit that the term *obscene* (when applied in a literal way in a sexualized context) is this kind of term, as is *hard-core pornography*. If you were, say, Allen Ginsburg or Gore Vidal in 1964, then you wouldn't find any masturbation aid "obscene," even if you might for certain purposes be able to adopt the stance of someone who would—for example, when discussing with your publisher whether your new book is likely to be censored. These days, in fact, the word *obscene* has almost become obsolete, at least with respect to its use in describing media; even people who are disturbed by certain depictions of the sexual or the erotic or the violent rarely perform their bemoaning using this term, which now sounds, at least to my ears, a bit quaint and naïve. The disuse of *obscene* may be a function of the fact that pornography, now easily available and for the most part consumed in private settings, is so ubiquitous that it has lost some of its power to shock, if not to alarm or unsettle or wound. And what counts these days as "hard-core pornography," is largely a matter of what you've gotten used to versus of what *retains*, retains for you, the power to shock. Experience suggests that there will be systematic differences in this power when it comes to certain demographics—say, today's adolescent boys versus their middle-aged mothers.

I need to underscore at this point that I do not intend here to be making any *ontological* claims. I'm not saying anything one way or another about whether obscenity or communist sympathizers or bitches or even women or wastebaskets *exist*, full stop. I'm not weighing in, to put the clarification another way, on any metaphysical debates about relativism. What I'm interested in is how what we might call a worldview or a set of investments and concerns, on the one hand, and the ways we talk about our experience, on the other, mutually inform one another.[4] As Justice Stewart's famous remark suggests, when a term plays a role in our mutually shared normative worldview, specifying the marks and features of a particular instance of the phenomenon it names will be no easier than specifying the marks and features of a wastebasket. But in cases in which a term that's important to my normative outlook does not play such a role in yours, it will be basically impossible for me to specify criteria for the term's application that, from your point of view, pick out any phenomenon at all.

I'm aware that I haven't said anything here to *justify* the claims I am making, and I'm afraid that, in this book, at least, I'm not going to make any progress on such a project. That is, I'm not going to be limning for you a philosophical theory of conceptual criteria. (Whether we need another such theory—whether we need *any* such theory—is a matter of debate.) What I *am* going to do is claim that the phenomenon of *sexual objectification* is like the phenomenon of obscenity: if the term *sexual objectification* is critical in helping you make sense of the world as you see it, then, more or less, you will know sexual objectification when you see it. Of course, there will be borderline, controversial cases, even among people who see the world very much the way you do. And there will be lots of questions to ask and claims to make—some philosophical—about the phenomenon of sexual objectification. But trying to specify its marks and features will only lead you down a certain philosophical garden path. Indeed, I believe, any attempt to lay out a set of criteria for what counts as sexual objectification will actually end up distorting the phenomenon.

Let me be clear that these are fighting words: there is a large literature in philosophy about what sexual objectification is and what makes it bad.[5] Strikingly, given where I'm coming from philosophically, this literature has been produced by people who find the term *sexual objectification* critical in making sense of their experience of the world. I am in effect arguing that this literature fails to track the phenomenon and that the ordinary intuitions of people who see the world roughly in the way these philosophers do—and, therefore, these philosophers' *own* experiences of being the victim of or otherwise witnessing sexual objectification—are more reliable. Furthermore, it seems to me that people who see nothing objectionable about the phenomena that strike some people as sexual objectification are going to be unmoved by a philosophical analysis of it. In other words, insofar as the philosophical literature sets out to delineate the marks and features of sexual objectification, it is unlikely to persuade anyone who doubts that the term "sexual objectification" names anything, or at least anything worrisome, in the world. This is something that philosophers, including feminist philosophers, who want to *change* the way that people (and not just other philosophers) think about the world, ought to care about.[6]

As far as I can tell, before feminists started talking about "sexual objectification"—which looks to be at some point in the late 1960s—the word *objectification* was not commonly used outside of the academy.[7] When it was used inside the academy, it was a technical term, ordinarily having to do with the way that an object was thought to express (in a literal or metaphorical sense of the term) something nonobject-like, such as an idea or a value. For example, Marx believed that human beings create value of various sorts by mixing their labor with what's in their environment, and he called this transformative process "objectification."[8] Along similar lines, Dilthey understood objectification as the expression of humanity as it manifests itself in the production of artifacts—everything from bodily gestures to buildings to social institutions.[9] And the neo-Kantians sometimes used the word *objectification* to refer to the process whereby intuition (the content delivered to our minds by our five senses) is transformed, via subsumption under the categories of the understanding, into the object of cognition. Note that in none of these cases is "objectification" something that in and of itself is a good or bad thing. Even in the case of Marx, "objectification" is simply something that is a natural part of human life; what determines whether it's a good or bad thing has to do with the social context in which people are laboring. The feminist concept of *sexual* objectification, on the other hand, has always had negative connotations. This is because it was coined as part of a feminist shift in how to understand the world and one's experience in it. According to this shift, *in a context in which women experience widespread, systematic, diachronic, structural disadvantages,* certain ways of perceiving and representing women tend to cause women direct or indirect material and psychological harm. Once you participate in this shift, the term *sexual objectification* will come to have purchase for you. It will "light up" the relevant phenomena, and you will see sexual objectification pretty much everywhere you look.

This metaphor of "lighting up" has become increasingly important to me as I have struggled to think about *sexual objectification* and other terms that make sense only in the context of one or another systematic normative way of understanding the world, that is, what I've been calling a "worldview." Lighting up in some cases may take the form of a conversion experience that consists in our seeing things that we simply didn't notice before, as though they had previously been cast into shadows. For example, after having acknowledged the subtle signs of suffering of a person you love, you might come to be struck by what you now recognize as the suffering of a person in similar circumstances, someone whom you used merely to ridicule or disdain or fear. (This, I take it, roughly describes the not atypical experience of a homophobic parent whose love for his gay child wins out over his longstanding revulsion.) Then again, it may happen that as our worldview shifts, we see exactly the same phenomenon as before, only now transformed for us in its valence or significance. What used to strike you as funny—say, a man wearing a dress—now strikes you as a brave and dignified way of being in the world. I want also to leave room for the possibility that the lighting-up experience may happen prior to a shift in one's worldview and simply because the way others talk about things becomes the norm. You may find yourself, for example, with a new perception of someone you used to think of as a *bum* simply because it becomes de rigueur in your social circle to abjure this term and call such a person *homeless*. You can have bonds of trust with people with whom you disagree that cause you to reconsider your views. In fact, there are lots of different ways to make the world light up—your particular experience in the world, yes, but also your experience of a piece of literature or, of course, of philosophy. It may be tempting to imagine that when a shift in perspective has occurred what has shifted is specifically (and only) the normative significance of the phenomena we saw all along. But it seems to me—and here I will only throw out a suggestion, without trying to defend it—that phenomenologically, at least, a new worldview transforms the phenomena themselves, that is, transforms not only our valuation of the phenomena but also what they *are* to us.[10]

I have claimed that if the feminist perspective makes sense of your experience, then the term *sexual objectification* will "light up" the relevant phenomenon, and you will see it everywhere you look in contemporary culture.[11] Recent examples of widely publicized sexually objectifying images include:

- an advertisement for Lynx Shower Gel featuring a mud-smeared woman in a teeny bikini, depicted head-on from her mid-thighs to just above her breasts, looking as though she is just about to pull the lower part of the garment off with her thumbs, the words "Wash me" drawn (presumably with a finger) on her belly.[12]
- an advertisement for the Burger King "BK Super Seven Incher" featuring the profile of a heavily made-up blond woman, her eyes and crimson lips wide open, staring straight ahead, zombie-like, the torpedo-shaped "seven incher" floating in mid-air about two inches away from her mouth, with the tagline "it'll blow your mind away."[13]
- an advertisement for a Max man's brogue shoe, pictured life-sized, photographed from above, the shoelaces of which are binding the hips, waist, and breasts of a Japanese woman,

dressed in a kimono, whose arms are stretched over her head
and wrists are bound to the heel of the shoe with the ends of
the shoelaces.[14]

- an advertisement for "the one and only Wonderbra" depicting
from the chest up a large-breasted, heavily made-up blond
woman, lips parted, her thumbs hooked into the straps of her
black bra, with the tagline "I can't cook. Who cares?"[15]

- an advertisement for a Cycles Laurent bicycle featuring an
image, from the rear, of a black woman dressed only in kitten-
heeled sandals, thong underwear, and a cropped cycling shirt
the banner of which reads *Osé* (meaning, in French, racy,
risqué, daring), tiptoes on the ground, bare derriere thrust
out, leaning over the bike's handlebars and looking back at the
camera.[16]

- an advertisement, for a used-car company called Ulster
Trader, depicting only a woman's large breasts, clad in a low-
cut white bra, with the cutline "Nice Headlamps. What do
you look for in a car?"[17]

- an advertisement for Tom Ford for Men "fragrance,"
depicting, from the bottom of the breasts to the top of the
thighs, a completely naked, clean-shaven woman who has a
bottle of the product lodged against her vulva and is holding
one of her hand on her torso and the pointer finger of her
other hand on the top of the bottle.[18]

If the feminist perspective I sketched above is your perspective,
then you will have experienced even my descriptions of these images
as instances of what you would call sexual objectification, even if you
couldn't exactly specify what marks and features these images have
in common. It is conceivable that you and I will disagree with respect
to one or two of the images, just in the way that we might disagree that
your CVS bag counts as a wastebasket rather than something that
you're using as a wastebasket. But for the most part, to the extent
that we share pretty much the same worldview, why all of the things
in the list I just ticked off count as instances of sexual objectification
will be no less mysterious or unclear to you than that what you are
breathing at the moment is air.

The philosophers I know who write about sexual objectification evidently do not agree with my claim that once one comes to see the world through feminist lenses it lights up in such a way that what counts as sexual objectification and the fact that it demeans and otherwise harms women become more or less obvious. These philosophers for the most part write as though both feminists and naysayers require an accounting of what constitutes sexual objectification and a compelling story about why, or when, it's a bad thing. The accounting is wont to take the form of a list of marks and features; the "why it's bad" story usually takes its cues from Kant's moral philosophy. These two projects—the list-making and the moral story—are intertwined: the idea is to start with a Kantian understanding of what's wrong with treating a person as an "object" and then to tick off the ways in which sexual objectification violates the Kantian moral law.

The project of explaining the badness of sexual objectification in Kantian terms became popular among feminist philosophers in the early 1990s, when Barbara Herman published a now-classic essay called "Could It Be Worth Thinking about Kant on Sex and Marriage?"[19] Herman in this paper proposed that Kant's general philosophical account of morality, combined with his specific remarks on sex and marriage, might help us construe the wrongness of sexual objectification as a failure to respect another person's humanity. On the Kantian account, the failure to respect another person's humanity is equivalent to a failure to respect the moral law. This claim is spelled out in the second formulation of the categorical imperative, the so-called Formula of Humanity, which enjoins us never merely to use other people as a means to our ends but always also, even when we do use others as such, to respect them as valuable ends in themselves. In her essay, Herman draws our attention to two of Kant's lesser-known works, the *Doctrine of Virtue* and the *Lectures on Ethics*, in which Kant argues that any form of sexual congress, even if it takes place in the context of a loving, mutually respectful relationship, inherently constitutes a violation of this formulation of the moral law. Taken by itself, he says, having sex "is a degradation of human nature; for as soon as a person becomes an Object of appetite for another, all motives of moral relationship cease to function, because as an Object of appetite for another a person becomes a thing."[20]

Alas, this view raises a pressing practical problem: if sexual intercourse is inherently immoral, then how can the human species perpetuate itself without violating the moral law? (Presumably, at the very least the man will have to make someone an Object of appetite in order to get into a state in which he will be able to contribute his genetic share in the making of a baby.) Kant's solution to the problem is marriage: what makes sexual intercourse morally tolerable despite its inherently degrading nature is the sanctification by the state of a couple's sexual union. When two people marry, Kant says, the law makes it the case that in effect the two become a single person, and this amalgamation of two parties into one makes the question of a moral relationship moot. The appetite one has for one's lawfully wedded spouse is in effect transformed into an appetite on the order of an urge to pass gas. Kant doesn't bother to say so, but the person that the man and the woman legally become when they are wed in a place with laws that make two into one has always been (surprise!) the man. So-called "coverture" laws were ubiquitous in Europe and elsewhere in Kant's day; indeed, they persisted into the twentieth century in certain locales in the United States.[21] Under such laws, for a woman to marry is for her to cede all of her rights and property, including any wages she might make, to her husband. She thus goes from being her father's daughter to being her husband's wife—never enjoying any degree of independent legal status. Kant's solution to the problem of taking someone else—even someone you love and respect—as an "object of appetite" therefore is coextensive with the erasure of women as autonomous beings. I use the word *autonomous* deliberately here, for in many of his lesser-known writings Kant makes clear his conviction that women are bereft of the capacity for practical reasoning and therefore incapable of following the moral law.

Unsurprisingly, many philosophers who write about sexual objectification—Barbara Herman included—find Kant's solution to the "problem" of sexual desire less than inviting.[22] At the same time, however, they often find compelling the *framing* of the problem, that is, the understanding of sexual objectification as something that happens when and only when the formula of humanity is violated in a sex-related way. This idea is at the heart of the locus classicus of this genre, Martha Nussbaum's 1995 paper "Objectification." Nussbaum begins with what she sees as a puzzle: while feminists (she points to Catharine MacKinnon and Andrea Dworkin) coined the term *sexual objectification* to point to what they saw as an unequivocally bad thing, it seems that objectification can in some contexts constitute a positive, even *essential*, part of a relationship whose signature features are equality, respect, and consent.[23] Your finding your partner super-hot may be an *expression* of your respect for her, rather than a nullification of it. Nussbaum thinks that we are "confused" here because we haven't yet "clarified" the concept of objectification: when we do, she says, we'll see that objectification in any given instance is composed of one or more of, as she puts it, at least seven distinct "notions."[24] These are:

1. *Instrumentality*: The objectifier treats the object as a tool of his or her purposes.
2. *Denial of autonomy*: The objectifier treats the object as lacking in autonomy and self-determination.
3. *Inertness*: The objectifier treats the object as lacking in agency, and perhaps also in activity.
4. *Fungibility*: The objectifier treats the object as interchangeable (a) with other objects of the same type and/or (b) with objects of other types.
5. *Violability*: The objectifier treats the object as lacking in boundary-integrity, as something that it is permissible to break up, smash, break into.
6. *Ownership*: The objectifier treats the object as something that is owned by another, can be bought or sold, etc.
7. *Denial of subjectivity*: The objectifier treats the object as something whose experience and feelings (if any) need not be taken into account.[25]

To this list, Rae Langton has added three more notions:

8. *Reduction to body*: one treats [the object] as identified with its body or body parts.

9. *Reduction to appearance*: one treats [the object] primarily in terms of how it looks or how it appears to the senses.

10. *Silencing*: one treats [the object] as silent, lacking the capacity to speak.[26]

Of course, any list of this kind is going to be a work in progress, and we should expect lots of tweaking as well as disagreements about when and in what places tweaking is needed. I don't, in general, have any problem with the tweaking enterprise; as we all know, any thinker worth her salt will welcome opportunities for improving her view.

However, I do have a problem with the fact that the tweakers do not want to touch Nussbaum's central claim. À la Kant she argues that no matter the form or forms of behavior that constitute it, "[i]n all cases of objectification, what is at issue is a question of treating one thing as another: One is treating *as an object* what is not really an object, what is, in fact, a human being."[27] Nussbaum argues, still in good Kantian fashion, that some cases of this sort of treatment are compatible with respect for another person's humanity. She gives as an example using one's lover's stomach instrumentally as a pillow. "There seems to be nothing at all baneful about this, provided that I do so with his consent (or, if he is asleep, with a reasonable belief that he would not mind), and without causing him pain, provided, as well, that I do so in the context of a relationship in which he is generally treated as more than a pillow."[28] The Kantian trick, it turns out (and as we know if we have read the *Groundwork of the Metaphysics of Morals*), is not to treat another human being *merely* as an object; and that is enough to avoid violating the Formula of Humanity. This is why, according to Nussbaum, some instances of sexual objectification may be morally permissible—"benign" to use one of her favorite terms of art. This can be true even when another person's autonomy is at stake. As Nussbaum puts the point, "Denial of autonomy and denial of subjectivity are objectionable if they persist throughout an adult relationship, but as phases in a relationship characterized by mutual regard they can be all right, or even quite wonderful."[29]

Unlike Kant, Nussbaum believes that objectification can be benign or even wonderful when it takes place in the context of a relationship in which the parties are roughly equal and when both consent to abandoning themselves to their carnality. By "rough equality" Nussbaum means that the parties mutually respect one another and clear-headedly consent to their arrangement. Her example of a potentially wonderful instance of mutual sexual objectification is that of the main pair of D. H. Lawrence's *Lady Chatterley's Lover*, in which the eponymous heroine, stuck with an impotent husband who shows little interest in her, and Oliver Mellors, the gamekeeper on the Chatterley estate and a man who has had serial extramarital affairs, fall deeply in love and begin a carnally redemptive affair, notoriously described in graphic detail by Lawrence. Even though Mellors is a working-class man, his respect for Connie Chatterley is such that, according to Nussbaum, we might regard their relationship as an instance of happy mutual objectification.

It's rather odd, however, that Nussbaum should take this view, since she is a major advocate of the idea that, in unjust social circumstances, people adapt their preferences to the shriveled space of possibilities in which they are operating.[30] Nussbaum does not suggest that adaptive preferences are false ones or that there's such a thing as a "pure" preference—that is, a preference that is not in some sense a function of one's circumstances. Rather, her point is that when frank social inequalities exist, people may shrink their expectations and desires to fit within the resulting constraints. What this means is that it's not obvious that mutuality of desire, respect, and consent is enough to ensure that a woman is not subject to sexual objectification of the noxious kind. The "rough equality" to which Nussbaum refers in her discussion of the Lawrence example therefore may not be enough to ensure that the objectification she discusses is "benign" or "wonderful." Indeed, what Nussbaum leaves out of her discussion of the *Chatterley* case is that a condition of Connie Chatterly's taking up with Mellors in the first place is that he is unusually well-educated and well-spoken for a member of his class. Nussbaum thereby sidesteps the question of what we should do with Lawrence's attempt to create "rough equality" between this man and this woman by suggesting that the man is not typical for a man of his class and that the woman has a reason not to be faithful to her husband.

My analysis of this example suggests that Nussbaum's way of understanding sexual objectification distorts the grassroots feminist concept, both by generalizing from the treatment of "women" to that of "human beings" and by drawing our attention away from the social circumstances that drive the phenomenon as feminists commonly understand it. Indeed, following Cass Sunstein, Nussbaum has argued that any type of behavior involving treating another person as a mere object, even in the context of an otherwise equal and loving relationship, counts as objectification. So carnally driven sex between life partners is an incarnation of sexual objectification, even though, in Nussbaum's terms, this is a "benign" or even "wonderful" species of the phenomenon. Of course I don't want to deny that lovers can enjoy the mere parts of each other's bodies; in another context, I personally would be inclined to argue that human beings can express very deep respect for one another by playing with power during sexual encounters. What I want to deny is that we can get a purchase on the phenomenon of *sexual objectification* that the feminist worldview in any of its incarnations lights up if we understand it to include any instance in which someone is not motivated in his or her behavior by the commitment to recognize the humanity of another person, even if that person in general does recognize the other's humanity.

By expanding the definition of sexual objectification to include such cases, Nussbaum empties the concept of political oomph. It becomes the philosopher's dummy concept, not the one that helps us make sense of the world in which we find ourselves living. Conceptual analysis as epitomized in Nussbaum's paper and employed by her many followers distracts us from the project of making sense of the persistence of sexual objectification as a social fact and thus from illuminating a phenomenon that the world as it stands gives us many reasons not to notice.

Of course, I am not the only feminist thinker who takes issue with Nussbaum's analysis of objectification. But most other theorists who worry about it disagree with Nussbaum because they *equate* sexism with sexual objectification. These philosophers—and I have in mind here Catharine MacKinnon and to some extent Rae Langton—think that, under "patriarchy," womanhood *amounts to* what men "project" on female bodies and that this projection is fundamentally sexual.[31] "Being a woman" on this account is in effect a secondary quality, that is, a quality that, though appearing to an observer to be inherent in an object of perception, is in fact imposed on an entity by its perceiver. According to MacKinnon et al., what people perceive when they perceive a woman is that she is a sexual object by nature, even though, in fact, this feature is a function of men's perceptual "gilding" of women, as Langton, adopting a term from Hume, puts the point. Even more insidiously, these thinkers claim, the content of men's perceptual standpoint is internalized by women. We are socialized to rise to the occasion and become, as it were, what we are told we are. But this is not what we really are. We are, all of us, living under a terrible delusion.

The problem with this view is that it oversimplifies women's experience of themselves. Even women who believe that their "nature" is in fact a function of the gilding phenomenon do not invariably experience men's sexualizing glances as uninvited or unwelcome or merely imposed, and they may strive to live up to the norms that are structurally imposed on them. In fact, women in all cultures are rewarded in many ways, some of them very basic and material, for objectifying *themselves*. An adequate account of sexual objectification needs to make sure that it is tracking this and other dimensions of women's actual experience and that it is painting with neither too narrow nor too broad a brush. In Chapter 4, I suggest that we find such an account in Simone de Beauvoir's *The Second Sex*.

4

Beauvoir on the Allure of Self-Objectification

$\mathcal{T}$HE CLAIM that norms of femininity and masculinity are not biologically or otherwise naturally mandated and that the absoluteness of their normativity makes them inherently oppressive lies at the heart of contemporary feminist philosophy. Judith Butler took this idea to a certain logical limit when she proposed in her landmark book *Gender Trouble* (1990) that gender, far from being a more or less static feature of a person's identity, bodily based or otherwise, is a kind of continuous apparitional impression that emerges and gets its intelligibility only from a person's endlessly repeated performances of masculinity or femininity as defined by the reigning gender norms. On Butler's view, further, "maleness" and "femaleness" are bogeymen concepts: we feel compelled to divide all human beings into two sexed types based on certain physiological criteria only as a way of attempting to anchor whatever gender norms happen to obtain. Our investment in reifying sex and gender, Butler argued, is a function of the punishment, in the form of socially sanctioned ostracizing and violence and the accompanying psychological anguish, that awaits those who dare to step over the lines that determine the fundamental meanings of our bodies.

In the twenty-year period during which Butler's position has entrenched itself in feminist philosophy, we also find a heartening loosening of gender norms in at least some parts of the world. Until very recently, to be properly gendered meant, first and foremost, to be heterosexual. But over the last couple of decades discrimination against gay, lesbian, bisexual, and transgendered people has been waning, however slowly and incompletely, at least in certain localities. And we might think that if progressive people in great enough numbers continue to expose the socially constructed nature of gender, then we can at least hope to arrive at a world in which gender norms lose their grip on us altogether.[1] This is the world that contemporary feminist philosophy for the most part aims to bring into existence—that is, a world in which there is no longer a need for feminist philosophy per se. Indeed, insofar as the enemy is now gender, rather than misogyny, and insofar as gender norms vary according to and intersect with other loci of oppression, such as racial classifications, social class, and norms of bodily ability/disability, it follows, as Butler observed long ago, that for feminist philosophy to privilege the goal of women's liberation or even to make claims about "women's lives" is for it to risk contradicting itself. While we can deploy the concept *woman* in the service of fighting injustice, we must never forget that to use this concept mindlessly is to reinforce the entrenchment of oppression.[2]

There can be no doubt that what you might call gender eliminativism has inspired some people who might not otherwise have been disposed to fight injustice—say, certain college students who come across the view in feminist theory classes—to take to the streets or at least to notice and question their own heterosexism. But our obsession with gender eliminativism and our queasiness about making claims about women's experience have also gone a long way toward ensuring the profound irrelevance of feminist theory in the real world. Those feminist philosophers who do worry in full voice about women are for the most part taking up positions that were well defined decades ago, such as Catharine MacKinnon's claim that pornography is at the heart of the social construction of women as mere sex objects. This is not to say that this sort of claim has become irrelevant. But discussions of such claims tend to proceed as though social conditions have not changed in any important ways since the pre-Butler era, that what life is like for women these days is fundamentally no different from what it used to be like. Antipornography arguments, for example, ordinarily do not even mention, let alone take seriously, the sea change that the development of the Internet has wrought. The apparent assumption is that the widespread and easy availability of photographs and films about every kind of sex act imaginable ought to have no effect on these arguments other than to underscore how correct they are. We find in the feminist philosophical literature pretty much no serious analysis of our now pornography-besotted world and no interest in engaging in anything other than the usual wrangling about whether pornography causes harm to women or constitutes harm to women or is only one factor in women's oppression or is neutral with respect to women or downright good for us.[3]

I am suggesting that in feminist philosophy today actual women's lives have gotten lost between two theoretical fetishes: on the one hand, we have gender eliminativism, the quasi-nominalist view that women, per se, don't really exist; on the other, we have gender reificationism, the idea that we know exactly what it means to be a woman.[4] At both of these extremes, the actual experience of women, as women, is invisible.

We may be tempted to imagine that this theoretical predicament is thoroughly postmodern. And yet it is precisely the state of affairs that Simone de Beauvoir described in 1949 in the very first paragraph of the introduction to *The Second Sex*. After identifying the *"querelle du féminisme"* of the previous century as "voluminous nonsense" and noting that it has not resolved the question of whether there is such a thing as a woman and, if so, what a woman is, Beauvoir writes, "One wonders if women still exist, if they will always exist, whether or not it is desirable that they should, what place they occupy in this world, what their place should be."[5] But these questions, she immediately goes on to claim, lose their grip on us once we pay attention to our everyday experience: "In truth, to go for a walk with one's eyes open is enough to demonstrate that humanity is divided into two classes of individuals whose clothes, faces, bodies, smiles, gaits, interests, and occupations are manifestly different. Perhaps these differences are superficial, perhaps they are destined to disappear. What is certain is that for the moment they exist with a blinding obviousness."[6]

Notice that Beauvoir in this passage in effect declares herself agnostic about the nature of the differences between men and

women. What she insists upon is the priority of our everyday sense
of these differences. As I have argued at length elsewhere, this priority is a function of Beauvoir's making her own experience as a
woman the background against which everything she claims in *The
Second Sex* must stand in relief.[7] Her own experience is intelligible to
her only as the experience of a woman, which is not to say that she
understands her experience to exemplify what it is to be a woman
any more than any other woman's life does. (Indeed, Beauvoir
expresses keen awareness, e.g., on p. xxxiii of the Introduction to
The Second Sex, that because her experience is that of a financially
independent intellectual woman, it is in many respects atypical.)
The bottom-line fact is that she is identified, by herself and others,
as a woman; and for her this means that her inquiry into what a
woman is must be answerable to this fact.

The Second Sex is a book about what it is for human beings to be
sexed, which means that as long as people understand themselves to
be sexed the book will not be vulnerable to a certain kind of obso-
lescence. No matter what social and political advances women and
other groups oppressed on the basis of their genders make in the
world, no matter how level the playing field gets, no matter how
strongly, to quote the very last words of the book, "men and women
unequivocally affirm their *fraternité*," *The Second Sex* will still have
something of the highest importance to say about what it is be a
woman—indeed, a sexed human being of any kind—and what it
takes for such a being to live a genuinely human life.[8]

I admit up front that this claim might well have exasperated
Simone de Beauvoir herself. As is well known, she was fond of denying that her main avocation was philosophy. More to the point, in
The Second Sex, especially in that concluding chapter, she is decidedly sunny about women's socioeconomic prospects and might even
be taken to be predicting the eventual irrelevance of her own point
of view. "It seems almost certain," she writes, "that sooner or later
[women] will arrive at complete economic and social equality"—
that is, that human beings will establish the conditions under which
women can become truly autonomous.[9] She further predicts that
this equality "will bring about an inner metamorphosis."[10] Beauvoir
doesn't say anything further about this metamorphosis, but it is
tempting to think that she means that once women are no longer

the second sex, men will stop understanding them as such and
women will not regard themselves as in any way inferior to men—
that, more broadly, it will make no difference to one's life whether
one is a woman or a man or, for that matter, some other sex. If we
stretch the point a little, we might say that Beauvoir makes room for
the goal that drives gender eliminativism. This possibility invites us
to ask: if the aim of *The Second Sex* is in fact to eliminate at least the
second sex, and perhaps by extension all sexes, as such, both socio-
economically and psychologically, and if that aim should be achieved,
then doesn't the book stand to become a document of historical
interest alone? Might it not, in fact, already have been eclipsed both
theoretically and in real life?

For some people, the answer to this question is yes. Though of
late there has been a renaissance of interest in *The Second Sex*, feminist theorists ordinarily do not take their bearings from it.[11] And, in
my experience at least, the default position for a good number of
young women, at least in the West, is to understand themselves to
be living in a post-second-sex world.[12]

We find evidence for this claim in *Alpha Girls*, a book written for
a popular audience by a Harvard psychologist named Dan Kindlon.
Kindlon argues that progressive social changes in the latter part of
the twentieth century have spawned a generation of girls who are
"reaping the full benefits of the women's movement," a movement
that, he implies, is now defunct.[13] Thanks to the feminism of previous generations, Kindlon believes, today's young women are now
entitled to do pretty much whatever young men are entitled to do.
Moreover, because these girls were born into their entitlement, they
are "fundamentally different from [their] sisters of previous generations": not only are they now equal to boys, but they also experience
themselves, Kindlon claims, as entitled to this equality.[14] As he puts
it, "Issues of sex and gender, dependence and independence, and
dominance and subordination are largely irrelevant to how [girls]
see [themselves] in the world."[15] Indeed, Kindlon, the father of two
teenage girls himself, goes so far as to quote the passage from the
last chapter of *The Second Sex* that I cited two paragraphs above and
then to declare absolutely flat out that "de Beauvoir's inner metamorphosis has occurred."[16]

Kindlon bases this conclusion on interviews he has conducted in recent years with American teenage girls who are highly successful by contemporary standards. One of them, a girl he identifies as "Susan," described to him what happened when she announced to her mother and aunt the names of the colleges and universities to which she intended to apply:

> "My mother and aunt sat me down for tea at the kitchen table", said Susan. "It took them a little while to spit out what they wanted to say. They felt that the schools to which I wanted to apply weren't 'feminist enough.' They wanted me to apply to Smith, their alma mater. 'But I'm not a feminist,' I told them. That stopped them in their tracks. My mom said that later, after I had left the room, my aunt began to cry because I didn't consider myself a feminist. My mother confessed that she, too, had been upset. I guess they felt that they had been unable to pass along much of what they had spent their lives fighting for. But they got over it."[17]

If, before they get over it, mothers and aunts are disposed to mourn the shape that their daughters' inner metamorphoses have taken, fathers, according to Kindlon, have reason to rejoice, since they themselves are now enjoying "a profound impact on the way many girls think and feel, how they interact with the world, and what they want and expect from life."[18] The implication is that while alpha girls and their fathers are living in the real world of today, their wives and mothers and aunts and grandmothers (at least those who are not turning in their graves) are stuck in the past. They are clinging to a picture of the world according to which issues of sex and gender, dependence and independence, and dominance and subordination are still very much alive.

And yet there are signs that even Kindlon does not think that we old ladies have completely lost our minds. In the preface to his book, he admits, in passing, that some girls still "lack self-confidence and are anxious, depressed, anorexic, or bulimic" and that "sexual harassment and date rape are real problems that affect too many women and girls."[19] And in the last chapter of his book, titled "Alphas in

Love," Kindlon quotes numerous girls talking about how much social pressure there is these days to provide oral sex to random boys—sometimes many different random boys at once. One girl tells Kindlon that this practice, which has come to be, for a not insignificant number of women, an integral part of what it is to have a social life on the typical American college campus, "results in a loss of self-respect for the girl and continued expectations on the part of boys"; another girl says that performing lots of oral sex on various boys turns girls into "sex toys."[20]

I wish I could find it remarkable that Kindlon doesn't see any contradiction between his acknowledgment that, on the one hand, a sizable enough number of girls still are anxious, plagued by eating disorders, sexually harassed, and willing to turn themselves into sex toys, and his conviction, on the other, that girls have now achieved parity with boys, both socially and psychologically. But in suppressing or repressing an awareness of this contradiction, Kindlon in fact epitomizes the so-called "postfeminist" mind-set. If you spend a lot of time talking to young women today, which, as the mother of girls in their early 20s and as a college professor, I do, you will see that they live this contradiction—and not just the ones who succumb to depression. The feeling that they are obliged to turn themselves into toys for boys sits side by side in their consciousnesses with their conviction that feminism is, at best, archaic and that the world is a place in which your gender no longer stands in the way of your success.

In my experience, college-aged girls (who these days do not refer to themselves as "women") are inclined to negotiate this contradiction, this split, by construing their way of being in the world sexually not as in tension with their postfeminist strength but as an expression of it. I first cottoned on to this logic about a decade ago, when, after a controversial column in the school paper made the issue a hot topic at my university, I invited students to come together to talk about "hookup culture." The meeting took place right before exam period, and it surprised me that dozens of students—girls and "guys" (as they get called) of varied sexual and gender identities and preferences as well as ethnicities and races—showed up. Most were there to extol the virtues of hooking up. I pretty much just posed questions and listened, though at times I could not maintain a poker face, as when I asked the students whether boys' performing oral sex on random girls was as popular as the other way around, and an especially independent-minded and articulate pro-hookups girl, after turning up her nose at the very idea of this switch, announced that before going to parties she always removed the hair from her vulva because "it's nasty down there." The intervention that epitomized for me the mind-set of most of the girls in attendance—no one seemed to disagree with the remarks I'm about to summarize— came from a girl who spoke eloquently about how hard both she and her family had to work to get her to college and how single-mindedly she was pursuing her goal to go to law school. This girl explicitly associated hooking up with feminism: she was not interested in "taking care of" some needy boyfriend, and yet she wanted to be sexually satisfied; hooking up allowed her both the freedom and the pleasure she sought. As it turned out, interestingly enough, most of her sexual experience consisted in unilateral oral sex performed on guys. In any event, I'll never forget the closing sentence of this girl's speech about why she was so high on hooking up: "I get all the benefits of a relationship without the responsibility."

I imagine that this way of thinking is familiar to those college girls who take things one or two steps further and are delighted to bare their breasts for the *Girls Gone Wild* video series. Lifting up one's shirt in the presence of a camera and a bunch of raucous, beer-drenched guys, and maybe French-kissing your fellow breast-exhibitors while you're at it, is understood as an act of autonomy: these girls are not allowing themselves to be exploited for the sexual pleasure of men; rather, they are exploiting for their own pleasure their singular sexual girl power, a power that, they have learned from the ur-powerful Madonna and her progeny, as well as, perhaps, certain postmodern theorists, is a birthright that could be taken up only once feminism became a thing of the past.[21] Lest this sound like prissy finger-wagging, I must stress here that it is absolutely critical for anyone who cares about these matters to *believe* young women when they say, as they routinely do, that this sense of power, the sense you get from making yourself attractive for and arousing men, is deeply pleasurable. In *Unhooked*, a recent book on young people's current sexual mores, Laura Sessions Stepp, while trying not to scold young women, argues that being in a monogamous, loving relationship is more conducive to happiness than a casual sexual encounter. This old claim, in my opinion, is a paternalistic canard on the order of the one that says that trying marijuana inevitably leads to a heroin addiction: it wears its speciousness on its face. By the time they are in college, all girls have experienced, either personally or vicariously, the pleasures that lording sexual power over boys yield. Being the object of the helpless desire of a boy you are about to fellate, especially when, at that moment, you're the only one around to fulfill it, can be—excuse the pun—a heady experience for a girl. And the pleasure is only intensified if it's quasi-sadistic. (As one of my students once put it to me, "There he is wanting it, and you could just get up and walk away"—though, of course, you don't.)

So there is pleasure in pleasuring guys, and this pleasure is real. And yet it is not unadulterated. For the stories the girls I've been discussing tell themselves about strength and power and pleasure do not, at the end of the day, cohere. Again, this is not a piece of moralizing on my part. It's a product of the other-shoe-dropping that the girls themselves, at least the ones I've talked to, almost invariably do. They tell you that the pleasures of hooking up, like the pleasures of getting really, really drunk—pleasures that often, it turns out, go hand in hand—don't last. There's fallout. There's what I've taken to calling the hookup hangover. You give the boy your cell number, but he doesn't text you later, which means that, unless he's suddenly gone celibate, it turns out that he's not interested in seconds, which means, at the very least, that your power to please him isn't unique. You run into him on the quad the next day and cringe in embarrassment, not just because you can't quite remember what happened last night, but because you've already doped out that he just isn't that into you. You worry that maybe he was one guy too many for you, that maybe in the eyes of the world, your world, you may have slid irrevocably over the line, which is as sharp and fateful as ever, from babe-hood into slut-dom. Then you might wonder whether exchanging a nice dinner for a nice blow job constitutes a fair trade, or why the players are usually guys and the sluts usually girls, or how some sexual Gestalt shift will actually come to pass, post–law school, so that guys will suddenly settle happily ever after for just one girl. Even if a girl never comes to suspect that the playing field may not be even, I am suggesting, she does not always experience her sexual way of being in the world as of a piece with her worldly "postfeminist" ambitions.

And here is a place where *The Second Sex* continues to have something useful to say to us. For Beauvoir's optimism about social change for the better leaves untouched her philosophical picture of the human condition, on which women's and men's achievement of parity with one another requires ceaseless vigilance. In the conclusion to *The Second Sex*, just a few paragraphs before she mentions that eventual "inner metamorphosis" that she predicts will follow in the wake of socioeconomic parity between women and men, Beauvoir reiterates a claim—a claim that is posed, restated, and argued for throughout her book—that every human being by definition struggles with what she calls "ambiguity": she is both a subject (a self-conscious being capable of moving beyond what nature and the world give to her, including her desires as they stand) and an object (an embodied being with characteristics, a style, appetites, and a history, all of which invite the judgment of others). It is fashionable these days to reject this dualistic, Cartesian metaphysic of the human being. But both Beauvoir and Sartre—convincingly, in my opinion—understand the subject/object split not as a mere fact of ontology, as Descartes is at least ordinarily taken to have argued, but more as a phenomenological dilemma.[22] In other words, they are interested not so much in claiming that the dualistic picture is true as they are in drawing our attention to the fact that our experience is one of dualism or, more precisely, of a tension between our drive to transcend ourselves and our drive to cement our identities in ways that we and others will find ceaselessly praiseworthy.

Of course, our tendency to deny this tension by pretending that we are only subjects (as when we wish to avoid what our histories seem to imply about us) or only objects (as when we fantasize that we are not ceaselessly bound actually to live our own lives) is what Sartre famously identified as "bad faith." Someone determined to regard Beauvoir as Sartre's philosophical handmaiden might understand her to be saying in *The Second Sex* that the way human beings have negotiated sex difference throughout history constitutes a massive collective act of bad faith: we pretend to ourselves, on a huge scale, that men are merely subjects and women merely objects. But this would be to miss a pivotal difference between *Being and Nothingness*, which pictures human individuals as endlessly avoiding their ambiguity through a never-ending chain of acts of bad faith, and *The Second Sex*, which construes the human condition in terms of bad faith so few times that attempting to find a dozen instances of the term in the book's 700-plus pages could preoccupy you for the better part of an afternoon. When Beauvoir does use the term, she very often is chiding those who think that women "are" inferior to men, in some timeless, absolute way. The verb *to be*, used in judgments about what people are like, she insists, must be read in what she calls its "dynamic Hegelian sense," that is, as meaning "to become."[23] If women are inferior to men at any given moment in history, nothing follows about what they stand to become. Indeed, I am not sure that readers of *The Second Sex* have grasped that we need to read the aphoristic line that launches Part II, "One is not born, but rather becomes, a woman," as a specification of this idea, which is laid out explicitly in the introduction to the book: when we say that a human being "is" something, we are talking about a stopping point that we impose on what is essentially a continuous process, that of living a life. To pretend that human beings are timelessly this or that, as a cloud, say, is essentially made of water molecules, is, Beauvoir will not hesitate to say, an act of bad faith. But then why does she decline to describe women who fail to object to their status as the second sex in these terms?

Abjuring Sartre's implicit moralizing, Beauvoir claims that from time immemorial human beings have on the whole found a certain satisfaction in exploiting inherently nonnormative biological facts to split the difference when it comes to the painful existential fact of human ambiguity: men, according to this way of thinking, will be the subjects, and women will strive to be objects. I put the idea in these odd terms to bring out what Beauvoir identifies as the incoherence of this plan: to "be" something, once and for all, is precisely not to be a subject; and to strive to be an object is precisely to demonstrate that you aren't one. If you're a Hegelian, what this means, in effect, is that the norms of sex difference are dialectically unstable. But then why have these norms been so intractable over the centuries? Why are women, as Beauvoir famously puts it in the introduction to *The Second Sex*, the "absolute" Other?[24]

Put simply, Beauvoir's answer is that the system works, to a very significant degree, for both women and men. Not only do both men and women benefit from the lopsided relationship between the sexes, but also, Beauvoir speculates, both may well be happier in this arrangement than they would be if things were otherwise. I trust that the payoff for men does not stand in need of another rehearsal. But it is worth recalling, from the introduction to *The Second Sex*, Beauvoir's take on why women are inclined not to fight their oppression: "To decline to be the Other, to refuse to be a party to the deal—this would be for women to renounce all the advantages conferred upon them by their alliance with the superior caste. Man-the-sovereign will provide woman-the-liege with material protection and will undertake to justify her existence; along with economic risk, she can evade the metaphysical risk of a liberty whose ends must be devised without help. . . . It is an easy path; on it one avoids the anguish and the strain of an authentically assumed existence."[25]

Beauvoir of course derives this notion of an "authentically assumed existence," as well as the claim that such an existence involves anguish, from Heidegger, to some extent via Sartre. But in her mouth, the words are not those of some overt or even hidden ethical imperative, whether it be to stop acting in bad faith or to resist the soul-numbing way of being-in-the-world of *Das Man* or, all on your own, just like that, to refuse to be party to the deal. Rather, for Beauvoir, an "authentically assumed existence" is one a person can take up only if she is afforded the material and psychological means to face the following facts: that she is inescapably on her own when it comes to the precise shape of her life; that the shape a life is taking at one instant does not guarantee or otherwise determine the shape or value that it might evince at the next; and that other people's lives are, radically, their own lives to live, which means that other people are metaphysically separate from her. For women, Beauvoir argues, the material means to face these facts must include true economic freedom for women—where the word *true* means that, in addition to ensuring on-paper salary equity, the world would have to provide for the particular needs of women and children (having to do with pregnancy, childbirth, child care, and family bonds), and the social mores of this world would have to be such that women experienced themselves as free to invest themselves fully in their work.

And the psychological means necessary for a person to assume her existence authentically? These are what Beauvoir has in mind when she writes about the "inner metamorphosis" that she expects human beings will undergo when socioeconomic conditions improve: people will no longer understand being a man or being a woman to entail a metaphysical division of labor. However, it is absolutely crucial to understand, contra the interpretation of the phrase implied by *Alpha Girls* author Kindlon, that this metamorphosis will necessarily have its limits. For, on Beauvoir's view, to be a human being is to be forced to grapple with a standing temptation to avoid, as she puts it, "living out the ambiguities of [one's] situation."[26] Importantly, Beauvoir thinks that it's in fact possible to avoid this temptation; indeed, in a stunning break from what Sartre says in *Being and Nothingness*, she even claims that, insofar as two people manage to bear their own ambiguity in relation to one another, each can experience both herself and the other person as a subject and object reciprocally, at the same time. (To put the point in Sartre's idiom: in Beauvoir's hands, the *pour-soi-en-soi* ceases to constitute a hopeless contradiction in terms.) Beauvoir makes particularly vivid, throughout *The Second Sex*, the attractions and possibilities of erotic reciprocity, which, she goes so far as to claim, can reveal us at our most human: "The erotic experience," she writes, "is one of those that discloses to human beings in the most poignant way the ambiguity of their condition. In it they experience themselves as flesh and as spirit, as the other and as subject."[27]

And yet, Beauvoir warns, any attempt on a woman's part to achieve erotic reciprocity with a man is bound to be "an enterprise fraught with difficulty and danger," not least because a woman cannot invariably count on a man to acknowledge and accommodate various facts about her physical vulnerability.[28] That female genitalia are not designed to penetrate men, that men and women reach orgasm differently, that a vagina does not have to be sexually aroused or otherwise in a state of physiological transformation to be penetrated, that women can get pregnant from intercourse—all of these facts can lead to a woman's experiencing herself as hopelessly at the mercy of her partner's sexual power. (I put the point this way to underscore the rigorously phenomenological nature of Beauvoir's philosophical method.) Regardless of whether socioeconomic parity between men and women becomes a reality, and regardless of how deeply men and women come to value this parity, women will always have reasons to succumb to the temptation of objectifying themselves—sometimes because being a sex toy can protect a woman from an even worse fate. (Indeed, one of my former graduate students, who wrote a dissertation on these matters, has suggested to me that this fact may help explain what motivates today's young women to perform so much unreciprocated oral sex on men.)

A great theme of *The Second Sex*—one that, alas, has yet to find sufficient resonance among feminists—is that the achievement of full personhood for women requires not only that men stop objectifying women in pernicious sexual and nonsexual ways but also that women care about abjuring the temptation to objectify themselves. For Beauvoir, indeed, the line between full personhood and complete self-objectification is whisper thin. A fully human being, Beauvoir thought, acknowledges her desire to be an actor in the world. She seeks the wherewithal to express her sense of what matters in the world; she dares to have a say in it. But there's a catch here. For part of being a subject, Beauvoir thought, is allowing yourself, and your say, to be the object of other people's judgment, rational or irrational: to risk being ridiculed or condemned or ignored or, worse, to find yourself convinced that the harsh judgments of others are true—or, maybe worst of all, to be confused about these judgments, to discover that, after all, you don't know who you are.[29] Here is where we are especially tempted to try to subvert the risk posed by other people's objectifying gazes by preemptively objectifying ourselves. And here is where *The Second Sex*, in making these temptations, as well as what lies beyond them, vivid, can help shore up our courage to resist settling for an adulterated form of happiness and to dare to hope for the satisfactions that might attend the anguish and strain of assuming one's existence authentically. To the extent we repress this fact—to the extent that we fail to read *The Second Sex* as a work of philosophy—we deny ourselves a certain wherewithal to resist the allure of self-objectification. And in our failure to acknowledge this allure, we make feminism irrelevant to our daughters and thereby increase their sense of being torn apart, of living in two worlds that they find they cannot always, or maybe ever, fit together.

5

How to Do Things with Pornography

𝓜Y TITLE is of course a twist on the one J. L. Austin gave to the series of twelve William James lectures he delivered at Harvard fifty years ago. And since my understanding of what is going on in Austin's lectures both deeply informs how I work philosophically and at the same time is pointedly at odds with the usual ways in which Austin is read, I think it best for me to start with some general remarks about how I read *How to Do Things with Words*.

Let's start by taking seriously Austin's entitling his lectures according to the conventions of an instruction manual, even though, of course, one won't even be able to make out the title unless one already knows How to Do Things with Words. Perhaps you are inclined to take this irony merely as an instance of Austin's legendary cleverness. (Let us not forget his *Sense and Sensibilia*, which involves a play both on Jane Austen's title and on the homonymy between his name and hers.)[1] But you won't take it so lightly if, like me, you are convinced that Austin's central concern was to show that his contemporaries in professional philosophy were theorizing about language as though they didn't know what they couldn't fail to know: namely, that we don't just *say* things with our words but also *do* things with them. Austin suggested in his lectures that philosophers had led themselves to focus exclusively on two aspects of our use of words, bequeathed to us by Frege: the *reference* of terms and the *meaning* of sentences (i.e., their "sense," understood as whatever it is that determines their truth value). What philosophers had failed to explore, Austin claimed in his lectures, is the extent—extremely great indeed, he argued—to which our use of words consists in more than claim-making: it gets things done. We use language not just to convey sense and reference, but also to apologize and to promise and to bet and to accuse and to forgive. To read the philosophy of his day, Austin implied, was to get the impression that philosophers had lost sight of this basic function of words and thus literally stood in need of an instruction manual, of being taught, or, better, retaught, how to do things with them.

The rebuke that Austin issued to his peers is ordinarily construed quite narrowly, as though his aspiration were merely to found a new subfield of what was just coming to be called the philosophy of language, the business of which would be to construct theories of how people *use* words—to do "pragmatics," as we now call it. But this understanding of Austin's legacy turns on an impoverished grasp of his ambitions and achievements. There is no sign in *How to Do Things with Words* that Austin sees himself as modestly gesturing toward a smallish expanse of unexplored philosophical territory adjacent to the vast swath that was being colonized by philosophers of language. To the contrary, there is every indication that he wishes to challenge the foundational premises of this incipient movement, most notably the assumption that well-formed sentences (or their parts) invariably and inherently possess, in some absolute sense, "literal" meanings on which stand and fall their linguistic powers to track or fail to track the truth. This challenge runs very deep—even deeper, I think, than many of Austin's admirers and fellow skeptics about the importance of "literal meaning" are wont to go.[2] For Austin's goal is not to argue that there is no such thing as literal meaning or to claim that it plays a more modest role in the workings of language than others had assumed. He does not, that is, wish to propound some counter-*theory*. Rather, he is worried about the very idea that there must be some one thing or other at the heart of language use, something that demands an overarching theory about how utterances say and do things. In effect, then, Austin is challenging the coherence and importance of the central project that philosophers of language understand themselves to be undertaking.

He is suggesting that doing philosophy—getting a productive philosophical grip on *how things are with the world*—does not require
that we be able to pin down the semantics of natural language in
advance of what Wittgenstein, at least here on the same page as
Austin, calls "looking and seeing."[3]

On my reading, then, *How to Do Things with Words*, addressed
quite explicitly to Austin's colleagues in professional philosophy
during the heyday in Anglophone circles of the idea that philosophy
was all about analyzing language, audaciously accuses philosophers
not just of failing at the enterprise of understanding how language
works but in fact of not knowing, or at least not acknowledging, the
first thing about it. The philosopher Austin has in mind disregards
not just what words in general can do, though that is true enough;
more specifically, such a philosopher never stops to ask himself what
he himself is (and perhaps more importantly is not) doing with his
words. The way back to philosophical sense-making will have to
rest on what he already knows, but to his peril has ignored or
repressed, about what words—and, in particular, *his* words—do or
fail to do.

How to Do Things with Words is not the only expression of Austin's
conviction that much of what passed for philosophy in his day was in
fact a kind of wheel-spinning. Elsewhere, for example, Austin takes
aim at the ideas—ideas that were absolutely central to the philosophy of his day—that (1) our perceptions of the world are mediated
by mental representations (in *Sense and Sensibilia*); (2) ethical theory
cannot proceed other than by attempting to pin down the meanings
of terms like *good* and *right* (in "A Plea for Excuses," "Ifs and Cans,"
and "Three Ways of Spilling Ink"); and (3) knowledge is to be
understood as incorruptibly true belief and therefore, since it is
never the case that our certainty with respect to the truth of a proposition is absolute, cannot be secured (in "Other Minds"). In all of
these writings, it is generally agreed, Austin is commending to our
attention not an *addition* to an established research program but, at
best, a *replacement* for it—or sometimes, as in the case of discussion
of "the problem of other minds," a call to abandon it altogether.
Though many people of course find these writings quite uncooge-
nial, no one misses the radical aspirations that are driving them.

And yet, curiously, *Words* is routinely taken "straight," as though here—and only here—Austin was perfectly content to till the same old philosophical soil and wished merely to draw attention to some adjacent virgin land.[4]

The repression that Austin points up in calling his book *How to Do Things with Words* thus finds its ironic twin in his inheritors' collective failure to grasp the nature of his (and, it follows, their own) enterprise—to discern the serious note in his clever title. My twist on that title is meant to mark what I see as a further repression in this inheritance, one that has to do with the way Austin has been taken up by certain contemporary feminist philosophers who are motivated by sympathy for the idea that the proliferation of pornography, at least under the current circumstances, constitutes a violation of women's civil rights. What concerns me is the *method* these inheritors of Austin are employing. Specifically, I am worried about "using" or "applying" what are taken to be Austin's ideas, or slight modifications thereof, in service of having a philosophical say about pornography. I am convinced that this strategy constitutes a problematic way to do feminist philosophy—problematic from the point of view of philosophy and, at least as importantly to me, of feminism. Second, this appropriation of Austin, insofar as it unquestioningly takes up the standard attenuated reading of *How to Do Things with Words*, obscures the various ways in which the book might genuinely help feminists think about how to combine philosophy with the furthering of our political aims. My aim here and in Chapters 6 and 7 is to make these two worries vivid or at least to provoke philosophers, feminist and otherwise, to think carefully about what our words actually say and do.

◖ To GRASP WHY feminist philosophers of a certain stripe have been attracted to his views, we will of course need to get clear on what Austin, in remarking on philosophers' failure to attend to the way words do things, is accusing his colleagues of overlooking; for he acknowledges early on in *Words* that he has a very specific phenomenon in mind. He concedes that some of his contemporaries had evinced interest, albeit "somewhat indirectly," in certain of the ways we do things with words, in particular the way we use them to *express* our attitudes or to *sway* other people to adopt those attitudes.[5] These philosophers had argued that, in Austin's words, "'ethical propositions' are perhaps intended, solely or partly, to evince emotion or to prescribe conduct or to influence it in special ways."[6] Here Austin is alluding to the central tenets of the forms of ethical non-cognitivism most prominent in his day, namely *emotivism*, which holds that our moral utterances, while apparently statements with sense and reference, are in fact devoid of propositional content and instead merely express a speaker's approval or disapproval of one or another view; and *prescriptivism*, which adds to emotivism's main thesis the idea that such utterances also contain an implicit thumbs-up or -down, in effect exhorting the speaker's auditors to follow suit. According to prescriptivism, when I say that euthanasia is wrong, I am not putting forth a proposition about how things are with the world—as I would be if I were to say, for example, that whether or not euthanasia is morally permissible is a controversial issue. I am merely giving the (emotivist) thumbs-down to euthanasia with the (prescriptivist) intention of getting my audience to give it a thumbs-down as well. In *How to Do Things with Words* Austin evinces virtually no explicit interest in the expressive powers of speech—that is to say, the dimension that engages the emotivist. On the other hand, he is directly concerned with the power of speech to sway an audience, the power that engages the prescriptivist, which he calls its "perlocutionary" force. And yet Austin's interest in the perlocutionary powers of language is limited. For perlocutionary effects—those consequences that I bring about *by* ("per") my locutions—are, he seemed to think, essentially a by-product of our utterances: depending on the audience and perhaps the time or place or other circumstances, the same utterance might generate very different perlocutions. (I *enrage* you when I say that euthanasia is wrong, but I *inspire* Fred.) Austin was interested not so much in the way that, at least on his understanding, words happen to do things—not, that is, in their perlocutionary force—as he was in the way they inherently do them.[7]

What the philosophers of Austin's day had not noticed, what Austin was trying to highlight, was the extent to which an utterance, delivered under the right circumstances, in and of itself constitutes a doing of something with words. When, for example, I say, "I forgive you," I'm not merely putting forth a proposition about the condition of my soul, nor am I merely expressing my feelings about what you've done or trying to get you to do or think or feel something. I am performing the act of forgiving you. When I promise you I'll meet you at five, I'm not just stating my intentions or expressing my commitment to you or attempting to get you to the church on time; I am, literally, giving you my word. When I say, "I christen this ship the *Queen Elizabeth*," I'm not just announcing the name of the ship or expressing my pride in it or trying to impress you; I'm christening the ship. Of course, not just any old utterance of the sentence "I christen this ship the *Queen Elizabeth*" will actually count as the act of christening the ship. Certain conditions need to be in place: I need, for instance, to be the person officially designated to christen the ship, and my utterance must occur at the right time and in the right place, and I need to have a champagne bottle in my hand. Admittedly, some of these conditions are more vital to the success of my act of christening than others. If I am the captain of the ship and smash a bottle of sparkling grape juice against its hull, all may be well; but it certainly won't be if I simply get it into my head to go down to the harbor and undertake to name some random ship. Similarly, if I swear I'll be there at five and yet lack any intention of meeting you, then my act of promising, like my ill-conceived christening venture, will be "infelicitous" or "unhappy," to invoke Austin's terms of art.[8]

A central goal of Austin's in drawing attention to what he calls the "performative" or, later in his lectures, the "illocutionary" power of speech, its inherent power not just to say but also to do things, is to disrupt philosophers' fixation on the idea that the only philosophically pertinent measure of our utterances is their truth value. Once we evaluate what Austin calls "the total speech act in the total situation," we see that the truth or falsity of an utterance (or, more precisely, the truth or falsity of the facts presupposed, implied, entailed by, or otherwise associated with that utterance) is only one dimension of the utterance's success or failure.[9] In addition to involving, first, the issuing of a "locution" with sense and reference, which implies a "truth / falsehood dimension," virtually all utterances will at least aim at the execution of a performative act ("illocution"), which is to be judged according to what Austin calls a "happiness / unhappiness dimension."[10] (An utterance often will also involve, third, the evincing of states of mind and behavior in ourselves and others; that is, it may have certain "perlocutionary" effects.) Because our utterances constitute speech acts, the things we say are not only "heir to [the] kinds of ill which infect all *utterances*" but also "subject to [the] unsatisfactoriness to which all *actions* are subject."[11]

Austin's intention in making such observations, as he says quite explicitly at the end of his last lecture, is to produce a "programme" for philosophers, one that must begin with their abandoning certain fixations and tendencies toward oversimplification—"which," he observes, "one might be tempted to call the occupational disease of philosophers if it were not their occupation."[12] At the end of *Words*, in his only example of how this new program might go, he discusses his contemporaries' tendency—quite dominant in the philosophy of the mid-twentieth century—to imagine that moral philosophy must start with a pinning down of the meaning of *good*. Certain influential philosophers had suggested, Austin notes, that "we use [this word] for expressing approval, for commending, or for grading. But we shall not get really clear about this word 'good' and what we use it to do until, ideally, we have a complete list of those illocutionary acts of which commending, grading, &c., are isolated specimens—until we know how many such acts there are and what are their relationships and inter-connections."[13] Here, clearly, Austin is accusing his colleagues of severely undercounting the number of acts that involve the use of the word *good*, of succumbing to the occupational temptation to oversimplify things. But how to generate a "complete list"? I suggested above that here is a place that Austin and Wittgenstein are in agreement: both think that finding one's way out of a philosophical dead end requires what Wittgenstein calls "looking and seeing." (A crucial difference here is that Wittgenstein seems to go out of his way to warn that no philosopher can avoid any given dead end once and for all.) But what does "looking and seeing" involve? Is it empirical work? Do I have to investigate how we use a word such as *good*, leave the proverbial study and concretely observe the way that other people talk? Or am I to stay in my study and proceed abstractly, by way of the logical analysis of concepts? Tellingly, Austin rejected both of these paths. His favorite method for generating lists of things that words do was to sit around a table with students and colleagues and float proposals.[14] The authority of the lists generated during these sessions—of, for example, the various categories of illocutions detailed at the end of *Words*—was therefore to rest neither on observations of other people talking nor on the inexorability of abstract logical thinking but on each participant's own experience as a user of English words—her or his own ear—as tested against other people's experience (and ears).

This procedure—a hallmark of "ordinary" language philosophy and of Austin, its avatar—has been construed by many philosophers, feminist and otherwise, as fundamentally conservative in every sense of the term, including the political one. On this popular construal, Austin was committed to understanding the meanings of terms as fixed by the way that "ordinary" people in "ordinary" life use them. Of course, different people using the same word in different circumstances might mean very different things: for example, a nonfeminist might use the word *woman* to refer only to people with XX chromosomes and the corresponding typical bodily characteristics, while a feminist might use the word to refer to any human being, regardless of her genetics or phenotype, who applies it to herself or who has had the identity "woman" imposed on (him or) her. But when we speak of the "ordinary" use of the term, we are bound—by Austin's lights, many philosophers seem to think—to pay attention to the way that the word is *typically* used, not to the fringe or progressive uses, as though what counts as "ordinary" is a matter of numbers. Since the nonfeminist use of *woman* is much more common than the feminist one, according to this understanding of Austin's "ordinary," ordinary language philosophy is, at best, of limited use to feminists.[15]

Austin, certainly, is often at pains in his writing to emphasize the surprising degree to which we are in linguistic attunement with one another. I ask you for a fork, and you hand me one; you ask me to multiply pi by ten, and I write down "3.14 x 10"; my boss orders me to do something I cannot conscience, and I (understand the implications and) refuse. Austin also issues numerous warnings in his writings that we should be careful not to jump to the conclusion that we are linguistically at odds with one another when we find ourselves using certain of our common stock of words differently. Here I have in mind his well-known discussion of the difference between doing something "by mistake" and "by accident," on which he makes clear that, though we often interchange these expressions, under the right circumstances we can easily discriminate between them as well.[16]

Austin saw that the power of words to do things was dependent on the extent to which we are both in and out of attunement with respect to our sense of what words can do in particular circumstances. He nowhere suggests that getting into attunement with one another is invariably possible, even in the most mundane of situations, nor does he imagine that his investigative procedures are guaranteed to produce this attunement. Indeed, he makes clear how fateful it is when our attempts to do things with even our non-politicized words, the meaning of which is tolerably uncontroversial, fail on account of our not being on the same page. A male boss tells his female assistant, "Be a love and get me a cup of coffee." Is he politely asking her to do something? Sexually harassing her? Condescending to her? Abusing his authority over her? This will be a matter of judgment, and Austin understood that our judgments will not always match. It is certainly true that Austin himself is disinclined, to say the least, to use politicized terms as examples in his philosophizing. However, there is nothing in his procedures to suggest that such terms are inapt for his procedures.

At the heart of these procedures is the requirement that the philosopher both articulate her sense of what certain locutions are doing and take the competing claims of others seriously, where "seriously" means neither digging in one's heels nor disavowing one's one sense of things—at least unless and until one finds oneself at loggerheads (for the nonce) with one's interlocutors. This requirement looks pretty generic: isn't this what all decent philosophers are supposed to do? The different is that for Austin, the requirement is not that you take stock of your own philosophical positions and subject them to the objections of others; it's that you take your own experience as a human being seriously and risk finding that you are unable to make this experience intelligible to other people and therefore, perhaps, ultimately, yourself. In rebuking his fellow philosophers for not knowing how to do things with words, then, Austin was in effect accusing them of avoiding their own experience and their own interpretations of that experience. This avoidance for Austin amounted to a failure on the part of his colleagues to recognize the locus of their authority as philosophers—that is to say, the authority required to speak in the voice of the universal, to make claims about how things, in general, are. Their commitment to the idées fixes that were preventing them from noticing how words do things was also distracting philosophers from noticing the ways in which their own words were not doing the things they intended them to do. *How to Do Things with Words* is therefore to be read as a plea for philosophers to pay heed not only to what people in general do with words but also to what they themselves are—or are not—doing with them.

❧ AS IT TURNS OUT, Austin would live to see very little of the response to this plea. He died in 1960, just a few years after he delivered the lectures that constitute *How to Do Things with Words* and before the lectures were published as a book. Given the unlikely places in which appeals to this work have surfaced in the meantime, I suspect that Austin long ago stopped turning over in his grave. Surely he did not anticipate that his lectures would come to preoccupy the likes of Jacques Derrida and the legions of deconstructionist literary theorists captivated by Derrida's views or to provide a centerpiece notion (that of "performativity") for the Foucaultian thinking that has led to the development of university departments of Queer Studies. More controversially, I would like to imagine that Austin might have been, if not surprised, then troubled by the interpretation and appropriation of his work that has gained ascendancy among his fellow analytic philosophers, an inheritance epitomized in the work of John Searle and others who understand themselves to be working on "pragmatics" in the philosophy of language.[17] By now, in any event, one can hardly imagine a use of *How to Do Things with Words* that would be shocking enough to disturb Austin in his eternal slumber. (As he himself says at the end of his BBC lecture on performative utterances, "life and truth and things do tend to be complicated."[18])

Given the colorful history of the reception of *How to Do Things with Words*, we perhaps ought not be surprised to learn of a movement within analytic feminist philosophy during the last couple of decades whose aim is to show how Austin's work might be deployed to bring pornography out from under the protective wing of free-speech law. The most well-known member of this movement is Rae Langton.[19] Langton starts with the fact that in a number of countries, perhaps most notably the United States, the production and use of pornography are protected on the grounds that curtailing its traffic would constitute a violation of a right to free speech.[20] The rationale for this protection turns on the assumption that pornography, like all speech in the legal sense of the term, is (mere) expression: it advances a certain opinion or point of view. But—and here's where Austin comes in—it's a mistake, Langton warns, to assume that a piece of speech is invariably just an expression of a view. What *How to Do Things with Words* shows us is that speech is often *performative* (or "illocutionary"), that it often accomplishes certain things in and of itself, that ordinarily to speak is to *act*.[21] Admittedly, certain conditions must be in place for any speech-act to come off as intended—to be "felicitous" or "happy," in Austin's argot; and the case of pornography is no exception. But if we can specify these conditions and establish the plausibility of the claim that they're in place in contemporary culture, then we can show that pornography does not merely express a certain set of opinions but in fact acts both to *subordinate* women and to *silence* them. And insofar as it inherently and differentially harms women, pornography constitutes a kind of sex discrimination and thus ought at least in principle to be actionable.

My discussion of this argument and others that evoke Austin's linguistic terms of art will focus on two of its features. First, there is a question about whether pornography has the *authority* that Langton concedes it must have in order to subordinate women by ranking them as sex objects.[22] Of course, as Langton concedes, individuals rank people all the time without materially *subordinating* anyone. For subordination to occur, the issuers of what Austin at the end of his lectures calls "verdictive" speech must have the right sort of authority in, of course, the right sort of circumstances.[23] (Indeed, though Austin doesn't quite say so, the power of a verdict will often depend heavily on the authority of an utterer.) But it's very difficult to say what sort of "authority" pornography could possess apart from an account of what authority, and especially the kind of authority that's not ceremonially invested in a person or group, is or could be. It's clear enough that the United States Supreme Court has the authority to strike down a law that a majority of its members deem unconstitutional. But it's certainly not obvious what it would mean for pornography or its producers or purveyors or consumers to enjoy "authority" in a culture at large. We cannot even count on agreement about what pornography *is*, although of course that might just indicate where we need to start in thinking through any question about its authority.

My second concern will be with an assumption that runs throughout the literature on this subject, namely, the assumption that pornography is speech.[24] To get my worry on the table, let me quote the first paragraph of "Speech Acts and Unspeakable Acts," Langton's most influential article on pornography and Austin: "Pornography is speech. So the courts declared in judging it protected by the First Amendment. Pornography is a kind of act. So [the well-known feminist legal scholar and antiporn crusader] Catharine MacKinnon declared in arguing for laws against it. Put these together and we have: pornography is a kind of speech act."[25] But why *should* we put these two things together? A great deal of pornography is not speech, *except* in the legal sense of the word.[26] Much pornography consists in photographs, still or pixelated, of actual human beings on display before a camera. If we are going to talk about the performative effects of pornography, then, we will need to know something about what Cavell, following André Bazin, has called the ontology of photography and film.[27] It's of course quite central to what Austin is doing in his lectures that, as the title indicates, he's talking about how to do things with *words*. And this is true even though, as Austin explicitly observes, we can achieve both illocutionary and perlocutionary acts nonverbally, as when we throw a tomato in protest (that would be the illocutionary act) and humiliate our speaker (the perlocutionary act).[28] So in drawing attention to the fact that Austin is talking about the phenomenon of human speech, I am not

denying that pornography might have both illocutionary and perlocutionary force. Rather, I am wondering *how* photography and film
do the things they do. To elide the legal and ordinary senses of
"speech" seems to me to occlude this issue from the start.[29] Austin
stresses in his lectures that "there cannot be an illocutionary act
unless the means employed are conventional."[30] If he is right, then
in order to determine what illocutionary act a photograph or film
might perform, we need to think about whether these media really
are governed by conventions and, if so, what they are. And even if
"convention" need not play a role in the performance of every successful illocutionary act, we still have an open question about how
the media of photography and film play on our sensibilities—how
they achieve the effects they achieve and how we understand the
role of the picture taker or director (or purveyor of pornography or
consumer of it) in the achievement of these effects.[31] This is to say
that the question of authority, or authorship, will be pertinent here
as well; it will be taken up in depth in Chapter 7.

 Why are Langton and others as invested as they are in the
specific project of using Austin to try to argue that pornography
constitutes a form of sex discrimination? An understanding of their
motivations will begin to emerge from a brief look at a signal
instance in the history of the feminist antipornography movement.

   In 1984, the city of Indianapolis attempted to enact an ordinance
making the traffic in pornography civilly actionable. At the heart of
the ordinance, authored for Indianapolis by MacKinnon and fellow
antiporn activist Andrea Dworkin, was the claim that "pornography
is a systematic practice of exploitation and subordination based on
sex which differentially harms women."[32] Without much ado, the
ordinance was struck down by a district court on the grounds that,
in the words in which Circuit Court Judge Easterbrook affirmed the
lower court's ruling, "the ordinance regulates speech rather than
the conduct involved in making pornography."[33] And of course the
regulation of "speech"—or, more specifically, of human beings'
attempts to express their opinions—is prohibited by the First
Amendment to the United States Constitution. But, oddly, Judge

Easterbrook at the same time explicitly agreed in this landmark decision, *American Booksellers Association, Inc. et al. vs. Hudnut*, that pornography is in fact a practice of exploitation and subordination. How, then, could he justify the idea that it is protected speech as opposed to harmful, and therefore actionable, conduct?

Perhaps Judge Easterbrook did not fully realize what he was doing in endorsing MacKinnon's understanding of pornography as a kind of practice. Indeed, a lower-court judge accused MacKinnon of lodging her claim that pornography might not just cause subordination but actually be a kind of subordination via "a certain sleight of hand."[34] The trickery would consist in MacKinnon's failure to flag an equivocation in her implicit characterization of, if you will, the ontological status of pornography. This characterization is expressed in three claims at the beginning of the ordinance, all of which Easterbrook seconds in *Hudnut*:

1. Pornography is a discriminatory practice based on sex which denies women equal opportunities in society.
2. Pornography is central in creating and maintaining sex as a basis for discrimination.
3. Pornography is a systematic practice of exploitation and subordination based on sex which differentially harms women.[35]

Claims one and three both say that pornography is a practice—of discrimination, of exploitation, and of subordination. If these claims are correct, then as a practice pornography is a form of sexism, just as discrimination, exploitation, or subordination on the basis of someone's skin color constitutes a form of racism. Claim two, on the other hand, is a claim not about what pornography is but about what it *causes*: namely, the use of sex "as a basis for discrimination." And, from a legal point of view at least, this looks to be a very different sort of claim, a claim about what a reader of Austin might be tempted to call pornography's perlocutionary effects. For if pornography (merely) causes sex discrimination, then, plausibly, it's (merely) a form of (legal) speech, albeit, perhaps, an extremely powerful one, as Judge Easterbrook—who fails to see any difference in status between claim two and claims one and three—opines:

We accept the premises of this legislation. Depictions of subordination tend to perpetuate subordination. The subordinate status of women in turn leads to affront and lower pay at work, insult and injury at home, battery and rape on the streets. In the language of the legislature, "pornography is central in creating and maintaining sex as a basis of discrimination. Pornography is a systematic practice of exploitation and subordination based on sex which differentially harms women. The bigotry and contempt it produces, with the acts of aggression it fosters, harm women's opportunities for equality and rights [of all kinds]." (Indianapolis Code §16—1(a)(2).) Yet this simply demonstrates the power of pornography as speech. All of these unhappy effects depend on mental intermediation. (*Hudnut*, section III)

Though Easterbrook explicitly identifies pornography as a "systematic practice of exploitation and subordination based on sex which differentially harms women," he in the same breath insists that pornography is ultimately to be characterized as "speech," that is, as a phenomenon whose "unhappy effects depend on mental intermediation." In Easterbrook's opinion, pornography, no matter how systematic its discriminatory effects, cannot be said to discriminate against women *in and of itself* and therefore must count, legally at least, as a protected form of expression.

Call this the "liberal" view of pornography. Not only is this liberal view encoded in American law, but it also has been vigorously defended by famous liberal philosophers, including, perhaps most influentially, Thomas Nagel and Ronald Dworkin.[36] The view is sometimes seen as having its roots in the second chapter of John Stuart Mill's *On Liberty*, "Of the Liberty of Thought and Discussion," in which Mill is taken to have argued that what tends in the liberal literature to get called the "free marketplace of ideas" is essential to the flourishing of humanity. Mill's arguments in this chapter are pretty much unabashedly utilitarian: he champions free speech—and thought—on the grounds that encouraging people to think and say what's on their minds is the only way that the ideas most beneficial to humankind—that is to say, the truthful ones—will come to the fore.[37] But in their discussions of pornography, both Nagel and Dworkin are careful not to endorse any utilitarian rationale, since they are of the same mind in judging that the proliferation of pornography is highly unlikely to bring about a better world. Indeed, for the sake of argument, Dworkin assumes that it will bring about a *worse* world. Nonetheless, he, like Nagel, argues that curtailing pornography would violate our *human* (and not just legal) rights.

Dworkin claims that human beings have what he calls a "right to moral independence," the right "not to suffer disadvantage in the distribution of social goods and opportunities, including disadvantage in the liberties permitted to them by the criminal law, just on the ground that their officials or fellow-citizens think that their opinions about the right way for them to lead their own lives are ignoble or wrong."[38] The legal right to free speech is a guarantor, then, of a *moral* right, if I can put the idea that way, to a certain lack of interference in one's private life. And Nagel argues that antipornography activists dangerously conflate the sphere of privacy with the sphere of what he calls "public space" and do so, he speculates (and so does Dworkin), because other people's sexual fantasies "disturb, disgust, or frighten" them.[39] Both Nagel and Dworkin suspect that those who would exempt pornography from the protection of free-speech laws are motivated by a revulsion for sexual fantasy—their own and others'—which interferes with their ability to acknowledge the line that any decent theory of human rights draws between the private and public spheres.

The liberal stance epitomized in the writings of Nagel and Dworkin is tailor-made to contest the view that the problem with pornography is that it's *indecent* speech, a view that has in fact been codified in US laws allowing communities to restrict public displays of what they deem "obscene."[40] To label pornography "obscene" is to suggest that it offends decent sensibilities to such a degree that curtailing its expression at least on the local level is legally tolerable. Now, according to the liberal view, any right you have not to be offended by what turns me on is going to be dwarfed by my right to privacy (figured, if you like, as what Dworkin calls "moral independence"). But the liberal argument doesn't touch the likes of

MacKinnon, at least not on this particular ground. For MacKinnon deplores the idea that what's wrong with pornography is that it's obscene; indeed, she finds this idea as odious as the phenomenon of pornography itself. The "obscenity" claim, according to MacKinnon, both reinforces the view that pornography is a kind of expression, so that its only badness could be its giving of a kind of offense (that is to say, to invoke the Austinian terminology, its having a certain per-locutionary effect), and diverts us from noticing that pornography is a *discriminatory practice that differentially harms women*.[41] It follows from MacKinnon's position that fighting pornography on obscen-ity grounds is a self-defeating way for feminists to proceed, since the very idea that pornography is obscene reinforces the funda-mental liberal claim that feminists ought to contest, namely, that porn is at heart merely expressive speech. Even if the obscenity objection were to result in a reduction in the traffic in pornography, its grounds, MacKinnon insists, are intolerable from a feminist point of view.

Like many antipornography feminists of a certain stripe, Mac-Kinnon is inclined to endorse instead a strategy that fits with her second claim in the Indianapolis ordinance about pornography's harms, the claim that "pornography is central in creating and main-taining sex as a basis for discrimination." This strategy is to adduce scientific evidence that men's use of pornography causes them to harm women in various ways, from viewing them with contempt and disrespect (and thereby, perhaps, not taking them seriously as workers or thinkers or human beings) to, some argue, raping or oth-erwise physically harming them. The most famous relevant investi-gations were conducted some years ago by Edward Donnerstein, a psychologist whose work is invoked frequently in the feminist anti-pornography literature. Donnerstein and his colleagues conducted a series of experiments in which they measured men's reactions—both verbal and, as it were, penile—to violent pornographic images. They found an association between men's pornography-related arousal levels and their sensitivity, or lack thereof, to violence against women; and they concluded from this data that some men who consume pornography may be more likely than other men to hurt women.[42] Notoriously, this rather weak conclusion entails a number of controversial assumptions, for example that men's use of pornography must be a cause of their desires and attitudes, rather than a symptom of them. Still, a very charitable reading of Donnerstein's conclusions might support the view that pornography causes some men to harm some women.

But that conclusion is not strong enough to undergird MacKinnon's understanding of pornography as a discriminatory practice that harms women. It is not enough, in particular, to defeat the liberal view of pornography as protected speech. In other words, MacKinnon's second claim, about the harms pornography *causes*, is bound to be trumped by the liberal argument against controlling the traffic in pornography. What needs to be shown, in order for MacKinnon to prevail, is how to make sense of the central idea in claims one and three of the Indianapolis ordinance: the idea that a bunch of magazines and films and books could constitute, in and of themselves and regardless of what effects they happen to produce, a subordinating and exploitative practice of discrimination against women. This is where Langton's work enters the picture.

∿ LET US NOW EXAMINE more carefully Langton's argument in support of what I will henceforth call *the subordination claim*, the claim that pornography can be seen as having "the illocutionary form of subordination."[43] Langton's proposal is that we recognize pornography, in Austinian terms, as (1) *verdictive* speech that "*ranks women as sex objects*" and (2) *exercitive* speech that "legitimates sexual violence" against them.[44]

Verdictives, Austin says, are "judicial acts" as opposed to "executive acts"; they are judgments about how things *are* that are based on *evidence*, rather than opinions about how things *should be* that are based on *preferences*.[45] Two of Austin's examples of verdictives are an umpire's ruling whether a ball is out of bounds and a jury's finding an accused party guilty or innocent—though, as Austin notes, a successful verdictive can be issued in an unofficial context, too; he lists "reckoning" and "calculating" as examples. In addition to their force as judgments, Austin observes, "verdictives have obvious connexions with truth and falsity, soundness and unsoundness and fairness and unfairness." For of course "the content of a verdict is true

or false": there is a fact of the matter about whether the ball was fair
or foul or whether the defendant committed the crime or not. And
yet, as Austin explicitly recognizes, verdictives, "as official acts,"
have the power to "make law" regardless of whether their content is
true; hence, their "connexions" with fairness and soundness. "A
jury's finding makes a convicted felon" even if the judgment that the
accused is guilty is wrong, unfair, and unsound.

In her argument that pornography performs the verdictive act of
ranking women as inferior to men, Langton is particularly interested in the implications of Austin's observation that an "official"
verdictive can, if I may put the matter this way, substitute a faulty
judgment for a fact of the matter—can make it the case that the
batter is "out" even if she in fact beat the ball to the bag.[46] Though
she does not quite say so explicitly, Langton wants to focus our
attention on cases in which the authority of a verdictive-issuing
judge is not patent. When it comes to ball games and murder trials
and other such public events, the fact of a verdict's having been
issued is obvious and the possibility that it is faulty is therefore made
salient. But when the power invested in the judge is not ceremonial,
the possibility of mistake, unfairness, injustice, or other forms of
unhappiness may not be salient. The judgment and the fact of the
matter may become hopelessly conflated, in which case the verdictive will have *created* the reality that the judge purports merely to
describe. The teacher tells Johnny that he is a failure, and so, in his
own mind, he becomes one (and, of course, the teacher's judgment
may then become a self-fulfilling prophecy). The evangelist declares
that homosexuality is an abomination, and so, in the minds of his
parishioners, it is. And, under the right circumstances, Langton
argues, pornography's ranking of women as inferior to men, as mere
sex objects as opposed to genuine human subjects, might be precisely what makes it the case that women are subordinate to men. By
"the right circumstances," Langton seems to imply, she means
simply that the recipients of the verdictive take the judgment of its
issuer to be (1) authoritative, which means, more specifically, that (2)
he is regarded as a reliable judge who (3) thereby induces the relevant
people to conform to the picture of the world of which the verdict,
if I may put it this way, is a snapshot. So insofar as pornography's

picture of the way things are is authoritative in this sense, it might actually *construct* women as the second sex.

Langton offers us a very similar story about the second way in which she thinks pornography plausibly subordinates women, namely, by functioning as "exercitive speech that *legitimates* sexual violence."[47] Here is what Austin has to say in *How to Do Things with Words* about exercitives, which, he notes, constitute "a very wide class": "An exercitive is the giving of a decision in favour of or against a certain course of action, or advocacy of it. It is a decision that something is to be so, as distinct from a judgement that it is so: it is advocacy that it should be so, as opposed to an estimate that it is so; it is an award as opposed to an assessment; it is a sentence as opposed to a verdict."[48] In this passage Austin implies, congenially enough for Langton, that an exercitive, when used by an authoritative person under the right circumstances, has the power to make the content of the utterer's judgment a reality. *Annul* is an exercitive verb, as are *veto* and *repeal*. Notice that all of these examples (unlike, say, the examples *entreat* or *recommend*) are typically associated with conventional procedures, and all can be felicitously used only in conjunction with the right kind of authority, ordinarily that of the state. Although Austin does not include Langton's *legitimate* in his examples, I think it fits the bill: to legitimate some practice, say, does indeed seem to constitute "a decision that something is to be so." To my ears, *legitimate*, while perhaps not as solidly associated with conventional procedures and civil authority as an exercitive such as *veto*, nonetheless seems to require that the party doing the legitimating cannot just be any old person: she or he must command a certain authority. To legitimate a practice, one must have the power to make that practice come to be, or rather come to be taken as, legitimate. I draw attention to the distinction here only to make explicit the obvious fact that an authority's declaring something to be legitimate does not automatically make it legitimate, in the sense that it would be if it were just or reasonable. Langton of course concurs: indeed, her argument implicitly rests on the claim that the pornographer's legitimation of violence against women is unjust and unreasonable, to say the least. What Langton needs in claiming that pornography is exercitive speech that legitimates violence against women is only the idea that an authority's legitimating of a practice provides its practitioners with an official, conventionally recognized justification for their action, should they find themselves in need of one.

So much, at least for now, for the two faces of the subordination claim. Let us turn to the second claim advanced by MacKinnon and famously analyzed in slightly different ways by both Langton and Jennifer Hornsby: that pornography has the illocutionary force of *silencing* women. The idea is that in addition to legitimating violence against women pornography performs a second exercitive function, that of *depriving* women of the background conditions that must be in place in order for their voices to be heard. Langton calls this silencing "illocutionary disablement."[49] It occurs when someone can utter the words she wishes to utter but is doomed to fail to do what she wishes to do in uttering them. A man says "I do" during a marriage ceremony; but his partner is also a man and so he fails to marry.[50] An actor trying to alert another character on stage to a pretend fire suddenly spots an actual fire in the back of the theater; he yells "fire!"; but the audience takes this as more dialogue and so he fails to warn. Linda Lovelace, the star of the notorious 1972 porn film *Deep Throat*, writes a book, called *Ordeal*, about her horrendous experiences making the film; but the book is routinely marketed as pornography, and so she fails to protest. A woman wishing to repel the sexual advances of a man says "No!"; but because pornography has made it the case that men hear this "no" as a "yes," she fails to refuse.[51]

Before I discuss in more detail this last and, for Langton and Hornsby, most pertinent example, let me draw attention to an important feature of the silencing claim, which is that it does not say that pornography has the *perlocutionary* effect of causing women not to speak—though of course one could argue that, in addition to silencing women in the way Langton and Hornsby think it might, pornography causes women to feel intimidated about uttering the words they are inclined to say. The claim at stake here is that pornography silences women at the level not of their locutions but of their illocutions: it makes it the case that some of the illocutionary acts that women attempt to perform are overwhelmingly likely to misfire.

Pornography, according to the silencing claim, denies women a reasonable chance of being able to make their auditors understand the force of certain of their utterances and thus to achieve certain acts—notably, the act of refusing sex. It makes it impossible, to put the point in the Austinian terms that Langton finds congenial, for certain of women's utterances to obtain "uptake."[52] Take the case, now, of a woman who wishes to refuse sex with a man. Except under unusual circumstances, she will of course be able to say "no" or its equivalent—to attempt to refuse the man. (If she can't, then it's because her powers of locution have somehow been curtailed.) However, the argument goes, if the man is conditioned not to recognize a woman's words as an attempt at refusal, then she will be unable to refuse, even when she uses conventional words—such as "*No!*"—to attempt to do so. And it's plausibly the case, according to supporters of the silencing claim, that pornography teaches men that, for example, to cite Hornsby's words, "women who do not behave with especial modesty or dress with especial circumspection are ready and willing to gratify men's sexual urges, but will feign unwillingness, whether through a pretended decency, or through a desire to excite."[53] More specifically, according to Hornsby, pornography might "create a *presumption* of [a] woman's being insincere."[54]

In a discussion of how pornography could be seen to produce women's illocutionary disablement by conditioning men in a certain way, Langton and a coauthor, Caroline West, try to understand exactly how the creation of such a presumption might come about. For, certainly, pornography does not proffer a verbal *argument* that when a woman says "no" she is in fact not refusing sex. Indeed, if it were to offer such an argument, we would have more reason to construe it as what the law calls "speech" than we have if it determines men's attitudes by a process of psychological conditioning.[55] To see how this conditioning happens, how certain presumptions get into men's heads, Langton and West ask us to consider a pictorial spread from *Hustler* magazine, the first photograph of which depicts a waitress being pinched by a male pool player "while his companions look on with approval."[56] The captions accompanying the spread reportedly read as follows: "Though she pretends to ignore them, these men know when they see an easy lay. She is thrown on the felt table, and one manly hand after another probes her private areas. Completely vulnerable, she feels one after another enter her fiercely. As the three violators explode in a shower of climaxes, she comes to a shuddering orgasm." Here, Langton and West observe, we have a case (a typical case, we might note) in which a woman is not represented as explicitly refusing sex—as saying "no." And yet, they argue, the most natural and obvious way of making sense of what is going on in the pictorial requires that one *presuppose* that the female waitress says "no" when she really means to consent to what's happening to her; that, despite her protestations to the contrary, she wanted to be raped and dominated all along; that she was there as an object for the men's sexual gratification; that raping a woman is sexy and erotic for men and women alike.[57]

Langton and West want the concept *presupposition* here because it allows them to understand the pictorial in terms proposed by David Lewis in his influential paper "Scorekeeping in a Language Game" (1979).[58] Lewis is interested in the way that certain things we *don't* say routinely come to play an important role in conversation. For example, suppose we are talking about the difficulty of an exam and I remark that "even Jane could pass."[59] Even though I don't *say* that Jane is incompetent, my remark introduces into the conversation the presupposition that she is. According to Lewis, conversation tends to be governed by a "rule of accommodation" that allows a presupposition like "Jane is incompetent" to be tacitly introduced and then, as long as no one explicitly challenges it, to exercise an influence over what can and cannot properly be said during the conversation thereafter. Lewis urges us to think of the tacit introduction of presuppositions into a conversation as a kind of "move" in a rule-governed "language game," a move that changes the "score" of the game. If none of my interlocutors challenges my remark about Jane, then the presupposition that Jane is incompetent is, to quote Langton and West's way of putting the matter, "immediately established as part of the score" of the language game and thereby makes it the case that saying "even Jane could pass" counts as a correct move in that game.[60] Moreover, this change of score may license, for example, the making of jokes at Jane's expense, the further disparaging of her talents, and so on.[61] Even more insidiously, Langton and West argue, because presuppositions are often implicit, they are less salient than explicit claims, hence more difficult to challenge, hence more *unlikely* to be challenged than overt attempts to change the conversational score.

With this picture in place, one can understand pornography as implicitly establishing rules in the various "language games of sex" by introducing presuppositions into these games—presuppositions that, because they are tacit, are more likely to go unchallenged than if they were explicit. Because the introduction of these presuppositions by and large in fact goes unchallenged, certain utterances in the language games of sex have come to be seen as counting as correct moves in those games. This is how a pornographic photo spread like the one from *Hustler* might contribute to changing the score of the language games of sex, despite its not making an explicit claim that that a woman's "no" should not count as an act of refusal. For by successfully introducing into the conversation, as it were, the tacit presupposition that a woman's "no" does not constitute an act of refusal, *Hustler*, along with other such pornographic speech, has made it the case that the rule "do not take her 'no' as an attempt at the illocutionary act of refusal" comes to govern what does and does not count as a correct response to a woman's "no"—has made it the case that men are, according to the rules of this particular language game, right not to take a woman's "no" as an act of refusal.[62] Insofar as pornographic speech sets up the rules in the language games of sex in this sort of way, Langton observes, it constitutes a particularly powerful kind of speech, namely, "speech that determines the kind of speech there can be."[63] And insofar as pornographic speech has this determining power, it will be able to disable women's attempts at refusal, to silence them at the level of their attempted illocutions.

What Langton and West are arguing, then, is that the presuppositions that pornography introduces into our cultural conversation about sex go unchallenged not just because they are insidiously tacit but because pornography has the authority to determine, via its own illocutionary acts, what sex *is* in the culture. Langton is fully aware of the pivotal role that this claim about pornography's authority plays in her arguments. In "Speech Acts and Unspeakable Acts," for example, she writes as follows:

If pornography sets up the rules in the language games of sex—
if pornography is speech that determines the kind of speech
there can be—then it is exercitive speech in Austin's sense, for
it is in the class of speech that confers and removes rights and
powers. We saw that the claim that pornography subordinates
requires the premise that pornography is authoritative speech,
otherwise it could not rank and legitimate. We can now see that
the claim that pornography silences requires the same premise:
pornographic speech must be authoritative if it is to engender
the silence of illocutionary disablement.[64]

The question now becomes: what is the nature of the authority that
pornographic speech must enjoy in order to subordinate and silence
women?

∾ THE ANSWER TO THIS QUESTION is not obvious. Even if we feel
morally certain that pornography is a thoroughly pernicious influence in the culture, we may well have difficulty cashing out this
influence in terms of the notion of authority. For since pornography
is not formally invested with whatever illocutionary power it has, we
need to think about exactly how it might possess the authority to
subordinate or silence women. This, it is important to me to note, is
something that Austin's antipornography appropriators do not do.
They simply claim that, in Langton's terms, "it may be that pornography has all the authority of a monopoly" for "hearers who . . . do
seem to learn that violence is sexy and coercion legitimate."[65] My
impatience with this claim stems not from a sense of its implausi-
bility or any dearth of evidence—I have no problem with the strategy
of putting empirical questions on the back burner—but from its
resolute avoidance of the question of what authority might amount
to in this instance. Ironically, at this crucial juncture in the appropriation of Austin we find a profoundly un-Austinian moment.
Austin's procedures are everywhere and always characterized by
dogged attention to the terms in which we are inclined to express
ourselves, by a sense of the fatefulness of how we count things and
how they count for us. If pornography's illocutionary powers rest on
its authority, then we cannot hope to understand these powers

absent reflection on what we have in mind in recurring to the word *authority*.

What form might pornography's authority take? Langton's claim that pornography (plausibly) has the power to legitimate violence against women suggests that perhaps what is at stake is a kind of *authorization*, a granting of permission to men to hurt women who appear to be refusing sex. (Notice that "authorizing" is a kind of illocutionary act.) Consider a certain type of adolescent boy cruising the Internet who comes upon some explicit photographs of naked men, presented in an explicitly affirmative context. It does seem to me that this boy's sense of relief—or of belonging, or of finding a concept for his longing, or of increased longing—might be construed as something that the site he is gazing at is authorizing. Note that *authorize* in this context would mean that the boy would understand himself to have reason to think that his feelings, of whatever kind, are shared by others and, hence, not inhuman. To put the point in a slightly different way, the boy would perhaps experience the fact of the existence of others like himself as permission to see himself as something other than completely—and disturbingly—sui generis. This feeling of authorization is likely to be even more intense for Internet surfers who have extremely unusual sexual desires. Indeed, there are websites devoted to people who are sexually aroused by blowing up balloons (for some, to the point of popping; for others, just before the popping point); by pretending that they have an amputated digit or limb; by expressing physical love for dolphins; by watching people in high heels step on bugs; and by having other people feed them (or feeding other people) to the point of gross obesity.[66]

But of course it is a very different question whether a website could possibly *justify* our dolphin-lover in his practices. True, a website might provide information about the formal permissibility in a given domain of sexual encounters with dolphins and so in that way reveal that certain types of human activities with dolphins are or are not (legally) authorized. But could a website give the dolphin-lover reason to construe his behavior and attitudes as authorized in some absolute, context-less sense? *Authorized* here would have to mean something like: absolving the dolphin-lover of responsibility for his fetish. But what or who in a culture has such powers of absolution *überhaupt*, that is to say, apart from the faith that individuals place in it or him or her?

Perhaps, though, these fetish cases are misleading. Perhaps we should be considering pornography that purveys and reinforces conventional discriminatory constructions of what it is to be a woman, pornography that portrays women as essentially sex-hungry beings who love penetration in all forms and who live to provoke men to orgasm. The authoritative force of such pornography, one might argue, comes from the sheer ubiquity of it: when men (and women) live in a conventionally pornographic world, when they are told over and over again that this is what women are like, then they will participate in the subordinating and silencing of women almost involuntarily. Consider the boy who searches the Internet for heterosexual porn and then (I mean subsequently, not, or not necessarily, consequently) presses sex on his girlfriend. Suppose that the boy has discovered and pored over lots of photographs of men forcing sex on resistant women. In this case, unlike that of the latently gay young man, we are not inclined to imagine the boy as experiencing an authorization of what he took to be his idiosyncratic desire to deny the humanity of his girlfriend. But this is because it is hard to imagine that the boy ever felt alone in conceptualizing women as mere sexual commodities, as bodies that are there for the taking. Unless one never sees magazine covers or billboards or watches TV or goes shopping for clothes, one cannot help but learn that huge numbers of people conceptualize women that way. So the boy who claims to feel authorized by pornography (alone) to conceptualize his girlfriend as a sexual object is being grossly disingenuous. There is nothing in the case to *be* authorized: the idea that women are essentially sexual objects for men, along with the idea that the happiest and most womanly women embrace this status, is ubiquitously accepted in our culture.

Still, imagine that the boy who assaults his girlfriend attempts to excuse himself by claiming that he did so because a pornographic website authorized the act. What are we to say? That, given our society's essentially pornographic outlook on women, the boy was in fact authorized by the website to assault her? But then we would have to accept his excuse. What we want to say is that *nothing* could authorize what he has done. This is not just because what he has done is horrific. It's not even just because, at the end of the day, we are loathe to absolve rapists of their crimes on the grounds that our society is insidiously or even explicitly rape-friendly. It's because no person or institution that is not formally invested with authority has such authority apart from individuals' granting it to them—because we understand sufficiently mature human beings as bearing responsibility for the way they see the world. We understand them this way because we wish to attribute to them the power to think for themselves—the power, that is, to be philosophical in the best sense of the word. (Not coincidentally, this understanding of what it is to be philosophical is, I take it, Austin's understanding; to do philosophy, for Austin, was to investigate what it is to be a human being not by conducting empirical research but by reflecting on what one's experience reveals as, for example, the difference between a mistake and an accident.)

Perhaps we still aren't working with the relevant sense of "authority." There is also the sense to which we appeal when we speak of authoritative editions of texts. But to call a text authoritative is simply to make a claim that this particular edition is more tightly connected with its *author* than any other. If one were to challenge the text's authority, a defender of it would tell a story that would end at the author's doorstep. The story might be fallacious or mendacious, needless to say; but the basis of the claim to authority would be clear. Consider now our use of the term *authority* to refer to an expert in a certain field. To call someone an authority in this sense is to claim that the person's views are, or ought to be, influential. And it's at least plausible that pornography might be authoritative in this fourth sense: it might have a very strong, even exclusive power to shape certain of people's beliefs and attitudes about the world and particularly about how we should construe sex difference.

But I doubt that this sense of "authority" can at the end of the day do the work that Langton et al. need it to do. What they need is a conception of authority on which pornographers can be seen to enjoy power to *fix* the conventional signification of pornographic images and words—or, if you like, the rules in the language games of sex. The power to fix conventions is a far stronger sort of power than the power, however great, to influence people's beliefs and attitudes. And it's not at all clear that any authority could possess the stronger sort of power, at least when we're talking about an entire culture's ways of understanding the conventional signification of some phenomenon. For the fixing of conventional signification rests, as David Lewis in his work on convention suggests, not (or not simply) on what some authority *ordains* it to be but on what those who abide by the convention *recognize and accept* it to be.[67] This means that the conventional signification of a piece of pornography—if indeed pornography has conventional signification—will be a matter not of the pornographer's authority to fix it but of consumers' acquiescence to the pornographer's point of view. Insofar as pornography's authority consists in its power to get us to acquiesce to the way it sees the world, its effects are not conventional, not what Austin might call illocutionary, but rather, if anything, perlocutionary. Ishani Maitra has recently suggested that one way we may be able solve what she calls the "Authority Problem" is by considering the extent to which speakers' authority is "licensed by their audiences."[68] I certainly agree that when authority is not explicitly invested in a speaker (e.g., when he is not invested with political, economic, parental, pedagogical, or some other sort of power), whatever authority he enjoys is going to be largely a function of his audience's willingness to *grant* him authority. But doesn't this suggest that we should shift our attention from the speaker's illocutionary acts to whatever it is that motivates his auditor to vest his words with a certain power—or not? One might be tempted to think that pornography virtually inevitably *makes* people see the world in a certain way. But even that is simply to say that it has a certain very strong perlocutionary force. The question then becomes: why?[69]

THE ANSWER TO THIS QUESTION surely has something to do with our culture's persistent misogyny, not to mention racism, queerphobia, ableism, and other sorts of entrenched prejudices, hates, and fears. But it also seems to me that Langton et al. have grossly underdescribed the way that pornography plays on human sensibilities. That pornography can be and no doubt frequently is influential in a pernicious, sexist way seems to be obviously true. But it is equally obvious that pornography meets the needs and desires of a huge number of people, both men and women; and the idea that it alone has manufactured these needs and desires is as implausible as the idea that the invention of the telephone has manufactured our needs and desires to talk to people who are not within shouting distance. This is not to suggest that the invention of the telephone has manufactured *no* new needs, nor is it to contradict the obvious fact that it has transformed certain old ones. Marx famously says that there is no such thing as a raw human need, that all needs take a culturally specific form.[70] And in *Civilization and Its Discontents*, Freud observes that apparent advances in civilization—and he singles out various technological developments, including the invention of the telephone—seem actually to have deepened human misery.[71] But Marx does not suggest that we have no inherent human needs, and it is one of Freud's goals in *Civilization and Its Discontents* to show that the new needs are permutations of the old. If the invention and proliferation of the telephone (and perhaps even more dramatically the mobile device and the Internet) mean that some of us can now bear to live farther away from our loved ones than we once might have, it does not mean that we never before longed to hear the voices of or see those loved ones when they or we did have to leave home. And if the proliferation of video technology means that some of us can now meet our sexual needs and desires more conveniently and more privately than we once might have, it does not mean that we never before longed for the various satisfactions that are peculiarly sexual (which is to leave open the question of the dimensions and terrain of the field of such satisfactions).

As the feminist film theorist Linda Williams notes in *Hard Core*, the pornographic use of film has been with us since the invention of the moving picture.[72] The first man to achieve the taking of photographs in fast enough succession to produce a primitive film, Eadweard Muybridge, produced hundreds upon thousands of sequences of naked men and women engaging in various activities. And the so-called "stag film," the crude, ordinarily black-and-white, ordinarily narratively sloppy films made for viewing in a booth in a sex shop or at a bachelor party, can trace its origins to the earliest period of film

history. These facts alone cannot of course prove the claim that pornographic film meets certain human needs. But we get closer to a
proof if we consider what Cavell says, in *The World Viewed*, about the
power of the medium of film to present us the human body as something that is "*dressed* . . . hence potentially undressed."[73] It follows
that when we see a desirable human being in a film—potentially *any*
human being in *any* film, Cavell implies—we are "looking for a
reason" for this human being's clothes to come off.[74] Cavell continues, "When to this we join our ontological status—invisibility—
it is inevitable that we should expect to find a reason, to be around
when a reason and occasion present themselves, no matter how con-
sistently our expectancy is frustrated. The ontological conditions
of the motion picture reveal it as inherently pornographic (though
not inveterately so)."[75] The implication here is that the desire to see
another human being naked is something that film is prone to
adduce, not to create. Again, this is to leave open the possibility that
in its adducing of desire, a particular film may reveal it for the first
time or transform it or make it stronger or show it to be in competi-
tion with a set of moral rules to which I thought I was eternally
committed. Indeed, it seems to me that unless you are open to the
idea that pornography has these particular powers, you will misunderstand whatever illocutionary force it has.

❧ AN ANTIPORNOGRAPHY FEMINIST PHILOSOPHER might object at
this juncture that the question of how pictures generally speaking have the power to arouse people sexually is orthogonal to an
exploration of the specific powers of pornography construed à la
MacKinnon and Dworkin—that is, again, as "a systematic practice
of exploitation and subordination based on sex which differentially
harms women."[76] It is understandable that certain thinkers are
attracted to the strategy of arguing that pornography (construed
thusly) is an illocution with subordinating and silencing power,
given the deep entrenchment in (at least) American jurisprudence of
the view that the effects of pornographic materials are what Austin
would identify as perlocutionary and that it is our duty to protect
perlocutionary speech that does not constitute a "clear and present
danger."[77] For by the lights of this jurisprudence, pornography is

merely a kind of expression and so by definition protected speech. On this understanding, expression is inherently *neutral* and its (perlocutionary) effects are unpredictable, which means that neither the utterer nor the auditor is automatically responsible for any failure of uptake. When an utterance has perlocutionary effects on others, it will be absolutely necessary to make one-off judgments about who is responsible for them. For in the domain of the perlocutionary we cannot rely on "convention" to sort out the question of responsibility.

In Chapter 6 I explore the idea that, contrary to the view I've just sketched out, there is a very tight connection between certain perlocutions and their effects and that it is possible to read Austin in *How to Do Things With Words* as having been well aware of that fact.[78] The power of expression to wound can be just as strong as the power to do things manifested by the illocution.[79] Expression potentially has this wounding power even when the last thing on the utterer's mind is to cause an auditor pain. (The teacher says to her students, "Terrific job, you guys: almost everyone handed in the assignment on time!"; and the students who failed to do so inwardly flinch.) Because it also has the power to offend or alienate, often in predictable ways, kids with typical social sensitivities learn over time not to say certain things even when they are true and their force is warranted. Take the expression "I'm bored," Cavell suggests. If it needs saying, "it may also be obvious, perhaps should be obvious, without saying; then saying it would place a demand that I may be unwilling or unable to face, a demand that you acknowledge the obvious."[80]

Even at its most literal, explicit, and forceful, speech sometimes has no power at all, as when a woman says "No!" to a man's sexual advances and he proceeds to assault her anyway. Let us construe this assault as, among other things, a form of silencing the woman, insofar as her words fail to do what she intended to do with them. This silencing is quite different from the silence of the kids who didn't turn in the assignment or the ones who hold their tongues when they're bored. The problem is not that the speaker failed to think carefully enough about the likely perlocutionary effects of her words or kept her feelings to herself rather than face the consequences of demanding an acknowledgment. What forces the woman's silence is the man's spectacular failure to acknowledge the absolutely clear and obvious. Can we imagine an instance in which the *only* way a woman is attempting to refuse a predatory man is by saying "no" (simply, flatly, with no note of fear or desperation or rage in her voice, with no accompanying body language)? The scandal is not, or not merely, that the man has not heard her "no" as a refusal, if indeed he has; it's that he no longer reads what she does in anything resembling conventional human terms. He no longer treats her as a human being. The woman's "no" strikes me as a desperate, and, in Cavell's sense, desperately passionate, utterance. Her failure to stop the man is a product not of the fact that the felicity conditions for the success of her illocution are missing, but the fact that there is not a human exchange going on here: the perlocutionary failure of the woman's utterance is, given this man's intentions, foreordained. Is it plausible to suggest that what has gone wrong is *only* that the man has been taught by pornography to ignore the woman's humanity, that pornography is the necessary and sufficient goad to his brutishness and brutality? The answer to that question must depend in part on what pornography is.

But we will not arrive at a meaningful understanding of pornography if we ignore the passionate power of expression, which means in this context its ability to take us into a no man's land of hurt and pain. The courts are wrong to conceptualize expression as inherently *neutral*, to take the fact that what it does is not always predictable in advance to mean that its utterers are not responsible for its perlocutionary effects. When an utterance has caused pain, it will be absolutely necessary for us—I mean, for anyone interested in what has happened, including the people directly involved—to make judgments about who is responsible for which effects. When we are in the domain of the perlocutionary we cannot rely on convention alone to sort out the question of responsibility. (I leave it to others to judge whether and how this observation might bear on any attempt to ask the courts to regulate pornography.)

All of this leaves unaddressed the question of whether pornography *is* a kind of expressive speech. This question might be unproblematic when it comes to pornographic *words*. But even if we can decide such a question fairly straightforwardly, we're left with the question of the nature of pornographic photographs and films. Developing an account of this nature will require an exploration of the erotic power of photographs of human beings. Developing such an understanding is a project for another occasion. Here, I will just simply suggest that such a project might start by juxtaposing Cavell's writings on photography with those of Linda Williams on pornographic film.

In *The World Viewed*, Cavell suggests that photography, as a medium, insofar as it has satisfied a human wish, has satisfied a wish peculiar to the modern world, a wish vividly expressed in Descartes's *Meditations*, for an escape from what he calls "metaphysical isolation."[81] Photography satisfies this wish, he says, "by *automatism*, by removing the human agent from the task of reproduction" and thus by maintaining "the presentness of the world by accepting our absence from it."[82] In *Hard Core*, Linda Williams suggests that what is sought in pornographic film is a confirmation of the existence of the woman's orgasm, which would mean of her sexuality, which in turn, I take it, would mean of the legitimacy of the man's sexual desire for her.[83] Cavell writes, "A photograph does not present us with 'likenesses' of things; it presents us, we want to say, with the things themselves."[84] Whether we can or will say this—that is to say, will rest content with this way of expressing our intuitions—is another matter. And Williams claims that the pornographic film "obsessively seeks knowledge through a voyeuristic record of confessional, involuntary paroxysm, of the 'thing' itself."[85]

What is the relationship between the quest for knowledge of the thing itself, or things in themselves, and human sexual desire? What sort of epistemological wish, if any, is involved in the desire to gaze at pornographic photographs and films? Whatever answer one might be inclined to propose, it is clear that this wish cannot be identified or accounted for simply by the idea that pornography is a kind of speech. One wants to ask: who is doing the speaking? The subjects of the photographs? (And are they subjects or objects—or both?) The pornographers? And what exactly is being said? And to whom? And why are people so aroused by looking at *photographs* and *films* of other people's naked bodies and their sexually explicit activity?

There is work to be done here. What surprises me is that none of the people on either side of the pornography debates appears to be interested in doing it. (Linda Williams's work, and the work that has followed in the wake of it, constitutes something of an exception, although absent important questions about what photography is and what film is, and so without aspiring to get to the heart of the matter.) Perhaps this is because what is required would be an honest accounting of our investments, both positive and negative, in the phenomenon of pornography, which might entail looking at a lot of pornography, if one hasn't already, and looking differently at a lot of pornography, if one has.[86] Austin's work reminds us philosophers that it is possible to look at something very familiar—ordinary words, in his case—in a new way, one that shows the perversity of our history of imagining that words bespeak themselves and stolidly wear their truth conditions (and nothing else) on their proverbial sleeves. The example Austin sets gives us reason to imagine that we will feel at least as much exhilaration as despair or shame when we recognize the depth of our own implication in what our words—and, I am suggesting, our pictures—say and do.

~ 6

What Is to Be Done with Austin?

> So far then we have merely felt the firm ground of
> prejudice slide away beneath our feet. But now
> how, as philosophers, are we to proceed?
>
> *J. L. Austin*[1]

Philosophical Illocutions

In their understanding of what Austin is up to in *How to Do Things with Words*, as I have been describing it thus far, feminist philosophers are far from unique. As far as I can tell, virtually all philosophers of language read the book pretty much as they do. According to the standard reading, Austin's goal is to lay out a theory of illocutionary force. This feature of language, the story goes, is one that Austin himself recognized to be dependent on other features of language that are theoretically more basic. For though the capacity of language to do things is not void of philosophical interest, the real business of philosophy is to produce a theory of how language works prior to any particular uses to which it gets put. You can't understand how language does anything until you understand its capacity to represent the world. *After* that, you can do what philosophers of language call pragmatics. Some philosophers of language understand Austin to have been pleading the case for putting pragmatics on a par with the more basic enterprises of syntax and semantics. But even those few who find this plea convincing agree that Austin himself was not doing anything more radical than theorizing about how "locutions" (Austin's term for stretches of language possessing sense and reference) tend also to be illocutions and perlocutions.

My view is that this understanding of Austin misdescribes in important ways both what he set out to do and what he achieved. Austin's aim, it seems to me, was not to enliven, enrich, or expand what philosophers call the enterprise of "pragmatics." It was to destroy the picture of language on which engaging in this enterprise makes good philosophical sense. "Illocutionary force," on my understanding of Austin, is not a fancy name for an aspect of pragmatics. To the contrary, Austin's term points to a dimension of our sentences apart from which they not only would not *do* anything but also would not *mean* anything, except, perhaps, in seriously impoverished ways. That is, they would not mean what we, as people who need and want to do various things with our words, need and want them to mean. *How to Do Things with Words*, on my reading, shows us that our being able to mean things with our words is a *function* of our being able to do things with them, so that attempting to put aside the "pragmatics" of language, even just—indeed, especially—at the outset of our philosophical work is bound to issue in massive failure.

An example may help establish the prima facie plausibility of the position that I am attributing to Austin here. I'm going to use the sentence "I'll see you at the pool at 8," but before I say anything in particular about it I need to lay out what I take to the be the standard way in which a philosopher interested in understanding this sentence is going to deal with it. On the standard picture, the first step is to get clear on the sentence's syntax and semantics. When it comes to the semantics of the sentence, philosophers need to theorize about the range of propositions that it might be expressing and the truth conditions for these propositions. One step in this theorizing will be to deal with pronominal antecedents, tense issues (i.e., the question of when the use of the sentence is or would become true), definite descriptions (e.g., "the woman who wrote the book *How to Do Things with Pornography*"), and so on. In other words, the philosopher will have acknowledged the dependence of what our sentences say on the context that the example brings to the fore. Once we get the semantics right, or right enough, then we can go on to talk about the pragmatics, including the question of what can be done with this sentence, given its semantic content. Of course, no one denies that these pragmatic dimensions of language use are very important to our verbal intercourse with one another. It's just that the pragmatic dimensions are essentially not just separate from the semantic and syntactical ones but also, to put the point metaphorically, at a "higher" level. If we do not understand what a sentence *means*, then we cannot do anything with it—or at least not anything reliable or systematic.

This picture seems to base itself in a thoroughly commonsense view of how language must work. It's a simple empirical fact that people with normal abilities to use language can decode, virtually immediately, what a wide range of sentences mean—and they can do so in a wide range of contexts or even when no context is provided. This is true of our sample sentence, "I'll see you at the pool at 8"; it's instantly perfectly clear what it might mean, even though I haven't provided a context for it. What philosophers of language are trying to do, in effect, is provide us with the mechanics of the process that yields this instant clarity. This project may or may not overlap with what theoretical linguists and cognitive psychologists interested in language acquisition and use are trying to do. If it does overlap, that would be a virtue: philosophy has a very long and distinguished history of getting clear on thorny problems and then passing them off to—or even generating—other disciplines.

One way to say what I think Austin is doing in *Words* is this: he's suggesting that there's no reason to think that the project I've just described could ever yield philosophically productive results about how, and why, people talk. This is because (1) the range of propositions that a sentence expresses cannot possibly be exhaustively specified by speculating about the scenarios under which the sentence might be used, since (2) the variety of circumstances in which a sentence might be used to mean what we ordinarily mean when we utter it is, if not boundless, at least dauntingly large, even though (3) precisely *because* we use sentences to do things, we are not brought up short when they are used in new or unexpected contexts.

Now let us look closely at the example sentence, "I'll see you at the pool at 8." I might use it to confirm a date we've made or to commit to seeing you or to suggest a plan of action or to predict when I'll arrive at the pool or to dodge your question about whether I'll actually take a swim or to politely but firmly turn down your plea that we

abandon our original plans because Freddy has announced that he'll
be at the pool as well. This much the semanticist may well be able to
predict. But then there are the varieties of nuances having to do with
the word *see*. Are we to eye each other from across the deep end? Or
will we be hanging out together? And then there's the question of
what will count in any situation as being at the pool "at 8." If the
speaker shows up at 8:22, does her utterance turn out to be false?
How far can we stray from 8 sharp and still have uttered something
that turns out to be true? Furthermore, there is a range of places that
speakers could be positioned and still be "at" the pool, some of which
will depend on exactly what is being picked out by the concept "at
the pool." (On the poolside concrete? Inside the pool's fence? At the
swimming club? In the locker room?)

My claim on behalf of Austin is not that the semanticist cannot
identify all of these possibilities in his analysis. It's that he doesn't
have a prayer of doing so for every use to which we might ordinarily
put this sentence. But let's suppose that I'm wrong about that. And
let's even accept, for argument's sake, that philosophers or linguists
or psychologists will be able to identify the exact mechanism in the
brain through which we do this. It will still be the case that inside
the semanticist's cupboard, we are by definition not faced with the
real-life challenge of attempting to correctly grasp what another
(complex) person is saying, which always requires paying attention to what she is or seems to be doing with her sentences. In real
life, and in good-enough fiction, we are constantly attempting—
admittedly with no guarantees—to construe what people are saying
according to what they are doing, or, sometimes, trying to do, with
their words and to make clear to others what we are attempting to
do with ours. Our attempts to do things with words and to construe
what others are doing with theirs is based not on the truth conditions of our sentences but on what we have learned about what
human beings are inclined to do, what human beings living in the
relevant time and place and circumstances are inclined to do, and
what the particular people we are interacting with in any given situation are inclined to do.

A fact that Austin took to be critical about language use is that
our own attempts to do things with words are often unhappy in

various ways and that our interpretations of others' attempts are prone to go astray. You're always prompt; I took you to be telling me that we'd get together at exactly 8 and feel irritated or alarmed if you're still not there at 8:21. When you tell me at 8:22 that you didn't mean that you'd be there at the dot of 8, I might not be able to decide if you're being sincere, or if I'm being persnickety, or if I know you as well as I thought I did, or whether my irritation is a function of my now-somewhat-embarrassing alarm, or whether I should forgive you. Then again, perhaps I thought we were making a date to spend our time at the pool party together, while you thought you were just confirming that you'd be attending. How I will interpret what you said when you told me you'd see me at the pool at 8 will be a function of how I construe the source of the misunderstanding—how much, and for what reasons, I cared about meeting you, your history of not keeping your promises, my insecurity about whether you really love me. If the extent of our interaction at the pool party is that you arrive as the clock is chiming 8, wave to me from the cabana while I'm swimming, and then depart, then my expectation that this was a date is dashed, and, for me, it has turned out to be false that we'd see each other at the pool, even if for you it's true.

It is in fact because our doing things with our words is so integral a part of the way we live (as human beings, as human beings in a particular setting, as the particular human beings that we are) that we may fail to see the power of words to do things *as the basis of our own philosophical theorizing*. For this basis comes sharply into view only when it is missing. This is why it's easy to take for granted everything that has to be in place in order for us actually to use language. In what follows, I will contend that, crucially, one of these circumstances, according to Austin, is that to speak is, ordinarily more often than not, to perform the illocution of committing yourself to your words. As Austin puts it early in *How to Do Things with Words*, "our word is our bond."[2] And to offer our bond is, always, to perform the further illocutionary acts of *inviting* others to grasp what we mean, *risking* being misunderstood, and *making ourselves vulnerable* to the judgments of others. (Hence, the slew of potential real-life ambiguities that uttering the seemingly banal sentence "I'll see you at the pool at 8" can bring into being.) In *How to Do Things with Words* Austin is claiming that because words must do things in order to mean things in any robust sense of *mean*, and because in doing things with our words we stake ourselves in the world and position ourselves with respect to other people, no philosophy of language that aspires to make a difference in the world can ignore the extent to which linguistic competence is, broadly speaking, an *ethical* matter. Or at least so I shall try to persuade you.

Illocutionary Force and Speaker Meaning: The Standard View

A central claim in what follows is this: it's best not to read *How to Do Things with Words* as a theory, of speech acts or of anything else. The enterprise of trying to support this claim seems doomed even before I flesh it out, however, since in *How to Do Things with Words* Austin identifies himself point blank as doing theory. Indeed, he says that he's constructing *two* theories, a *general* theory of illocutions and a *special* theory of what he calls "performatives," that is, illocutions that explicitly announce themselves as illocutions, such as "I hereby pronounce you husband and wife."[3] But my claim is not that there is no theory in *How to Do Things with Words*. Rather, the claim is that the theory that Austin apparently takes himself to be construct- ing is less philosophically interesting or momentous—in my bolder moments I believe that that *Austin* thinks it's less momentous—than what he is *doing* in *How to Do Things with Words*, which is proposing that the way we talk is in large part a function of our capacity for taking responsibility for what we do. The theory, I submit, is a means for us to grasp something philosophically deep about what it is to use words, not a philosophical end-in-itself. This means that even if the theory turns out to be wrong-headed in its particulars, it might still do something important philosophically.

I am claiming, to put the point in another way, that Austinian theory, in its aims and achievements, is very unlike the sort of theo- rizing that predominates in present-day philosophy of language, whose raison d'être is to provide the right story about how noises and marks can represent the world. More specifically, contemporary semantic theory aims to provide the apparatus for identifying the truth-conditions of well-formed sentences taken literally. In order eventually to throw my own reading of Austin in relief, I'm going to start by comparing it with the largely dismissive understanding of Austin's project that contemporary semanticists are inclined to accept. Philosophers who subscribe to what I'll call the "standard reading" are of course primed to read *How to Do Things with Words* as a theoretical end-in-itself. Austin's ground-floor theoretical claim, it is supposed, is that your garden-variety utterance involves the issuing of a locution (something that has meaning), an illocution (something that constitutes an act), and a perlocution (something that has an effect on its auditors); and that these three facets of the utterance are at least in principle distinct. This means that, theoretically, at least, what an utterance means is determined independently of what it does and of what effects it has on its auditors.

The foundation of this understanding of Austin strikes its adherents as screamingly obvious, not even worth justifying: that whatever a speech act actually does in the world must be "parasitic" on what it says. If people don't grasp the "locutionary act" that a coherent utterance effects, then nothing is going to get done with it.[4] So, regardless of what his philosophical aspirations may have been, Austin cannot be doing more in *How to Do Things with Words* than attempting to extend our philosophical attention beyond the project of pinning down the semantics of natural language to the question of how locutions end up getting things done.

It will perhaps be useful for me to schematize Austin's theory of speech acts as it's ordinarily understood:

1. Locutionary acts are the production of sentences with meaning. This implies, given the intimate relationship between meaning and truth, that the main dimension along which locutionary acts are to be judged is their truth or falsity. A viable semantic theory will explain how true locutions are true.
2. Illocutionary acts are acts that a speaker accomplishes in her production of a locutionary act, that is, a sentence with meaning. However, unlike locutionary acts, illocutionary acts are fundamentally dependent on a speaker's intentions. For various reasons, speakers sometimes fail to convey their intentions or

else they convey intentions they do not have; in Austin's terminology, illocutions are sometimes "infelicitous." An illocutionary
act will be felicitous when a speaker successfully employs certain conventions associated with the act he wishes to perform
and when his auditors recognize him as having so done. Again
in Austin's terminology, this latter requirement amounts to
there being "uptake" with respect to a speaker's intentions.[5]
So, for example, I felicitously carry off the illocutionary act of
betting you $5 that my horse will place if and only if: (a) I intend
to bet you $5; (b) I say something that conventionally counts
as betting you $5; (c) certain circumstances associated with
betting on horses are in place, such as that a particular horse
race is to be run in the near-enough future; and (d) you grasp
from my intention and from the conventional locution and circumstances that I wish to bet you $5 that my horse will place.

3. Sometimes, illocutions are expressed via explicit performative
utterances, which are ordinarily couched in the form of the
present indicative active first-person singular grammatical
form. The illocution of promising to be at a meeting, for
example, may be successfully achieved by uttering the sentence "I promise to be at the meeting"—when, of course, the
right conventional circumstances obtain.

4. We cannot theorize about perlocutionary acts, since they are
by definition unpredictable. People can have any of a huge
number of reactions to any utterance. This means that one can
never guarantee that one will bring off a perlocution merely
by uttering a performative formula in a conventionally appropriate setting in which uptake is achieved.

On the standard view of what he is doing, then, we have no reason
to construe Austin as mounting a formidable challenge to the idea
that semantic theorizing is the fundamental task for philosophers of
language. Indeed, on a charitable reading, we can understand him to
be expanding the domain of that theorizing. In any event, there is
no doubt that producing a theory of illocutionary force, or at least a
start on a theory, is the main business of *How to Do Things with
Words*. Or so the standard reading would have it.

What Austin Does with Words

My guess is that even people who engage regularly with Austin's writings do not remember, or perhaps care, that his title at Oxford was "White's Professor of Moral Philosophy." Of course, having a certain title does not commit you to any particular philosophical neck of the woods. Still, it seems to me that there is something of a parallel between our having forgotten Austin's title and our disinclination to read him as attempting to change the direction not just of how we think about language but of what moral philosophy ought to look like. A little bit of evidence here is to be found in Austin's papers "A Plea for Excuses" and "Three Ways of Spilling Ink," in which he marvels at how much of our discourse consists in our attempting to justify ourselves to one another—or, even more often, to get others to excuse our shortcomings—and calls for philosophers to take this fact seriously in thinking about what is demanded of us as social beings.[6] I read *How to Do Things with Words* as of a piece with this project.

In this section, I'm going to sketch out a way of thinking about what Austin does in this book that contests the standard reading. My recommendation about what to do with Austin is going to proceed from a series of claims about what he himself is doing in *How to Do Things with Words*, that is, about the illocutionary force of his writing. I start with the claim I sketched out above, namely, that, in philosophizing about language, Austin is primarily interested not in producing a viable theory of linguistic competence or a description of the conventions and quasi-conventions that govern illocution in natural language but in drawing our attention to the human capacity to make various commitments to and in the presence of others. He is especially interested in the human capacity to make judgments, to justify judgments, to enforce judgments, and to evade judgments.

We find evidence for this claim at the very end of *How to Do Things with Words*, where Austin sketches out five classes of what he calls "illocutionary forces of an utterance."[7] This project is ordinarily taken by Austin's readers to be an attempt at a finer reticulation of the theory of speech acts. But note that Austin himself says that the point is "to play Old Harry with two fetishes, which I admit to an inclination to play Old Harry with, viz. (1) the true/false fetish, (2) the value/fact fetish."[8] Characteristically, Austin here indulges a fondness for the clever and perhaps even the flip. But the serious point he is making is that our utterances are not well understood if we confine ourselves to speaking about them in terms of truth and falsity or value and fact. For these utterances are intimately tied up both with our power to justify or enforce them and with our tendency to reposition ourselves with respect to them when we are challenged. In order to drive this point home, I ask you to indulge a brief rehearsal of the five classes of illocutionary acts Austin identifies.

First, there are what he calls *verdictives*, which are acts of judgment about how things are and what things are worth. By definition, these judgments are vulnerable to contestation and controversy and are binding only in proportion to how much power the judge has been granted or appropriates. What gets done when I judge from the bleachers that the pitcher's cut fastball was in the strike zone is different from what gets done when the home plate umpire makes the same judgment.

Second, we have *exercitives*, which are judgments not about how things are and what they are worth but about how things will be. The aim of a person who issues an exercitive is not, or not primarily, to be correct or right or justifiable (as the issuer of a verdictive aims to be) but to exercise power or influence. We can of course do this poorly or well, in practical or moral terms, according to our lights or others'. When I issue exercitives, I position myself in particular ways to other people, as when I *urge* my partner to get new hearing aids or *order* my son to go to bed. It will be fateful if I do not have the power or influence over my auditors necessary for my exercitive to be successful. It will also be fateful if my auditors fail to construe the exact nature of the exercitive I intended—or fail to acknowledge the power I wield.[9]

The third class of illocutions comprises the *commissives*, which commit their utterers to "a certain course of action," as when you *promise* to do something or *oppose* a certain way of proceeding or are *inclined* to go forward.[10] A person who enacts a commissive thereby exposes himself to the judgment of others—and potentially puts himself in the position of having to excuse or justify himself not just to others but to himself as well—if he in fact ends up undertaking a different course of action.

Fourthly, Austin calls out a class of *behabitives*. In uttering a behabitive, Austin says, you "adopt an attitude" toward other people and their accomplishments, failures, and subjections to twists of fate.[11] We *apologize, congratulate, commend, condole, curse, blame*, and so forth; in other words, behabitives betray our judgments of others.

Finally, there are the *expositives*, which "make plain how our utterances fit into the course of an argument or conversation."[12] We *affirm, deny, question, doubt, revise, understand, conclude by*. In enacting an expositive, as in enacting a verdictive, we invariably leave ourselves vulnerable to a failure of "uptake" on the part of others, who may misconstrue, perhaps for good reason, what we take ourselves to be doing.

My rehearsal of these classes of illocutionary acts is meant to support the claim that, for Austin, much of what we do when we use words is not best characterized as representing the world truly or falsely or proposing that various things in the world are valuable or not. Rather, Austin is drawing our attention to the frequency with which we *position ourselves with respect to other people* when we speak. Of course we say things that are sometimes true and sometimes false. Of course we pass judgment on the goodness or badness of things. Of course both the degree of truth of an utterance and the degree of value of an object of discussion are often very important. But, for Austin, the philosophically interesting feature of this talk is not so much whether we're correct in these judgments (though of course our being correct or not is often enormously important) but how the utterer's position in the social world, and the nature of that world, is or stands to be changed by them.

I have been trying to show that, contrary to what the standard reading suggests, the aim of Austin's work is not best construed as part of the enterprise to produce a viable theory of linguistic competence. I now put into question the compatibility between Austin's views and three presuppositions on which the standard reading of these views rests, *viz.*, (1) the idea that you can't talk about illocutionary force until you get the semantics of sentences right enough, which will demand your attending to their "literal meaning"; (2) the

idea that Austin's distinction between locutionary and illocutionary
acts is an obvious and important theoretical one; and (3) the idea
that what essentially controls the type of act that an illocution constitutes is a speaker's intention and what determines the "felicity," as
Austin put it, of the illocution is the audience's uptake of this intention. I specify these three presuppositions separately, though it
becomes obvious very quickly that they are intertwined in the standard reading of Austin.

First, literal meaning. Austin to my knowledge uses this phrase only
once in his writing, and this use is consistent with the idea that there
is no reason to talk about the "literal meaning" of a sentence except
when we have a specific figurative use of the same sentence in mind.[13]
He never uses *literal meaning* as a technical term in philosophy, that is,
as belonging to a theory in which it plays a more foundational role
than any other semantic aspect of language. Austin would deny that
ascertaining the philosophically critical aspects of an utterance can
proceed in neat stages. The philosophical elucidation of an utterance
will demand that we look at what he calls "the total speech act in the
total speech situation."[14] Therefore, even if it makes sense to distinguish between the "literal meaning" of an utterance and its illocutionary force, philosophy has no general need of this distinction.

If Austin rejects *literal meaning* as a technical term, then it should
come as no surprise that he doesn't need to draw a sharp line between
locution and illocution. Austin simply isn't interested in what sentences might mean when they are detached from consideration of
the ways that people use words. Here we find another reason for
Austin's desire to "play Old Harry" with the "true/false fetish."
Again, it's not that the truth or falsity of our assertions is unim-
portant. It's just that what philosophy should be looking at is what
role truth and falsity play in the way we talk with one another, which
includes our: claiming that things are true and false; contesting that
what counts as true, in the world at large, or with you, is really true;
pointing out that saying that something is true, even if you're right,
is not always appropriate; worrying that what we take to be most
true is in fact a mere matter of taste . . . and so on.

Furthermore, Austin suggests, contrary to the standard reading,
that a speaker's intentions may not be pertinent when it comes to

ascertaining what someone is saying and doing. The extent to which a person doing the ascertaining (an interlocutor, a reader, a philosopher, the speaker herself) ought to take a speaker's intention into consideration in deciding what she has done with her words is ordinarily a matter of ethics, not of semantics.

This is a very important point. In the last few years, as I have pored through the literature on "speech acts," I have been amazed at how often one comes across the claim that intention always plays a major role when it comes to illocutionary force.[15] Let us reflect on a well-worn example.[16] Suppose a woman walks into a coffee shop desiring exactly one dry-measure cup of coffee beans and tells the waiter, "Bring me a cup of coffee." Alas: he brings her a cup of brewed coffee. On the standard view, the best way to explain the communication problem here is in terms of the waiter's not grasping the woman's intention to order a cup of coffee beans, for her intended illocutionary act was to order the waiter to bring exactly one cup of coffee beans. But it seems to me that central to Austin's take on this case would be the woman's *not* doing what she in fact intended to do. For when you ask for a cup of coffee in a coffee shop you are, by convention, ordering a cup of brewed coffee. It doesn't matter to what the customer did that she intended to order a cup of beans. If this strikes you as wrong, just try to imagine what would happen if the woman's next move were to say to the waiter, "I'm sorry—I meant I wanted a cup full of beans." It's highly unlikely that the waiter would construe himself as having made an error and that any apology he issued would be sincere. Indeed, it's hard to say what would happen, precisely because we don't know more about the "total situation" in which the woman's apology (if that's what her "I'm sorry" comes to) might be delivered. This is why, if I were to stop now and let you think about this example, you would surely take it in different ways if you were to imagine what the utterance would be saying and doing were it to occur in a film comedy and how its meaning would change in a film tragedy.

My discussion of the role that intention does or does not play in our talking to one another is closely related to the question of the importance of "uptake" in determining both what it is that we are doing with our words and what is necessary for them to do what we

want them to do. Hornsby, for one, has suggested that all that's necessary for an illocution to be felicitous is that a speaker's audience
grasp her intentions—in Austin's lingo, that (what she thinks he
means by) "uptake" occur. To see that this analysis will not do, let's
tweak that last example a little bit, so that the woman ordering the
cup of coffee wants, well, a cup of coffee, and the waiter brings her
a dry-measure cup of beans. Would it be illuminating to say that the
woman failed to order a cup of coffee because her attempt at exe-
cuting the illocution of ordering a cup of (brewed) coffee failed to
achieve uptake? Or is it the case that sometimes "uptake" is beside
the point when it comes to the question of whether a certain act has
been performed?[17]

One more example in this category. Suppose that a man has been
seeing the same woman for three months. One night, while they are
having a lovely time tarrying over dinner in a romantic setting, he
tells her that he loves her. Now imagine that soon afterward the
woman learns that the man is also seriously dating someone else.
She confronts him. He says, "Well, when I said that I loved you I
just meant that I am fond of you. I didn't mean that I was *in* love
with you." Let us suppose that the man is absolutely sincere, that he
intended to tell the woman that he was, merely, fond of her. It
remains the case, of course, that the woman has a right to feel
deceived. But notice that this is not because of either (a) her failure
to grasp the literal meaning of "I love you" or (b) her failure to grasp
the man's intentions. What the man intended when he said "I love
you" to the woman under these circumstances is beside the point.
What he said is a function of what it is to say these words under
these circumstances. If it were not, if an analysis such as Hornsby's
were correct, then, from the point of view of the philosopher of
language, the only thing to say is that there has been a failure of
uptake or, in more colloquial terms, perhaps, a misunderstanding.
What I'm suggesting is that this analysis is too shallow to help us get
a purchase on what the man's utterance has done.

Of course, how the man and the woman go on under the circumstances I've imagined for them is up for grabs. The woman can
respond to the man's failure to mean what he said in any number of
ways. Even absent the man's offering the woman an apology or a

reason for his thickness or treachery, the woman may be the sort of person who is inclined to forgive him, perhaps because she has a damaged sense of her own worth or because she is afraid of men in general or of this particular man or because she's a generous person. Regardless of how the couple proceed, the resolution of the mess the man has made could go on for quite a while. Indeed, as a rule, we spend enormous amounts of time attempting to get our intentions across, dealing with responses that seem to register that we didn't entirely succeed, attempting to grasp other people's intentions, getting exasperated with other people for thinking that their intentions matter more than what they said or did, and so on. It's a fraught business, and perhaps that's why philosophers are tempted to imagine otherwise, to insist that intentions ordinarily control illocution.

Now, Austin himself suggests that what an illocution does is in large part a matter not of intention but of "convention." Much has been made, by both his admirers and detractors, of Austin's leaning on this notion, both to characterize illocutions and to distinguish them from perlocutions. If you are interested in Austin as a theorist of speech acts, then, it seems to me, you have a right to take Austin to task on this front—as, for example, Derrida so mercilessly does in "Signature Event Context" and his subsequent ugly and painful exchange with John Searle.[18] Someone who reads Austin as a theorist charitably might concede to him that in ritualized situations, such as christening a ship or getting married or placing a bet, the borderlines of the concept are clear enough (though Austin himself notes that even here they are fuzzy, as when we wonder whether we can baptize a dog).[19] And our charitable reader might further concede that certain everyday practices, though not formally ritualized, could plausibly be said to exploit conventions, as when, for instance, we order cups of coffee in coffee shops never imaging that we might be presented with a cup of beans.

And yet, surely, the person who reads Austin as a theorist, albeit charitably, will say, there are oodles of things that we do with our words when it seems a stretch to say that we rely on the sort of convention that would have to be integral to an Austinian theory of speech acts. Suppose that you are my superior at work. I rely on my job to get by. You don't seem to like me very much, and you don't take criticism well. I notice that you've made a mistake on some project that you have to present to our higher-ups. I bring it to your attention as delicately as I can, but you dismiss what I have to say and I give up. Later on, you get called on the carpet for the mistake and you are furious with me for not alerting you to the problem. Do you have a point? Did I alert you? Did I try to alert you? Are there conventions here? Is the notion of conventions going to help us decide these questions? I ask these rhetorical questions because it seems to me that they may be hard to answer definitively in a case such as the one I've sketched out.

And then there is the question of whether convention is really what distinguishes illocution from perlocution. A woman is about to give a speech in front of a thousand people, and five minutes before-hand her dearly beloved husband informs her that he is leaving her for another woman. Perhaps we don't want to say that the husband commits the act of causing his wife distress by "convention." But aren't we very close to this territory? That is, don't we expect the husband to know that this act is almost guaranteed to devastate his wife?

These sorts of problems about the notion of convention are virtu-ally inevitable, I think, if you are out to evaluate *How to Do Things with Words* as a piece of theory. But they recede in importance if we resist the temptation to sublime Austin's use of the concept of con-vention, to take it as a technical theoretical term. Conventions of language for Austin are, roughly speaking (and Austin continually reminds us that he sees himself speaking "loosely" and "roughly"), what we are inclined to say (and do) in certain circumstances, not what is stipulated or set in stone. By convention, colloquium presen-tations in the Philosophy Department at Tufts take place on Friday afternoons at 3 p.m. That they may sometimes happen at other times does not touch this fact. When Austin distinguishes illocu-tion from perlocution using "convention" as a pivot, what he is saying is something like this: if you want to perform a certain illo-cutionary act, you are as likely as not to find that there are certain conventions for doing so at your disposal. If you want to warn your boss that he has made a mistake, you can avail yourself of the con-vention of using the explicit performative formula, "I warn you:

you've made a mistake there." That you are ill disposed to do this, that your attempt at warning is far more subtle, means only that there will be some fuzziness about exactly what act you have undertaken. But that's exactly the outcome that the person with the jerky boss wants—and that we should therefore expect.

What about the idea that perlocutions are not "conventional," when we reflect on this idea nontheoretically? It seems to me that when Austin makes this claim he is not gesturing at the idea that there are no almost-certain ways to provoke people in the ways you might wish to provoke them. Rather, he is pointing at the extent to which, when it comes to perlocutionary effects, there are no conventions about *how we assign responsibility* for what has happened. This is why different jurors hearing the same evidence for and against a defendant can reasonably disagree. It's why using words in general is as complicated as it is. You order your young child to go to bed, and he starts to sob. How do you construe what has happened here? Did you succeed in your intention to order? Or did you do something else? Whose fault is it that the child is so broken up? Is it appropriate to bring up the notion of fault under these circumstances? (And what are the criteria for appropriateness here?) Is the sobbing a reasonable response to the order? (And who decides what counts as reasonable?) Does the sobbing demand a response from you? Are you obliged to respond with sympathy, of any amount or kind? How does one decide what counts as an explanation of what has happened?

How to Do Things with Words suggests that these are the sorts of questions that are pressed, at every turn, on those of use who are consigned to use language. Indeed, it follows from what Austin says that anyone who does not recognize implicitly that such questions bear on what exchanging words with other people amounts to, or has no idea how to handle such questions, may be at a loss genuinely to use language at all.

Illocution and Meaning

It's conceivable that what I've said here will have convinced a philosopher of language that Austin cannot be construed merely as a philosopher who did "pragmatics" in a certain way. But I imagine that I will not have convinced, or maybe ever could convince, such a philosopher to take seriously that last claim I made, about what people have to be able to do genuinely to use language at all. In what follows, I wish only to make more patent why I care so much about these matters.

I'm going to start by telling you a true story about a boy I know. He has an incapacity, perhaps locatable at what gets called the "high-functional" end of the autistic spectrum, that's characterized by what I would describe as an attenuated ability to ask or answer questions about what people are doing with their words. Like many such children, Johnny has a huge vocabulary and an impressive ability to perform all sorts of calculations, even though he has a certain difficulty finding his way around in social space. Once, for instance, a few summers ago, when Johnny was nine years old and my family and his were on vacation together, he began to pick flowers from the hotel's quite magnificent garden. His grandmother said to him, "Johnny, you're a big boy; you know that you shouldn't pick those flowers." But Johnny did not understand what she was saying. He took her to be stating facts about how things are in the world: he's a big boy; he possesses a piece of knowledge about his lack of a right to pick the hotel's flowers. So of course he continued to pick the flowers because he didn't understand that someone who says "you shouldn't pick those flowers" means "stop picking those flowers." His grandmother, realizing that he hadn't understood, said, firmly, "Johnny, stop picking the flowers." To this, Johnny turned around and giggled. He took what was said to him as a witticism, on the order of "stop being so cute." Now, at this stage in his childhood, as he observed and processed the ways in which other people were different from him, he was beginning to understand that sometimes people say things to which the concept *ironic* applies. Trouble is, he had tremendous difficulty distinguishing ironic from non-ironic uses of language. Sometimes, he used people's reactions as a way of figuring out what was going on. But other times he just preemptively guessed. And when he was wrong, as he often was, and as he was in this instance, he couldn't figure out what happened.

Johnny's troubles were heart-rending. Often when he did grasp the illocutionary force of an utterance correctly—that is, when his understanding of an illocution raised the same issues as it does for people who don't have the disability he has—it was because he had *figured out* what someone's words were doing. This means that, though it is not flat-out wrong to say that he understood what someone was saying—he did so, I'm inclined to put it, at a distance, as though he were a scientist studying a phenomenon rather than a participant in it. He got it, sometimes, that he at first didn't get it, that he had had to think about it and use other cues to understand what was going on, that he hadn't gotten it directly. And this indirection often translated into a certain failure of responsiveness; when he did have a sense of what his next move should be, it often came off, to recur to one of Austin's terms of art, as hollow.

I have claimed that the usual appropriation of Austin's thought, even by people who are keen to endorse it, ironically rends imperceptible to such people the illocutionary force of their own speech and writing. Now I can say: it's as though they willfully put themselves in Johnny's position. Sometimes, the problem is that, in their zeal to theorize, they exempt themselves from the task of attempting really to see what is going on, as though they couldn't possibly be surprised again and again by the phenomena they are writing about. For political purposes, it may be necessary to take a certain stance on an issue—say, to declare that pornography is harmful to women. But if philosophers desire to get people who strike them as obtuse or cruel or brainwashed or apathetic or just plain wrong to reconsider their views, then, for political purposes, we are going to have to think about whether developing theories to defend stances is what we are called to do. This is not because nonphilosophers are wont to find theory boring or esoteric. It's because in failing to attend carefully to how real people actually speak or what phenomena in the world (pornography, say) are actually like, what we say is, at worst, wrong and, at best, hollow.

Sometimes, the problem is not so much theory-mongering as it is a profound lack of interest in the illocutionary force of philosophical discourse. Actually, it's worse than that: it does not occur to contemporary philosophers to ask themselves: what are my words doing? This is in part a question about the audience for philosophical work. But it also concerns the issue of what sorts of illocutions philosophy is suited to perform, of the role of what you might call *style* in philosophical writing.[20] These days, anyone who thinks about this issue is told that she is doing "metaphilosophy." This is not quite a dirty word, but the attitude of the profession for the most part is that regular old in-the-trenches philosophy, preferably performed cottage-industry-style, is what produces results. Doing metaphilosophy is, at best, a lower priority. This stance, I'm suggesting, rests on the idea that I take Austin to be contesting in *How to Do Things with Words*, namely, that you can understand what words mean without grasping what they're doing. It's like claiming that the attenuation in Johnny's capacity to grasp what others' words are doing do has no bearing on his understanding of what they mean. Only what is a disability in Johnny's case is, I am judging, a failure on the part of philosophers. And insofar as this failure consists in a robust lack of interest in what actual people's utterances mean in actual circumstances, it amounts, to say the least, to a willingness to empty our own discourse of illocutionary force and, therefore, of human weight.

Postscript

At least in its analytic incarnation, philosophy these days is a decidedly theoretical enterprise—so much so that its practitioners are likely to wonder what the point of saying that philosophy is a decidedly theoretical enterprise could possibly be. What I intend to do here is make plain the point and why it bears pondering.[21]

In using the word *theory* I have in mind something pretty rough and ready: an attempt to describe and explain phenomena systematically in an internally consistent way that mandates or predicts what should or will happen in relevant future cases. So a systematic story about how human beings (or maybe "rational" beings), present and future, ought to act counts, on my definition, as a normative ethical theory. A story about how languages, analyzed into their generic component parts, do what they do ("hook on to the world," refer, bear meanings, accomplish things) counts as a theory of language. And so on.

Philosophers at present have a great deal of confidence in theory. Specifically, they trust that theory in philosophy (1) is possible—

that is, that it's reasonable to think that we might arrive in philosophy at a theory that is just as potent and as likely to produce an impressive degree of convergence among experts as is a good scientific theory—and (2) is important—that we will be able to know or do something that it is desirable to know or do if we develop a good philosophical theory.

Philosophers do not like to dwell on the fact that several millennia of work have not produced any theory on which there has been an impressive degree of convergence, that is, one that is best explained by the conjecture that the theory is true.[22] Philosophers also do not like to ask themselves what exactly might be gained by the production of such a theory. Indeed, they tend to get testy when you ask them to think about these issues, though occasionally they venture to do so.

One such venture was recently undertaken by Timothy Williamson, who currently occupies what is probably the most distinguished chair in the universe of professional philosophy, namely, the Wykeham professorship of logic at Oxford. In an article in an anthology called *The Future for Philosophy*, Williamson makes much of his chair and notes with pride that he has inherited it from the likes of A. J. Ayer, Michael Dummett, and David Wiggins, all of whom, he thinks, have made great strides in the enterprise of preparing human beings to make serious philosophical progress. Williamson claims that the present lack of a certain kind of theoretical progress in philosophy can be explained by the relatively recent development of its most powerful tool, predicate logic, which provides us with "a sharpness of philosophical vision unobtainable by other means."[23] Williamson is convinced that as we get more adept at using this tool, certain age-old tough nuts will get cracked—for example, the problem of vagueness. To show how helpful logic is at making theoretical progress with respect to such problems, Williamson considers the following example:

Suppose that there was once plenty of water on the planet Mars; it was clearly not dry. Ages passed, and very gradually the water evaporated. Now Mars is clearly dry. No moment was clearly the first on which it was dry or the last on which it was not. For a long intermediate period it was neither clearly dry nor clearly not dry. . . . We may wonder whether it was either. We ask ourselves: Was Mars always either dry or not dry?[24]

This question, Williamson notes, is "simple, non-technical, [and] non-metarepresentational."[25] And yet "in order to give an adequately reflective answer" to it, he tries to demonstrate, we must "adjudicate between complex, technical [i.e., logic-driven], metarepresentational theories." Williamson's contempt for anyone who would deny this conclusion is unvarnished: "Impatience with the long haul of technical reflection is a form of shallowness, often thinly disguised by histrionic advocacy of depth. Serious philosophy is always likely to bore those with short attention-spans."[26]

When he introduces the Mars dryness issue, Williamson observes that we can take an interest in it not because solving the problem will serve any "urgent practical purpose" but because "we should like to know the history of Mars."[27] But I do not think it is going out on a limb to claim (1) that no philosopher interested in vagueness is interested, *as a philosopher*, in the specific question of whether Mars was always either dry or not dry; and (2) that no one interested in the history of Mars is going to be worried about whether Mars was neither dry nor not dry during what Williamson calls the "long intermediate period." The nonphilosopher might well be interested in whether Mars could support life during that period, or whether and why the water dried up in an irregular way, or whether the amount of water waxed and waned. But the question of whether Mars was always either dry or not dry is an instantiation of a general philosophical problem that holds no interest whatsoever for Martian history buffs, per se.

Despite the window-dressing, then, Williamson has not motivated his attention to the problem of vagueness. He simply assumes that it is a real problem and that it is philosophically interesting. Williamson is of course welcome to take an interest in anything he likes and hasn't the slightest obligation to justify his interests to those who don't share them. But he certainly has not earned his rebuke toward those who are impatient "with the long haul of technical reflection." These impatient folk may not have short attention spans or suffer from boredom with serious philosophy or be of shallow character. They may simply not understand why Williamson and his fellows are willing to devote many hours to solving problems the interest and solvability of which are not manifest to them.

Let us put the solvability issue aside for the moment and ask whether the interest of the problem of vagueness can be made more manifest than Williamson has made it. The problem of how to understand what's going on with vague predicates has been around for almost the entire history of Western philosophy, since Eubulides of Melitus, a contemporary of Aristotle's, first articulated the so-called Sorites paradox. This fact alone might provide at least preliminary support for the idea that vagueness is an interesting and important problem.

The Sorites paradox (the word *Sorites* means "of heaps" in Greek), famously, is this: one grain of sand does not constitute a heap; neither do two or three. But how many grains do you have to add until you get a heap? Where do you draw the line? Is it plausible that *n* grains do not a heap make, but *n* + 1 grains do? Now suppose that you have something you'd be willing to call a heap. Take away one grain, and it's still a heap. Eventually, you're not going to be willing to call it a heap anymore. But, again, where do you draw a plausible line?

Before I respond to that question, I want to underscore (contra Williamson, in his attempt to motivate the Mars-dryness problem) its complete lack of practical importance. In real-life instances, we sometimes are not sure, or disagree about, where to put the line between *x* and not-*x* or the lines between *x* and not-*x* and neither-*x*-nor-not-*x*. But such cases are not generic. We do not resolve them—we are not tempted to try to resolve them—by appeal to a *theory* of vagueness. Neither does their resolution yield such a theory. For the philosopher, any "vague predicate" will do; favorites include baldness, human tallness, and childhood, as well as heaps and dryness. But what determines how real-life cases get settled is invariably specific. Thinking about vagueness is general gets us nowhere. Rather, what matters, always, are a case's specific features, such as what the people involved care about, what's at stake, what's fashionable, and who has the power to decide such things.[28]

Take the question of when a child legally becomes an adult. The case is obviously Sorites-like insofar as it involves the application of a predicate the borderlines of which we feel obliged to sharpen, even though there are no indisputable criteria for doing so and even though no one believes that a person becomes drastically different the minute she becomes an adult in the eyes of the law. We feel pressured to establish a sharp legal line between childhood and adulthood not because we have a general interest in keeping the boundaries between these concepts sharp but because we (or at least many people) feel we need to put limits on when people can drive, vote, buy alcohol, and so forth. We know that there are lots of places at which we could draw such a line—that there is a range of ages within which locating the line would be tolerable and ranges outside of this range at which it would not be. However, the relative arbitrariness of the place at which the line is drawn is something we understand we all have to live with. The drawing of a line does not strike us as intolerably arbitrary, in the way that drawing a line in the $n + 1$ grains of sand problem does. This is in part because we (or at least the powers-that-be, past and present) feel that we *need* a line between adulthood and childhood and in part because we have ways of getting around the line when need be—as when we allow the courts to try a teenager "as an adult" or when we abstain from condemning or punishing a mentally challenged adult who does not have the cognitive capacity to understand that what he just did was wrong.[29]

Indeed, for every one of the philosopher's examples of vagueness, there's a potential real-life cognate that will have nothing in common with the philosopher's generic use of the relevant predicate. Suppose I ask you to put a heap of mashed potatoes on our guest's plate, and the tablespoon you give him strikes me as not making the grade. It's inconceivable that any theoretical apparatus could ever settle the question of whether you in fact did what I asked you to do. Instead, what you and I might talk about are things like how much people typically eat, what it's polite to serve a guest, what *heap* usually means when it is used to talk about how much food to give someone, and so forth. We may not be able to resolve our difference, but neither one of us will be tempted to look for answers in a general theory of vagueness.

The point is that anyone who takes an interest in the Sorites paradox is going to do so not because life calls for a theory of vagueness but for reasons that are completely internal to a certain way of proceeding in the practice of philosophy. Despite its ancient history, however, the reasons people worry about the Sorites are not as deeply entrenched as philosophy students these days may be led to believe. It may surprise those who find the Sorites and other problems and paradoxes of vagueness unavoidable to learn that we find no discussions of these issues throughout most of the history of Western philosophy, from Aristotle until the early twentieth century. (I will not speculate about the reasons for this absence but will point out only that it indicates that the problem of vagueness did not exercise humankind for at least two of it's 2.5-millennia existence.)

Williamson's agenda in his Mars paper renders unsurprising the revelation that what revivified the problem was the development of predicate logic, which allows you to cast the following argument in formally valid terms (and in various forms of those terms):

Premise: One grain of sand does not a heap make.
Premise: If x grains of sand do not a heap make, then $x + 1$
grains do not a heap make.
Conclusion: Therefore, 100,000 grains of sand do not a heap make.

The conclusion here seems obviously false. But where does the argument go wrong? The first premise seems indubitable. But if we reject the second premise, then we are committed to the implausible claim that there is some precise x such that $x - 1$ is not a heap but x, $x + 1$, $x + 2 \ldots x + n$ are.[30] A nonphilosopher might find this problem to be of a certain intellectual interest. But for a contemporary philosopher of language, it constitutes a threat. The reason is that the contemporary philosopher of language is interested in coming up with a formal theory—that is, one that works with predicates with precise extensions—that explains how natural languages do what they do. Because there are lots and lots of vague predicates in language, the Sorites looms everywhere. So if we can't solve the Sorites, then the theorizing enterprise appears to be threatened.

The early logicians—Bertrand Russell in particular—did not feel this threat because they had more modest aspirations than do contemporary philosophers of language. Frege and Russell had no interest in generating a formal semantic theory of *natural* language. Their goal was to use logic to develop an *ideal* language. In his 1923 paper "Vagueness," Russell says,

> In an accurate language, meaning would be a one-one relation; no word would have two meanings, and no two words would have the same meaning. In actual languages, as we have seen, meaning is one-many. (It happens often that two words have the same meaning, but this is easily avoided, and can be assumed not to happen without injuring the argument.) That is to say, there is not only one object that a word means, and not only one possible fact that will verify a proposition. The fact that meaning is a one-many relation is the precise statement of the fact that all language is more or less vague.[31]

For Frege and Russell, then, the Sorites problem was a nonissue. *Of course* (thought they) expressions of natural language are vague. But if you aspire to use logic to come up with a general theory of natural language, then the Sorites will loom large for you.

This brief discussion of the Sorites suggests that for contemporary philosophers of language the interest in the vagueness problem is a function of a deeper interest in the project of using formal logic to generate a general theory of natural language (and not a function, that means, of various particular real-world interests in the history of Mars, the age of consent, hirsuteness, and so on). But now the impatient person that Williamson has in mind has reason to ask why he or she ought to find *this* project interesting.

~ 7

On Philosophical Authority

$\mathscr{I}$N CHAPTER 6, I argued that philosophers have under-estimated the radicality of Austin's project in *How to Do Things with Words*. Austin, as I see it, was not trying in that book to point to an interesting project—"pragmatics"—that one might pursue after, or in tandem with, the project of doing natural-language semantics, conceived as the project of limning the literal meanings of all sentences of English or any other language. For Austin, there is no such thing as the literal meaning of a sentence—I mean, the literal meaning *simpliciter*, as something that every well-formed sentence of a natural language possesses prior to its employment in some context or another. (To speak of the literal meaning of a sentence is, for Austin, to have at least one contrasting metaphorical use in mind.) Indeed, for Austin it's precisely talk of the "literal meaning" of sentences that leads philosophers to imagine that semantics is something that can be done a priori. As I put it on p. 88 of Chapter 6, Austin's aim was not to enliven, enrich, or expand what philosophers call pragmatics. It was to destroy the picture of language on which an independent enterprise called "pragmatics" makes any sense at all.

Austin launches *How to Do Things with Words* on the premise that at least some sentences, those he calls "constatives," have literal meanings that are indeed productively analyzable apart from pragmatic considerations. Such sentences are to be contrasted with what he calls "performatives," a vital feature of which is their capacity to do things when used in the correct context. But—crucially—Austin finds after a few chapters that this distinction is unstable, that no sentence is inherently a constative or a performative. He then calls for what he calls a "fresh start" to "help us out of our tangle" and begins talking about the various dimensions of *all* of our sentences.[1] He homes in on their (inevitable) performative aspect, which he now calls their "illocutionary force." But this is *not* a fancy name for what pragmatics is interested in.[2] To the contrary, it identifies a feature of our sentences apart from which they not only would not do anything but also would not *mean* anything. All meaningful utterances, Austin suggests, are at least attempts at illocutions. Perhaps Austin's understanding of illocution will not, at the end of the day, turn out to merit our endorsement. But when it comes to reading Austin, it's not even the beginning of the day: as a profession, philosophy has yet to grasp what Austin is claiming—and, thereby, according to his lights, doing—let alone to provide grounds for dismissing his view.[3]

In Chapter 5, I discussed some of the ways that Austin's work has been taken up, along the standard lines, by philosophers who see in it a ground of support for Catharine MacKinnon's oft-maligned claim that pornography discriminates against women by subordinating and silencing them and therefore should not be protected by free-speech laws.[4] Simply put, the project is to use *How to Do Things with Words* to vindicate the coherence of the idea that pornography not only says problematic things that lead to the harming of women but also inherently constitutes a form of harm—a form, these philosophical supporters think Austin helps us see, that is a product of its illocutionary force. My goal in the present chapter is not to weigh in on the viability of MacKinnon's position. Rather, I wish to draw attention to the question of what exactly the philosophers who wish to use Austin to defend the coherence of this position are in fact doing. My view is that their thoroughgoing lack of interest in the illocutionary force of their own words prevents these philosophers from noticing the extent to which these words are not doing what they assume they are doing. This would mean that in their attempts to use Austin to argue that pornography is inherently harmful these philosophers have, ironically enough, evinced the same ignorance or repression about how words do things that, as I argued in Chapter 6, it was Austin's central project to combat.

In worrying about the illocutionary force of the words of philosophers who want to vindicate MacKinnon by drawing our attention to the illocutionary force of pornography, I do not mean to be suggesting that the project these philosophers have taken on is more problematic than the projects of other philosophers who have imagined that a good thing for philosophers to do when it comes to policy debates is challenge or support the coherence of a given position. For it is now common for philosophers to assume that pretty much all positions stand in need of a kind of justificatory bolstering and that this activity is the special provenance of the philosopher, who brings a singular sort of expertise to the enterprise. The philosopher's particular talent is to clarify what exactly is at stake in a debate, to point out the lack of soundness and validity in arguments, to bring to light the questionable assumptions on which a position is based.[5] I do not know of an instance in which a philosopher writing about pornography has articulated or otherwise acknowledged the assumption that the position he endorses will not be fully shored up apart from his exercise of skill. Indeed, philosophers routinely write as though there is no question as to the importance of their acts of attempted justification for their arguments and positions.

We see the same attenuation of thoughtfulness that, I am about to show, MacKinnon's philosophical supporters evince about what philosophical speech is and does throughout the range of attempts to "apply" philosophy to various real-world debates—and, for that matter, throughout philosophy period. I focus here on the attempt to lend MacKinnon a philosophical hand only because, in their appropriation of Austin, an attenuated appropriation that I am claiming is typical, the writings I have in mind bring out the ramifications of the philosopher's lack of interest in how philosophy does things—and in how, at least on Austin's view, it could do things—with particular force and clarity and with respect to a set of issues on which I wish we philosophers could weigh in more helpfully, namely, those concerned with women's sexual experience, autonomy, and safety.

 ❧ I DON'T SUPPOSE that anyone will deny that most philosophical writing these days has little to do with the vicissitudes of public policy. But I don't think we generally construe this fact as a threat to the theoretical integrity of what we do. After all, there are at least two sets of circumstances external to what it is to do philosophy that might account for philosophy's modest influence. First, there is the current state of the world. We live in an era in which people are bombarded with effusions of culture that are almost invariably more seductive and easier to digest than is philosophy. Perhaps in part in response to this bombardment, people seem more and more to be taking refuge in fundamentalisms of various forms and are therefore becoming even more deadened than usual to the power of reason. Second, there is the state of the profession of philosophy. As philosophy over the past one hundred years or so has become increasingly sophisticated and specialized, so has philosophical writing, which is now unavoidably beyond the ken of nonprofessionals, who lack not only the training to grasp it but also a familiarity with "the literature." The *New York Times* "Stone" philosophy column aside, those of us who have the aspiration to find a way of reaching the public are likely to be waylaid by the heavy demands of academic life, not least those that must be met if one is retain a foothold in one's profession. In any event, these observations appear to entail a counterfactual: if people would and could pay attention to philosophy, they would recognize the unique and vital way in which it grounds ethical and political positions.

My position is that this counterfactual is false. I regard the effeteness of our position-bolstering activities as a sign that we philosophers have, to our own and our culture's peril, lost sight of what philosophy is, what it is good for, and what it can do. Our persistent attempts to buttress one or another political or ethical position with philosophical argumentation ironically divert us from having a say in the world. I have emphasized in my writing on Simone de Beauvoir— from whom, on my view, we still have much to learn about the relationship between philosophy and social criticism—that our failure even to recognize the irrelevance of contemporary philosophy in the culture at large is especially lamentable when it comes to feminist interventions in the discipline.[6] For to be worthy of the name feminists must care deeply about making the world a less sexist place, must be committed to serious and thoroughgoing social transformation. A feminist therefore cannot afford to commit herself, consciously or mindlessly, to a form of writing that systematically fails to constitute genuine, and genuinely efficacious, cultural criticism.

This means that feminist philosophers cannot afford to write in the way the profession encourages, that is to say, as though our authority as thinkers were somehow identical with our cultural authority, as though the sheer rationality of our ideas and argumentation ought to be enough to effect change. Crudely put, the attitude—the unexamined, unexpressed attitude—that feminists must consciously reject is this: if rationality can be shown to dwell beyond doubt on the side of a certain viewpoint, then all rational creatures ought to be won over to that viewpoint; those people who resist it are, regrettably, either deficient in their cognitive powers, stubbornly incoherent, or otherwise beyond the reach of reason.

This attitude is a version of scientism, on which the job of the philosopher, like that of the scientist, is to pose and then solve various problems in such a way that all well-informed and reasonable people will converge on the revealed truth. Whether any version of what I am calling scientism is appropriate for science itself is not my subject. All I need here is the simple fact that, in sharp contrast to the state of affairs in the sciences, no substantive thesis proffered in the history of the Western incarnation of our craft has enjoyed anything resembling universal assent. And yet we willfully ignore the fact that no philosopher has gotten a "result" on which the rest of us, even in any given era or by the lights of any given philosophical "paradigm," agree. We remain relentlessly scientistic even in the face of philosophy's stunning lack of success by the lights of any science. In assuming that our writing is contributing to philosophical progress—in assuming that there *is* such a thing as philosophical progress, at least construed on analogy with scientific progress—we render ourselves insensitive both to the present effeteness and the potential power of our words.[7]

But if we are not making scientific progress when we philosophize, then what are we doing? We find a compelling alternative understanding of philosophy at the very inception of the practice, in Plato's early dialogues, in which Socrates suggests that the goal of philosophy is to get people to see the value in attending to and questioning their settled understanding of what they are doing in and with their lives. It follows that the task that the philosopher should aim to become especially good at is not theorizing about what rationality demands but finding ways to attract individuals, idiosyncrasies and all, to undertake for themselves the task of investigating what it is to be rational. This task is described in particularly memorable terms in the famous "allegory of the cave" in Book VII of the *Republic*. "Education," Socrates claims,

> isn't what some people declare it to be, namely, putting knowledge into souls that lack it, like putting sight into blind eyes. . . . The power to learn is in everyone's soul. . . . The instrument with which each learns is like an eye that cannot be turned around from darkness to light without turning the whole body. . . . Education is the craft concerned with doing this very thing, this turning around, and with how the soul can most easily and effectively be made to do it. It isn't the craft of putting sight into the soul. Education takes for granted that sight is there, but that it isn't turned the right way or looking where it ought to look, and it tries to redirect it appropriately.[8]

Here Socrates characterizes philosophy as aiming not to "put knowledge into souls" but, rather, on the assumption that "the power to learn is present in everyone's soul," to *redirect* the soul's sight. It's not that the soul of one who stands to benefit from philosophy is defective or deficient; it's that such a soul is turned the wrong way, toward the darkness rather than the light. Philosophy, which Socrates figures as a kind of education, is the craft of effecting this turning.

The conversion that Socrates is calling for in Book VII of the *Republic* is not one of faith. It is a turning from mindlessness to thoughtfulness, from dogmatism to self-scrutiny, from habit to deliberateness. To become invested in this kind of conversion is not to adopt a new outlook on the world once and for all but to understand oneself as standing in endless need of discovering what rationality demands in one's own case, in one's own thought and life, and thereby to attempt to avoid succumbing to the temptations of smugness and self-petrifaction. On Socrates' understanding, the philosopher's special talent, her singular role in the world, is not to produce arguments that buttress one position or another on any given issue, arguments that can be packaged and sold to those interested in speaking on the side of reason. (The philosopher is not, as Socrates would put it, a mere sophist.) Rather, the philosopher is to understand rationality as something that each individual must discover in and for himself, in his own time, on his own terms.

Plato's Euthyphro, for instance, will not moved by any generic argument about what piety is. For he has a massive investment in a conception of piety that will exonerate him from charges that he acted impiously in accusing his father of committing murder. Socrates will not, therefore, employ argumentation either to bolster Euthyphro's position or to lay out and defend a new one. Instead he will attempt to *lead* Euthyphro, in all his specificity, to see the irrationality in his own conception of piety. Of course, more times than not, and certainly in the case of Euthyphro, Socrates' success backfires: his confounded interlocutors (and, often, frustrated readers) turn on him with rage and demand that he give them an account of the phenomena they now find themselves flummoxed about. One can draw from this response the moral that Socrates is himself a poseur, someone who either knows nothing and therefore has no business rattling other people or who knows something but ironically, perversely, refuses to share it with others. The implication here is that a "philosopher" like Socrates does not deserve an audience. But I understand the figure of Socrates to stand for the warning that philosophy cannot assume an audience for itself—cannot, in other words, count on the sheer force of reason, construed in generic terms, to guarantee its authority.[9]

The cultural authority that philosophy enjoys, or fails to enjoy, I am claiming, rests on nothing more—or less—that the individual philosopher's powers to incite interest in thinking. Philosophers abrogate these powers when they write as though their authority were coextensive with the authority of reason itself and therefore self-evident. And this abrogation of philosophical authority, this debasing of it, is often evident in the manner in which philosophers weigh in on the subject of pornography.

Let me turn again to the paper of Rae Langton's titled "Speech Acts and Unspeakable Acts," one in a series that Langton has written on how to understand what pornography is and does.[10] I am interested in this paper for two reasons. First, it exemplifies what, at least by the current standards of the profession, a philosophy paper is supposed to be. This is to say that it (1) articulates a question of precisely circumscribed scope ("Is MacKinnon's position incoherent?") and then (2) provides an answer to this question ("No") via a thorough and comprehensive argument that never strays beyond the bounds of what reason itself might be said to demand. The paper also (3) anticipates and responds to potentially serious objections, all the while (4) reminding the reader of the important issues that lie beyond its scope and its author's expertise. Second, Langton—now a philosophy professor at the University of Cambridge and one of the relatively few women who have enjoyed real success in the profession—demonstrated remarkable courage in bringing her analytic talents to bear on a highly controversial issue of importance to feminists. Indeed, in her writing on pornography Langton has been expressly interested in taking on certain very powerful men in the profession—specifically, Thomas Nagel and Ronald Dworkin—who had accused MacKinnon not only of incoherence but even of squeamishness about sex.[11] I admire, more than I can say, Langton's considerable talent and bravery. My concern is that these virtues are perhaps being channeled in the wrong direction.

It may be helpful for me to get a sketch of what exactly worries me on the table before filling in the details. First, there is the fact that Langton explicitly understands herself to be underwriting a particular political position. Second, Langton's act of underwriting takes the ironic form of her straightforwardly "applying" bits and pieces of J. L. Austin's *How to Do Things with Words* to the question of how pornography does whatever it does. (This form of appropriating Austin—and it is the typical form—is ironic because it amounts to the application of familiar forms of philosophical argumentation and technical terminology to new "problems"—precisely what, as I argued in Chapter 6, Austin is decrying in his book.) Third, although Langton has much to say about the authority of pornography, she does not ponder the nature of the authority that would allow her or any other philosopher to weigh in on the pornography debates. This is surprising, since she is explicitly interested in the question of what it is to have authority in the culture and what can and cannot be done with that authority. In particular, she sees that everything she says about pornography's ability to constitute a kind of subordination and silencing depends fundamentally on pornography's (or sometimes she says pornograph*ers'*) cultural authority. But she evinces no interest in thinking about the role of her own arrogation of authority in the attempt to undermine the authority of pornography. In other words, her explicit interest in what cultural authority is and how it is appropriated does not extend to an interest in understanding the cultural authority she is out to arrogate via her own act of writing.

Recall what Langton takes herself to be doing in "Speech Acts and Unspeakable Acts." She begins by accepting the definition of pornography proposed by MacKinnon and other feminists in various attempts to make pornography's production and proliferation civilly actionable. Pornography, on this definition, is material that depicts women

> dehumanized as sexual objects, things or commodities; enjoying pain or humiliation or rape; being tied up, cut up, mutilated, bruised, or physically hurt; in postures of sexual submission or servility or display; reduced to body parts, penetrated by objects or animals, or presented in scenarios of degradation, injury, torture; shown as filthy or inferior; bleeding, bruised or hurt in a context which makes these conditions sexual.[12]

MacKinnon's claim is that in depicting women as such, pornography not only depicts their subordination but in fact *constitutes* "the graphic sexually explicit subordination of women in pictures or words." In a parallel way, she insists that pornography not only causes women not to speak up for themselves but *constitutes* a curtailment of their freedom to speak.[13] These two claims—that pornography in and of itself subordinates and silences women—have come under heavy attack. And Langton's goal is to "exploit" the work of Austin in *How to Do Things with Words* to "vindicate an argument that has been dismissed as philosophically incoherent," to show that rationality is in fact on MacKinnon's side.[14] What Austin shows us is that we use speech not just to express our opinions and attempt to persuade others to fall in line with them. He shows us that virtually all coherent stretches of speech have "illocutionary force": they routinely do things other than simply express opinions, and they do these things in and of themselves, apart from any audience reactions they happen to elicit.[15]

Now, by the standards of professional philosophy it must be counted a virtue that Langton evidently sees herself as playing a very carefully circumscribed role with respect to a certain feminist antipornography position: what she imagines she can do, in her capacity as a philosopher, is, simply, to remove a stumbling block—a charge of philosophical incoherence—from the path of MacKinnon and like-minded activists. In fact, Langton says at the end of the introductory section of the paper that she is aiming for a "modest result," namely to show that "the twin feminist claims [regarding the silencing and subordinating acts pornography inherently performs] are certainly coherent, and, granting some not entirely implausible empirical assumptions, they may well be true."[16] And yet, I submit, anyone who is committed in advance to the view that pornography should not be regulated is bound to find holes in generic arguments against this position, just as a Catharine MacKinnon is going to find any generic arguments in favor of it beyond the pale. Each camp is working with a radically different understanding of what the world is like and what role pornography plays in it. If you insist on framing one side's picture in terms of premises, the other side is bound to reject them. I am about to say more about why I make these claims. But first, notice that I am *not* claiming that there is no way to get someone in one of these camps to change his or her mind. Nor am I claiming, à la Richard Rorty, that the only realistic way to change minds is through some method that must be identified as lying outside the purview of philosophy.[17] Rather, I am calling for philosophers to invest or perhaps reinvest themselves in a grander vision of our profession, our capacity to speak in an authoritative voice in our culture, our capacity to call ourselves and others to the task of serious reflection.

As Austin warns, and as Langton acknowledges, just saying a stretch of words does not guarantee that they will have illocutionary force. When, a number of years ago, my then-ten-year-old daughter's best friend intoned, "I now pronounce you husband and wife," while my daughter was dreamily staring at a photograph of Johnny Depp in *People* magazine, no act of marrying was achieved. Circumstances can be such that an illocution *misfires* or is *infelicitous*, to use Austin's terms of art. If circumstances had not been awry—if her best friend Zoe had been licensed to perform marriages in the state of Massachusetts, and if Anneliese had been unmarried and of age, and if Johnny Depp had also been unmarried and had been game to show up at the altar, as it were—then the words "I now pronounce you husband and wife" would have constituted, in and of themselves, an act of marrying. Unfortunately for Anneliese, however, circumstances were not in fact on her side.

As Langton readily acknowledges, just depicting sex, or even what some may regard as sexualized discrimination or violence, does not entail that the depictions have the illocutionary force of subordinating or silencing women. Even if pornography without question glorifies violence against women and ineluctably depicts women as inferior to men, it can't legitimate this violence or make its ranking count and thereby directly subordinate women except to the extent that it enjoys a certain authority in the culture. "Does pornographic speech have the authority required to substantiate MacKinnon's claim?" Langton asks.[18] Her answer at that juncture is that this is "not really [a question] to be settled from the philosopher's armchair." What we can't see from that chair, she specifies, is whether pornography is authoritative in "the domain of speech about sex," particularly for people who "want to know which moves in the sexual game are legitimate."

For Langton, when it comes to the question of whether pornography subordinates women, philosophy has done a respectable job once it has established the plausibility of the following claim: *if* pornography depicts women as ripe to be victims of violence and as inferior to men and *if* the views of pornographers are authoritative, then pornography can coherently be said to subordinate women. *Whether* pornography so depicts women and whether pornographers enjoy the requisite authority is a matter of (extra-philosophical) empirical investigation. This might sound straightforward enough. But exactly what sort of empirical investigation does Langton have in mind? How do you decide, "empirically," what pornography depicts? Obviously, you look at a lot of pornography. But of course people who have looked at a lot of pornography disagree dramatically about what they see. My point is that "empirical" investigation will get us nowhere when it comes to this question of deciding what pornography depicts.[19] Notice that this is not necessarily because there is no fact of the matter here. I'm not, that is to say, suggesting that at this point we run up against some sort of relativism. Rather, the problem is that whatever the fact of the matter is, no amount of disinterested investigation of the world will reveal it. The question of what pornography depicts and what it does is a matter of judgment, of how one sees what one sees. (If you are a contemporary philosopher, you might think that these matters are outside philosophy's purview. If you are Socrates, you will think that this is where philosophy starts.)[20]

Because empirical investigation is of course beyond the scope of her paper and her expertise, Langton suggests that we might shed light on the nature of pornographic authority if we analogize it to the authority of a sports referee: "Just as the speech of the umpire is authoritative within a certain domain—the game of tennis—so pornographic speech is authoritative within a certain domain—the game of sex."[21] Let us try to unpack this comparison. A game of tennis has institutionalized rules, for example, that when one player in a singles game hits the ball out of bounds after a successful serve, the other player gains in the score. The job of the umpire, again by virtue of the formal institutional position she holds, is to uphold the rules. To do this, the umpire has to judge what is going on in the game, to bring her powers of judgment—her skills and authority— to bear in specific instances. If the people who have the power to hire and fire her judge that her powers of judgment have declined, they may well relieve her of her duties.

Now, how to understand the analogy with "the game of sex"? We of course will need a vivid picture of what this term could mean. But whatever this picture turns out to look like, we can say in advance that "the game of sex" obviously has no institutionalized rules and appoints no institutionalized authority to set or judge them. If pornographers have some control over the game of sex, then their position of authority to set and referee its rules will be of a de facto sort; it will simply be the case that they will provide the norms that at least certain people—perhaps the majority of boys and men, even—follow as they make their way through the world sexually. An example of such a norm might be: "It's permissible for a man to force sex on any woman at any time because, despite appearances, all women secretly want them to do so." But then of course the question becomes: what makes men accept this norm? Given that sexual norms are not institutionalized in the way that tennis rules are, why would a man adopt a norm such as this instead of, say, "Rape is absolutely unacceptable"? Why would any man bestow authority on pornography? Once again, I submit, no amount of "empirical investigation" will yield a definitive answer to this question. Notice that I'm not saying that empirical investigation might not lead to some drug that prevents men from, for example, raping women. (Not that I'm holding my breath here.) What I'm saying is that to the extent that we view the issue in terms of bestowing authority, as Langton insists we must, no set of experiments is going to do the job. What is needed is a vision of how things are with the world that gives us to understand the sway certain people allow pornography or, for that matter, any entity not invested with institutionalized power—philosophy, perhaps?—to hold over their conduct.[22]

What kind of authority is necessary for a philosopher's vision of how things are with the world to hold sway? What is necessary, to put the question in Austinian terms, for the successful execution of a philosophical speech act? More fundamentally, what is a philosophical speech act? What sort of illocutionary force does a felicitous philosophical speech act wield? Under what conditions is such a speech act felicitous? Let us pose these questions in light of one of Langton's philosophical speech acts. At the climax of "Speech Acts and Unspeakable Acts" Langton writes: "The claim that pornography subordinates has good philosophical credentials: it is not trickery, or 'sleight of hand'; it is by no means 'philosophically indefensible.'"[23] What act is being attempted in this passage? Well, at this juncture in her article Langton is *epitomizing* a claim that she has been trying in the article to defend. She is also engaged in a further act of *claiming* (that the claim that pornography subordinates has good philosophical credentials). If we inspect the felicity conditions for such an act, we will not find that having authority is one of them. But we can say more about Langton's speech act than that she is lodging a claim. For isn't she trying to *legitimate* MacKinnon's view of the relationship between pornography and sexual subordination, to *rank* this claim as better justified than the claims that would purport to undermine it, and perhaps even to make it the case that the lodgers of these would-be undermining claims are *silenced* at the level of the success of their own illocutions—that their attempts to extol pornography will come off as unauthoritative? If so, then by her own lights these actions will misfire to the extent that she lacks the requisite authority. But what *is* the requisite sort of authority? What authorizes philosophical speech?

The obvious answer is: reason itself. But this answer begs the question of how reason, on any construal of the notion, gets its authority in the culture. All you have to do is look around to conclude that, contrary to the assumption that appears to pervade philosophical writing these days, the culture does not take reason's authority to be self-evident. Plato, for one, felt this state of affairs to be intolerable: on his view, any philosopher worthy of the name was obligated not just to commune with the forms but to come down from the mountaintop and attempt to attract the citizenry to the sublime, if almost imperceptible, beauty of reason. It was not enough for the philosopher to churn out journal articles on the mountaintop and hope that the hoi polloi would at some later date decide to take an interest in their acts of legitimating, ranking, and so on. To be a philosopher for Plato is to provide a vision of how things are with the world and to attempt to attract people to the project of recognizing themselves—or not, as the case may be—in this vision.

Aristotle agreed with Plato. So did the medievals, and so did any number of modern philosophers. In fact, it was not until the midtwentieth century that philosophy seems to have beaten a retreat to the proverbial ivy tower. Part of the impetus, of course, has been the increasing specialization and institutionalization of the discipline. But philosophers' relatively recent reluctance to worry about our authority in the culture also has nobler roots. It is to some extent a product of horror at the way their colleagues' work had been exploited by dangerous ideologues—how Marx's investment in humanizing humanity had given way to Stalinist Russia, how Nietzsche's celebration of human nature had provided grist for the mill of Hitler. The young Rudolph Carnap alludes to this horror in the preface to the *Aufbau*, as we see in the following passage:

> We cannot hide from ourselves the fact that trends from philosophical-metaphysical and from religious spheres, which protect themselves against [a scientific, rational, and anti-individualistic conception of philosophy], again exert a strong influence precisely at the present time. Where do we derive the confidence, in spite of this, that our call for clarity, for a science that is free from metaphysics, will prevail?—From the knowledge, or, to put it more cautiously, from the belief, that these opposing powers belong to the past.[24]

Vigorously progressive in his politics, committed to the ideals of socialism, and horrified by the elitism he saw in the metaphysics of, most prominently, his contemporary and compatriot Martin Heidegger, Carnap passionately believed that he was morally and politically obliged to treat philosophy as an at least potentially rigorous science. It is understandable, then, that Carnap in his day and age felt that the cost of philosophizing in the old way—the cost of attempting to arrogate cultural authority by the sheer act of writing—was simply too high. Philosophy was instead to take its carefully circumscribed place in a new world, one grounded not on the philosopher's personal metaphysical vision but on pure reason itself. The philosopher's goal, Carnap thought, was to employ reason to make progress on fundamental scientific questions of universal interest and importance. The social and political cost of construing the cultural role of philosophy otherwise, he claimed, was simply too high.

Carnap is to be lauded for his relentless thoughtfulness about what he was doing, within both philosophy and the wider world. My beef is neither with Carnap nor with the style of philosophizing he bequeathed to the next century. My worry, rather, is that Carnap's conception of philosophical reason has come apart from the reasons for his investment in it—that we have inherited his thought but not his thoughtfulness. (Crucially, I could say exactly the same thing about Freud or Wittgenstein or Kant as an ethicist.)

What I am in effect worrying about, then, is whether we can afford to continue to cleave to the narrow conceptions of philosophy we have inherited and their implicit claims to self-evident authority. I am not suggesting that we dumb philosophy down in order to rescue the masses. I am not advocating a return, or forward leap, to any particular style or form of philosophizing. I am not denying that we take tremendous political, social, and moral risks when we attempt to provoke other people to unsettle their settled opinions. I am not encouraging us to aim too high. But I *am* calling for us to commit ourselves to a grander, more ambitious, and more explicit expression of interest in the question of what it is that we *are* doing and what licenses our doing it. What would it look like for philosophy to issue an audible call for genuine thinking, to compete, that is, with the penchant for self-anesthetization that contemporary culture encourages? What would it look like for us to aspire above all to have a say in the world?

∼ 8

Getting Things Right

$\mathscr{I}$N THE FALL of 2011, Harvard University hosted a conference on "Philosophical Progress," which included a somewhat notorious and rather unpleasant session featuring Jason Stanley and Carlin Romano.[1] Stanley, at the time at Rutgers and now at Yale, is a well-known and influential philosopher who has worked mostly in the philosophy of language and epistemology. Romano, who holds an MA in philosophy from Yale, is a writer/critic who served as a book reviewer at the *Philadelphia Inquirer* for twenty-five years and was at the time of the conference critic-at-large for the *Chronicle of Higher Education*; he had also taught philosophy classes off and on and recently had been appointed appointed as a professor of philosophy and the humanities at Ursinus College.

The title of the Stanley–Romano session was "Philosophical Progress and Intellectual Culture," and the participants' charge was to talk about the relationship between professional philosophy and the wider world. Stanley spoke first and focused on how to understand the uneasy relationship that professional philosophy seems to have with the rest of the humanities. He stressed that philosophical topics and concerns are different from those of the other humanities, which makes communicating across disciplinary borders challenging. For example, when a metaphysician like Kit Fine talks about *essential* properties, he has in mind a meaning of the word that's different from its political inflection in nonphilosophical humanistic discussions of whether members of a certain social group—women, say—share some kind of essence, for example, being empathetic and nurturing.[2] Non-philosophers are therefore wont to misconstrue or fail to grasp the import of the matters that concern us philosophers and won't understand why we care about what we care about.

Most people, Stanley claimed, are not in a position to appreciate the progress we have been making in academic philosophy, which is in large part a function of the sophisticated technical tools that we've been able to develop in the relatively recent past.[3] The nature of the philosophical problems these powerful tools allow us to address is very difficult to communicate to the masses, not least because the connection of these tools to the everyday world is not patent. In fact, some of the progress we philosophers make, according to Stanley, takes the form of our proposing arguments that are in effect in search of an empirical basis—as when, for example, Jerry Fodor proposes a theory of mind that catches the attention of scientists who then make it their business to investigate whether the theory in fact has explanatory power, or when Ned Block's work is taken up in debates about the relationship between IQ and race, or when the metaphysical theorizing of Dean Zimmerman or Ted Sider influences theologians.

Stanley's articulation of this perspective seemed to exasperate Romano, who—by his own admission going somewhat off-script—vigorously took issue with Stanley's faith in the value of contemporary professional philosophy. Romano's goal, it seemed, was to deny that philosophy belongs to professional philosophers. Any person with the interest, he said, can engage in philosophy; announcing that he was quoting a recent UNESCO report, he claimed that "philosophy is anyone's business and no one's property."[4] At the same time, Romano implied that, ironically enough, (real) philosophy is *not* the business of professional philosophers, at least those who work in the "analytic" vein epitomized by Stanley's work. Accusing analytic philosophers of "intellectual fraud or phoniness" and hand-waving, literally and figuratively, at one of Stanley's books, Romano claimed that professional philosophers these days are failing to take account of the world as it is. You guys are talking only to each other, he said; you are arrogant and condescending, you write terribly, and what you do is pseudo-science. Professional philosophy is just plain *stupid*—as, Romano noted with glee, the Nobel Laureate physicist Richard Feynman was fond of saying.[5]

In an attempt to provide an example of professional philosophical knuckle-headedness, Romano quoted a sentence from Stanley's book. But in his mocking of Stanley's sentence Romano made two errors that were obvious to anyone with a decent training in the philosophy of language (and a fortiori to many of the conference attendees). He conflated two technical terms in philosophy (*implicate* and *imply*), and he seemed to either misunderstand or be ignorant of the work in philosophy of language that lies behind the passage he was exploiting.[6]

Not surprisingly, members of the audience, composed largely of philosophers residing in Stanley's intellectual neck of the woods, were in various ways offended by Romano's uninformed and contemptuous dismissal of Stanley's work and lashed out at Romano during the Q&A.[7] My own reaction was complicated. On the one hand, I had found Stanley's talk frustrating. I felt that he was preaching to the choir: laying out the usual defense of the value of doing philosophy the way it's done at the most powerful departments and published in the most prestigious journals in the profession—and avoiding engaging with the concerns of people whose approach to philosophy runs on another set of rails or with serious critics of the mainstream philosophical enterprise. On the other hand, I was frustrated and even a bit mortified by Romano's intervention, which struck me as an invitation to Stanley and fellow travelers to congratulate themselves on their rectitude and superiority.

I also felt some guilt. For in the early stages of putting the conference together the organizers had thought that it might be a good idea for *me* to be part of this session's mix. I think the idea was that, like both Stanley and Romano, I had written some journalistic pieces for the wider world (indeed, my first job out of college was reporting for *The Boston Globe*) and had spent a lot of my professional time thinking about what philosophy is and what it's good for. But unlike Stanley, I was explicitly worried about a certain intellectual myopia among mainstream professional philosophers—our tendency to imagine, without argumentation or perhaps even awareness, that when we use words in the everyday lexicon, such as *knowledge* or *truth* or *meaning* or *mind* or *morality*, in a technical sense we are talking about the phenomena that these words in their

everyday usages name. And unlike Romano, I was mostly a philosophy professor, rather than mostly a journalist, and therefore more
likely to be able to recognize and engage with, say, a claim about
conversational implicature.

So I could see why my being on the Stanley–Romano docket had
made some sense to the organizers. But when one of them had proposed the idea, I ran screaming in horror—though I phrased my
concerns somewhat more judiciously in declining the invitation:
"My guess is that, though the combo of CR, Jason, and me almost
certainly would be entertaining, and might even be enlightening, it
also could get pretty ugly. Not for personal reasons: Jason and I are
of course friends, and I've never met Romano. It's just that I imagine
that Jason and Romano will not be on exactly the same page, to put
the point mildly; and I'm a little worried about being the girl in the
middle trying to make peace."[8] What I was worried about, to put
the point less figuratively, was that both Stanley's and Romano's
talks would be inflected by a species of arrogance—distinct in each
case—that would overshadow whatever I said or did. Romano's
ignorance of and raw contempt for the topics that preoccupy contemporary professional philosophers was well known to me from his
writings.[9] Stanley's arrogance takes the form, in both his talk and
his work, of an implicit and undefended claim that it is not incum-
bent on—or at least critical for—professional philosophers to make
our work intelligible to other humanists, let alone to the hoi polloi.
To his credit, in recent years Stanley has begun writing essays for
popular audiences and, as I write, is working on a thought-provoking
book—draft chapters of which I have read—intended for a broad
audience on the subject of propaganda. But in speaking of "making
our work intelligible," I am talking about the assumption that what
is most central to what we as philosophers are doing—perhaps
because it relies on technical notions—is not worth trying to convey
to people who are not trained in our discipline.

What was bound to be at stake between Romano and Stanley at
the conference was essentially whose arrogance was worse. This, from
my point of view, was a tough call. Romano's well-known boorish-
ness was an easy target. But I'm also very much troubled by the common view in analytic circles that philosophy's incomprehensibility to

many outsiders is a function of its sophistication and not of its prac-titioners' intellectual priorities.

I'm not a young woman, and I don't make a habit of referring to myself as a "girl." My point in using that word in the email I refer-enced above was to suggest that if I were to say what I wanted to say about philosophical progress—namely, that one of its hallmarks is an acknowledgment of the arrogance that theorizing about funda-mental issues on the basis of "reason alone" courts—people would be likely to see me merely as a finger-wagger asking the boys to stop being so jerky.[10]

The downside of my declining to play that role was that I was given my own conference session, which meant that I had to produce a more substantive paper than I would have had to present as a panel member. This paper turned out to be difficult to write, in part because, aside from Romano, I think I may have been the only invitee who was not certain that the style of philosophizing for which people are paid the biggest salaries in the most illustrious philosophy depart-ments is superior to other ways of construing the enterprise. I felt I had to tread lightly, even though I was determined to say what I really thought about the state of our profession and to reflect seri-ously on what sort of progress philosophizing affords. At the same time, I wanted to think about the potential pertinence of questions about the gender gap in the history and profession of philosophy to the subject of the progress that our discipline can hope to achieve—and to the arrogance that, in my view, thwarts this progress. This determination to discuss the place of women in the profession turned out to be as daunting as the challenge of addressing my paper to an audience that, I imagined, might stand to greet what I had to say with coldness or—perhaps worse—indifference. It was only at the very end of the process of writing my paper that I began to see a way to articulate how the question of progress in philosophy and the ques-tion of women in philosophy intersect. In the version of the paper I pulled together for the Harvard conference, there's only the barest hint of a confluence. I was able to develop my thoughts on the occa-sion of speaking, in February 2012, to the Gender and Philosophy workshop at Yale.[11] What follows is a third attempt to make the case that resisting the arrogance that seems to haunt the enterprise of philosophy is essential to changing the millennia-old demographic homogeneity of the profession, a change itself essential to the making of a certain important kind of philosophical progress.

✎ IN RECENT YEARS, TIMOTHY Williamson—one of the most influential of all contemporary philosophers—has had a lot to say about the nature of philosophical progress.[12] Philosophy, Williamson suggests, is tricky: it differs in certain important respects from other kinds of inquiry. One difference is that you can't always tell in advance which philosophical questions are worth pursuing; indeed, new philosophical questions often initially seem "hopelessly elusive or naïve."[13] And yet by trying out methods for addressing even a very rough question, we give ourselves the opportunity to refine and clarify the nature and object of our investigation. This means that, somewhat paradoxically, even if the original question turns out to have been a pretty dreadful one—because it's confused, perhaps, or stated in the wrong terms or unanswerable as it stands—tackling it head-on stands to lead to philosophical progress.

Williamson believes that, ultimately, philosophy as an enterprise makes the same sort of progress as science does, at least when, as he puts it, philosophical work is properly "disciplined."[14] Disciplining our philosophizing, according to Williamson, requires making "a systematic conscious effort to conform to the deliverances" of, ideally, more than one set of the rules or standards bequeathed to us from, for example, semantics, syntax, logic, common sense, the findings of other disciplines, imaginary examples, the aesthetic norms of theory-making, including simplicity and elegance—and so on.[15] In the recent past, Williamson claims, we have made significant progress in philosophy. We have, for example, improved our theoretical understanding of possibility and necessity—and of truth. And, like Stanley, Williamson believes that this progress is largely a result of our committing ourselves to the careful use of the new and excellent disciplinary (in both senses of the word) tools that the development of modern logic has bequeathed us.

I agree with Williamson that what he calls "discipline" is an essential part of sound philosophizing and also that there is more than one type of constraint or set of standards that might do the job.

I am going to suggest, however, that his list of such standards needs to be broadened and that this is true even for the type of philosophy that he favors. And I am in effect going to disagree with him about two other things.

First, I do not think that he has decisively made the case for the claim that philosophical progress ought to be measured in scientistic terms—that is, as a function of the success of philosophical theorizing. (This claim figures heavily in what Williamson calls his "metaphilosophical writings," though to my knowledge he takes its truth for granted and doesn't seem to believe it requires any justification.) I don't deny that the use of the methods Williamson extols has led to a certain kind of progress and even stands to make more of that kind of progress, as he predicts. I know, for example, that philosophers working in the gray area between, say, philosophy and linguistics or philosophy and public policy have produced results of value to their colleagues on the other side of the disciplinary line. And as my (philosopher) husband enjoys reminding me whenever I worry out loud about the value of the contemporary philosophical enterprise: the modern history of the academy is in part the story of how philosophical enquiry has spun off new debates, lines of theoretical and empirical enquiry, and even disciplines, and there's no reason to think that things are any different now from the way they've been for at least the past four centuries. It's undeniable that philosophy continues to be of academic service by, for example, framing theoretical problems in a precise enough way that they can be handed off to people in neighboring fields. Still, as Ernest Sosa has recently observed, it's sobering to think of how few even minor questions in philosophy are settled. As Sosa puts the worry, "On one important question after another, a troubling number of us fail to agree with the rest."[16] In light of this fact, I will propose that there is another kind of progress that philosophers, regardless of their conception of philosophy or interests or methods or metaphilosophical commitments, can make and should strive to make.

In addition to being skeptical of the assumption that the scientistic model of progress that determines what counts as "research" in the modern university is the best, or at least the only, model that ought to be guiding those who profess philosophy, I worry, secondly, that this model may actually be forestalling this other kind of philosophical progress. I have in mind the human progress that results when people—and not just professional philosophers—commit themselves to the task of making their own most deeply held assumptions (and not just their views on particular issues or questions) visible and subjecting them to scrutiny. In my view, universities, and not just undergraduate colleges, need to acknowledge that the professing of philosophy—and not just in the classroom—often has a much higher value than the quest for philosophical research results. It is an essential part of what it is to philosophize well, no matter the methods or standards to which one cleaves.

I use Williamson as a stalking-horse here in part because he is expressing a view about the value of philosophy as it is currently practiced by the most powerful people in the profession but also because of the striking normative tone of his remarks.[17] In "Must Do Better," for example, he expresses a deep contempt for people who doubt that philosophy ought to be in the business of theory-making. Failing to hold themselves to the same high standards of rigor that the best philosophers demand and yet accusing such philosophers of asking senseless questions, these "mockers and doubters"—and, Williamson stresses, they have been around at least since the days of the Presocratics—are indulging in "a feeble and unnecessary surrender to despair, philistinism, cowardice or indolence."[18]

Williamson makes a similar normative point, albeit apparently aimed at a somewhat different audience, in a paper called "Past the Linguistic Turn?"—written at about the same time as "Must Do Better." In "Turn" he claims, "The rise of modern logic from Frege onwards has provided philosophers with conceptual instruments of unprecedented power and precision, enabling them to formulate hypotheses with more clarity and to determine their consequences with more reliability than ever before."[19] Those who balk at this judgment, Williamson claims, suffer from "impatience with the long haul of technical reflection," which is "a form of shallowness, often thinly disguised by histrionic advocacy of depth." Analytic philosophy "at its best," he says, "uses logical rigour and semantic sophistication to achieve a sharpness of philosophical vision unobtainable by other means. To sacrifice those gains would be to choose blurred vision." And for good measure he adds: "Serious philosophy is always likely to bore those with short attention-spans."

Williamson appears to be aiming his piquant terms of criticism at two different camps. First, there are the philosophers of his own ilk who participate in theoretical debates while failing to hold themselves to what Williamson calls "high enough methodological standards."[20] Indeed, this is surely the target audience for "Must Do Better," which began as a closing commentary on papers presented at a four-day conference on "Truth and Realism," held at the University of St. Andrews in 2004, and whose last paragraph begins with the sentence "In making these comments, it is hard not to feel like the headmaster of a minor public school at speech day, telling everyone to pull their socks up after a particularly bad term."[21] Williamson calls for philosophers to move slowly, to aim for absolute precision, to choose and describe examples with great care, and to provide explicit and perspicuous arguments for their views; and he warns us to beware of the "shoddy work" that is often "masked by pretentiousness, allusiveness, gnomic concision, or winning informality." To succumb to the temptation of aiming for depth by indulging in "an agonized rhetoric of profundity" is, paradoxically, to blind oneself to philosophy's "deepest difficulties." Doing philosophy well requires the "unglamorous" virtues of patience and austerity. "The fear of boring oneself or one's readers is a great enemy of truth," Williamson writes. "Pedantry is a fault on the right side." The highest virtue for a philosopher, he suggests, is precision, for precision is the handmaiden of perspicuity, which in turn provides us with the best chance of catching errors. For this very reason, cultivating in oneself the virtue of precision requires the courage to be wrong. But as payment for our virtue and compensation for our defeats, we must remember that "precise errors often do more than vague truths for scientific progress," which implies that we must have the humility to give others the best possible chance to expose our own errors. In sum, as Williamson puts it, "Although we can make progress in philosophy, we cannot expect to do so when we are not working at the highest available level of intellectual discipline. That level is not achieved by effortless superiority. It requires a conscious collective effort."

The second group in Williamson's crosshairs, the ones at whom he is wont to aim the heaviest rhetorical artillery, are the aforementioned "mockers and doubters." These are people, he seems to suggest, who think that "technical minuteness"[22] is flat out the enemy of philosophy. They embrace obscurity. They think that philosophers ought to be oracles. They want depth without rigor and precision. They revel in obscurantism. And Williamson implies that this is at least in part because they do not have the patience to do philosophy: they are easily bored, they have short attention spans, they are histrionic. It's not clear whether Williamson thinks that you can be one of these people and genuinely have the right to call yourself a philosopher. Perhaps he has in mind your garden-variety "Wittgensteinian" or continental philosopher or deconstructionist cultural critic; perhaps he is gesturing more broadly at the hoi polloi, the sort of people who, rolling their eyes, attack a *New York Times*' Stone blog post after skimming the first half. In any event, he seems to be insinuating that the only real philosophers are those who worship the one true god of rigor and precision.

The split between the sorts of philosophers Williamson admires and the sorts of professors of philosophy he rebukes is, I think, taken for granted among those who share his views about how to make philosophical progress. We find another characterization (though not an endorsement) of this dichotomy in an August 2011 post on the NewAPPs blog, written by Eric Schliesser. The post begins like this: "Analytic philosophy was self-consciously founded (a) against the great man approach to philosophy [let's call that 'the magisterial approach'], and accepting, by contrast, (b) the division of intellectual labor, such that (c) philosophy is a collective enterprise. The rhetoric that accompanied these moves appealed to success of the sciences. . . . One self-conscious byproduct of this approach is that from (some baseline) progress is *possible*. As in the sciences, even refutations and lack of confirmation can facilitate progress. Everybody's efforts matter."[23] Schliesser is here describing what he takes to be the "founding myth" of "analytic philosophy," namely, its self-conscious commitment to the idea that philosophy practiced as a collective, science-like enterprise allows for the possibility of progress in a way that the "great man" or "magisterial" approach does not.[24] As this myth would have it, (1) the only alternative to the analytic approach is the great man/magisterial one; (2) only the analytic approach has a chance of making real progress, since magisterialism is marked by grandiosity and sweeping claims, rather than hard, precise, peer-reviewed work within a community of other researchers; and (3) as its dubbing implies, the great man/magisterial approach is somehow *morally* bad or dangerous, perhaps because it's elitist or undemocratic or available only to benighted egotists whose proclamations about how things are do not lend themselves to scientific confirmation or disconfirmation by a jury of peers.

What inspires Schliesser in these reflections is a review by Mark Schroeder of Derek Parfit's magnum opus, *On What Matters*, in which Schroeder is struck by Parfit's declaring that if the metaethical view of moral normativity that he is defending (a form of "non-naturalist cognitivism") is wrong, then his life's work will have been in vain.[25] At least three times in volume II and once in volume I of *On What Matters*, Parfit says that if naturalism turns out to be true, then he and his metaethical fellow-travelers, such as Sigdwick and Ross, will have—and this is a quote from Parfit—"wasted much of our lives."[26] Schroeder argues that Parfit was moved to make this dramatic claim because what matters more than anything for Parfit is that "moral progress" is possible.[27] In arguing for the possibility of this progress, Parfit does not mean to refer only to human beings' behaving more virtuously, though he is clearly interested in that outcome and in fact argues that humanity has already made headway on this front.[28] He is also talking about the possibility that philosophers will discover and agree on the existence of a set of distinctly moral, nonnatural, non-reductive facts—in other words, about the possibility of a kind of *philosophical* progress.[29] Obviously, if there are no discoverable, distinctly moral facts, then Parfit's quest to discover these facts is hopelessly misguided—a waste of his life. In other words, Parfit is suggesting that what would make one's life as a philosopher a waste would be to be *wrong* in one's basic philosophical orientation.

Thus, Parfit, in his own distinct way, via his own philosophical preoccupations, joins Williamson in endorsing the idea that the point of doing philosophy is to *get things right*. Both Williamson and Parfit are convinced that getting things right is possible in philosophy—that there are philosophical facts and that we can discover them—even though, compared with how things go in at least some sciences, the results may be slow in coming. Williamson seems to believe that a major enemy in philosophy of the quest for truth is Great-Man-ism. Either you strive with a community of serious, humble, patient, open-minded others to define and struggle with a philosophical problem using the best tools at your disposal, or you proclaim, all by yourself, magisterially, how things are and what matters about how things are. Parfit speaks of philosophers who cleave to different normative ethical views as climbing a mountain from different sides; using this metaphor, we might picture Williamson's Great Man as someone who on the basis of nothing other than hubris fancies himself to be able to leap to the top of the mountain, completely on his own, without ever having done the hard work of trying to climb it or giving himself the advantage of learning from other mountaineers' successes and failures.

Schliesser and Williamson help us in somewhat different ways to identify the various distasteful aspects of magisterialism. Williamson brings to the table the worry that people who don't have the will or patience for this long reflective community haul will be unable to see the virtues in it and will resort to bombast or obscurantism or demagoguery in the name of saying something deep. And Schliesser's story about the founding of analytic philosophy (which he of course intends to be just-so) implies that magisterialism has the effect of excluding people from the philosophical conversation, thus reducing our opportunities to learn from our mistakes and to create a robust community of researchers supporting each other in our quest to understand the most basic questions human beings can ask. Parfit, on the other hand, seems to think that you can somehow in effect chart a middle course between scientism and magisterialism, one that involves a commitment to making progress in a community and avoids both demagoguery and elitism. You can do this by devoting yourself exclusively for years to constructing a comprehensive, wide-ranging philosophical theory that nonetheless takes seriously what a lot of other smart people have said and—if the acknowledgments are accurate—decisively outdo Descartes by asking almost 250 of them to read and criticize your manuscript.

But doesn't Parfit's worry about wasting his life suggest that there's more to his apparent commitment to magisterialism than interacting with others now and then while fundamentally charting your own way up the mountain? I think we can construe what Parfit is saying in a way that it doesn't come out as an expression of egoism. As Parfit readily acknowledges, lots of people have argued, or assumed, over the years that there are ethical facts and that these facts don't reduce to facts about the natural world. They have found it significant that it's not uncommon for utilitarianism, Kantianism, and contractualism to reach the same conclusions about what *sorts* of things are morally wrong, even if they tell different stories about how and why. Parfit has devoted the last couple of decades to trying to come up with a new way to prove that these conclusions about moral wrongness are correct. Doing this work comes at a high opportunity cost. Given the subject matter that has gripped him for nigh on half a century, he must care very deeply about another way of getting things right, namely, *doing the best thing he possibly can with his life*. After all, he could perhaps have spent a career writing for the *New Yorker* "Talk of the Town" section or writing poetry or photographing buildings—all things he evidently has done or, in the case of the photography, still does, rather well—instead of devoting almost all of his waking hours to philosophy.[30] I'm suggesting that we might read Parfit as worrying that he may have wasted his life not, or not just, because he failed to be the Great Man figuring out the truth in philosophical ethics all by himself but because, given the gifts that life has handed him, he might have been of better service to the world, if you will, had he chosen a different path, maybe even a different path as a philosopher. This is a noble worry.

Indeed, it's a worry with which all professional philosophers are familiar, at the very least from our graduate school days, when it becomes clear how hard it is to find one's way in philosophy. As PhD candidates we learned that one has to settle for *aiming* to get things right, since we so rarely, if ever, *do* get things right and since what counts as getting things right is so wildly variable across the discipline. Even if you are very talented—and very lucky—the signs that you may at least be on your way to getting things right are less than entirely reliable: your committee likes the first chapter of your dissertation; you get an article accepted in a decent journal; you get invited to the fun conferences with the heavy hitters; your school moves up two or three places in the departmental rankings. For most of us, these moments, if we even have them, are few and far between. Far more often, we find ourselves wondering not only if we *can* make the grade, but if we even *want* to, if perhaps there's something else we can do that we love to do almost as much as we love to read philosophy and write philosophically but without the nagging sense of self-doubt, the apparent amnesia of our teachers about what it's like to be a graduate student, the secret conviction that we haven't read enough, the fear that we won't get a job. In other words, we experience in prospective the Parfit worry that entering the profession of philosophy may not be a promising way for us to channel our time and effort.

These sorts of anxieties are often tamped down, when they are tamped down, by our peers, from whom, proverbially, we learn the most as graduate students. But what usually *saves* us is the exemplarity of a mentor, who in his or her practice of the philosophical profession makes us want to join it enough to push past our various doubts and defeats. The challenge then becomes to distinguish yourself from your mentor, to learn how to become yourself as a philosopher. The way that academic philosophy allows you to do this is to find a problem of manageable size in or neighboring your mentor's philosophical area of expertise, master the problems and the jargon, read all of the relevant literature, identify a position or claim you disagree with, figure out and articulate with precision what's wrong with it, and suggest your own "positive" view. In other words, you are supposed to aspire to find a place in the community of scientistic philosophy. For some people, those who are talented, tenacious, and lucky, this process will ultimately turn out to be a pleasure. And it may well lead to at least a modest sense of confidence that will allow a fledgling philosopher to take up new challenges not just in her chosen area or areas but in philosophically foreign territory. Others will not be so lucky. Some simply will not find a role model in their particular philosophical world. Others, fairly or not, will be deemed mediocre at the task of getting things right; they may make too many errors of reasoning or be unable to circumscribe a problem precisely enough or be good at naysaying but not good at proposing viable alternatives to a beleaguered view. They may be asked to leave their programs, or they may, as many do, just fall by the wayside.

Of course, something like this happens in pretty much every academic discipline. Standards are established by what are regarded by the majority of people in the profession as its most successful practitioners, that is, the ones who get the best results. (There is some circularity here, since in many disciplines what count as the best results are by definition the sorts of results that the most powerful people in the profession get.) Though outliers of various stripes may be able to hang on at the margins of the profession, those who accept and meet its central disciplinary standards are most likely to succeed in it and have an influence on it. As people enter the profession and try to find a place in it, a kind of invagination happens that eventually leads to the spawning of more and more new cottage industries. Some of these cottage industries border on other disciplines; if you're in philosophy, pretty much all of them do. One way to deal with the problem of interdisciplinarity is to get yourself trained up in the methods and standards of the relevant neighboring cottage industry. Another way is to scramble to respond to a top-down order from your dean to figure out how to cross the divide.

Notice that there's no room in this picture for magisterialism, except perhaps in the outlands (the minor universities, the small colleges, the fourth-tier academic presses). Schliesser is right that analytic philosophy was "self-consciously founded against the Great Man approach in philosophy." As I noted in Chapter 7, a major hero in this founding story was Rudolph Carnap. Carnap was motivated in significant part by a thoroughly admirable and deep determination, forged in the face of the horrors that were happening in Europe in the 1930s, to avoid the sort of philosophical obscurantism, especially about matters of human value, that might be exploited to provide fodder for political monsters. He believed—understandably, I think— that in his time and place no philosopher could afford to aspire to be a Nietzsche. Philosophy had to conduct its investigations scientifically, embracing the standards of science *mutatis mutandi*. The standards

Williamson claims define the discipline of philosophy—logical precision, clarity, attention to relevant outside disciplines, common sense, Occam's razor, and so on—are the standards of a certain kind of intellectual caution, one that there can be no doubt was called for during the era in which analytic philosophy established itself—which, not coincidentally, was the same era in which the university as a whole was articulating and raising its own professional standards.

I do not mean to be insinuating that these standards are not called for now. But I do want to think about what we lose both by embracing them to the exclusion of other, non-scientistic standards and by suggesting that the only alternative to them is magisterialism. This dichotomy is a false one. I will say more about why it's false momentarily. But for now let me just observe that you do not have to aspire to be a Great Man in order to worry that there's more to being a philosopher than getting things right. There is, for example, the obligation we have to make ourselves intelligible to the people who allow us to draw salaries. Even those of us who think that Williamson in his metaphilosophy gets it exactly right will agree, I imagine, that *eventually*, at least, the significance of our philosophical findings in principle ought to be rendered intelligible to nonphilosophers, which is a way of saying that their *human meaning* ought to be real, deep, and articulable—and not just in the areas of ethics and political philosophy. It seems to me that as a profession we are in effect waiting for good enough results before we let our fellows in on what we're doing. We have cut ourselves off from our roots in Socrates's practice in the Athenian marketplace; we do not feel pressured, as a profession, to converse with the hoi polloi, except insofar as they are forced, or elect, to take our classes. Socrates was put to death in part for allegedly corrupting the youth; but in today's world, it's far more likely that philosophers will be put to the death—departmentally, if not individuals—to the extent that we are *failing* to unsettle the young. There is no doubt that many philosophers at all different kinds of institutions work very hard to make what we do intelligible to and (to use the current buzzword) transformative for our students. At some schools, it's explicitly all about the teaching. But the reward systems at the institutions in which the trendsetters and kingmakers in our profession work make very clear that bad teaching, especially at the undergraduate level, is a minor sin, one that merits at worst an uncomfortable chat with the dean or a half-percentage docking in our salary.

The cost of this attitude—which is pressed upon us by the particular way in which philosophy has been institutionalized in the contemporary academy—is very high, in both human and philosophical terms. In human terms, we are missing opportunities to attract people to the rewards of examining their settled views. This is happening at a time in which the sheer volume of news and information and opinions we are asked to digest puts tremendous pressure on people to hold on for dear life to whatever dogma appears to have the power to prevent them from getting swept away. Not every human being has the luxury of not being a fanatic. But no one who has had a successful experience in a classroom of philosophical neophytes can fail to know the satisfaction, and not just the pain, of watching students struggle to develop the skill of reconsidering their own opinions and thereby identifying, sharpening, and securing interests they didn't know they had or were perhaps afraid to explore. Those of us who have written for the *Times'* Stone series (including Stanley and Williamson) have learned that despite our best attempts to communicate as clearly and carefully as we can with the masses, we are likely to be held in contempt by people who feel no obligation to make sure they understand what we're saying before they attack. We need to remember that the problem here is not only that human beings are stupid and that the Internet makes it worse. It's also that people aren't used to hearing signals from our particular planet and might (1) resent that fact and (2) not know what to make of us.

Furthermore, it's not just the nonphilosopher who benefits from a trip to the agora or the modern-day classroom. The philosopher puts himself in intellectual harm's way by holing up in the ivory tower. What I have in mind here is the danger that our use of jargon courts insofar as we help ourselves, in our philosophical argot, to words that people use all the time outside of philosophy—words like *knowledge* and *mind* and *person* and *meaning.* In using these words as technical terms, we can feel tempted to imagine that our work is automatically going to be relevant to, if not flat-out about, the phenomena to which our everyday uses of the words refer. We do not feel a standing obligation to measure the distance between the range of everyday meanings of these words and the meanings we philosophers impose on them.[31]

Take the word *gender* as it gets used these days by feminist metaphysicians of various stripes. The dominant view is that *gender* is the name of a product of social forces (norms, ideology, circulations of power/knowledge) that mark human bodies in various more or less oppressive ways. Some feminist philosophers do not deny that bodies are naturally sexed, though, in view of the phenomenon of intersexuality, many deny that there are only two biological sexes. Others see the very idea of *biological sex* as itself a "socially constructed," politicized notion that acts to draw our attention away from and thereby license the extent to which gender controls the meaning of our anatomies, assigning each human body to one of two essentially arbitrary groups and then policing the border between them.[32] But both camps—those who think that bodies are naturally sexed and those who challenge this "commonsense" view—hold that insofar as being a man or a woman is in significant part a function of being gendered, whether a person is a man or a woman is fundamentally not a function of her or his physiology.[33]

This way of understanding things seems so obvious to theorists working in feminist metaphysics that for the most part we don't notice how difficult it is actually to *live* this view. It often doesn't occur to us that our discoveries about the metaphysics of sex and gender do not mesh in obvious ways with people's *experience* of their and other people's bodies. Take, for example, the experience of a child with XY chromosomes and the usual anatomical manifestations of this genotype who from an early age identifies as a girl. Needless to say, this child, like every other, will be subjected to all sorts of gender norms no later than birth, and probably earlier. Dysphoria with respect to her social gender assignment—in other words, "male"—may take the form not only of her rejecting the norms of masculinity but also of discomfort with her own primary and secondary sex characteristics. Should we philosophers understand this discomfort as essentially a function of oppressive gender norms that determine the social meaning of human anatomy? Maybe.

But it's not obvious that or how this understanding connects up with a transgendered child's conviction that her having a penis, for one thing, is fundamentally *a mistake of nature*. The social constructionist explanation suggests that absent our oppressive gender norms, the child might not be experiencing bodily dysphoria. But this explanation sits uneasily with the transgendered person's sense that her or his anatomy is just *wrong*, since it implies—potentially condescendingly and insultingly—that, in a different world, her anatomy might well be a matter of indifference to her.

I need to make clear here that I am in no way trying to argue that this gap between philosophical discourse and the ways people speak in nonphilosophical contexts is fundamentally problematic or unbridgeable; nor am I suggesting that philosophers should abandon the use of specialized discourse. My point is that there are important reasons for us to care about building these bridges on a regular basis as a way of ensuring that in our theorizing we are not illicitly imagining, when we shouldn't be, that we are making discoveries about real-world phenomena when in fact we have turned an ordinary word into a technical one and therefore have more or less changed the subject.

I have been arguing that the lack of widespread interest among philosophers in attempting to make ourselves intelligible in the wide world is related to what I have claimed is a false choice in our philosophical methodology and aims between "scientism" and "magisterialism." I have in effect just been laying out a worry about scientism in philosophy, which is that it can both lead to an esotericism that interferes with our social duties as philosophers and mislead us about the scope and significance of our results. Up to this point, however, I have said very little about magisterialism. Williamson's beef against it is that it yields very bad philosophy—in the same way, presumably, that a scientist who did not keep abreast of the latest methodologies, findings, and equipment, allowing nothing other than his intuitions about the things that interest him professionally to guide him, would do very bad science.[34] Another obviously worrisome feature of magisterialism is indicated by Schliesser's other name for it in his blog: the "great man approach." One of the attractions of understanding philosophy as a science-like discipline—that is, with a special range of problems and methods, proposed and refined within a community of open and cooperative peers working together to make progress—is that it creates space for a variety of people, from a variety of backgrounds and intellectual schools and with a variety of interests, to enter the profession of philosophy. You don't need to be a Hegel or a Nietzsche or a Wittgenstein or a Hume; to inflect the point in a certain important direction, you don't need to be a white, European man. This fact matters quite a bit in a world in which white men are grossly overrepresented in the professional philosophical world. A scant 20 percent of philosophers employed full- or part-time as such are women; even more scandalously, only about 1 percent are black.[35]

In recent years, with increasing urgency, the profession has begun to ask about these embarrassing statistics. A major impetus for the growth of interest in this question was the appearance in 2008 of Sally Haslanger's paper "Changing the Ideology and Culture of Philosophy: Not by Reason (Alone)," which begins: "There is a deep well of rage inside me. Rage about how I as an individual have been treated in philosophy; rage about how others I know have been treated; and rage about the conditions that I'm sure affect many women and minorities in philosophy, and have caused many others to leave."[36] Haslanger adds to personal anecdote a good deal of psychological research and hard data (including the abysmal record of seven of the top philosophy journals in publishing articles by women as well as the almost total exclusion of feminist work in these publications) to make the claim that philosophy as a profession is deeply inhospitable to women generally speaking (and also, she suggests, to non-white men). In her analysis of women's situation in philosophy, Haslanger relies on well-known work by Virginia Valian, one of the first psychologists to claim on the basis of experimental results that even when people—including women—consciously and actively abhor and fight sexism in academia, they often harbor significant unconscious ("implicit") bias against women.[37] Valian argues that much of human interaction is mediated by "gender schemas," sets of largely unconscious beliefs about men and women that condition our perceptions and expectations. Conflicts between the stereotypes and norms of femininity, on the one hand, and the characteristics necessary for success in academia, on the other, can result in the neglect or undervaluing of women's work, with predictable consequences for women's careers. Moreover, when women work in areas in which they are a distinct minority, they are vulnerable to "stereotype threat," a kind of self-stigmatizing anxiety that has been shown to degrade individuals' performance in a variety of tasks. But if Valian is making a point about academia generally speaking, then there seems to be a further question about why philosophy in particular is so much more inhospitable to women than most other disciplines, including chemistry, mathematics, and astrophysics.[38] Haslanger suggests that the explanation for the dearth of women in the philosophy is fairly simple:

> I don't think we need to scratch our heads and wonder what on earth is going on that keeps women out of philosophy. In my experience, it is very hard to find a place in philosophy that isn't actively hostile toward women and minorities, or at least assumes that a successful philosopher should look and act like a (traditional, white) man. And most women and minorities who are sufficiently qualified to get into graduate school in philosophy have choices. They don't have to put up with this mistreatment. Many who recognize that something about choices is relevant have explained to me that women choose not to go into philosophy because they have other options that pay better or have more prestige. This may be true for some, but this doesn't sound like the women I know who have quit philosophy (and it sounds a lot more like the men I know who have quit). Women, I believe, want a good working environment with mutual respect. And philosophy, mostly, doesn't offer that.[39]

I certainly agree—as, I'm sure, do many other women philosophers. At the same time, many of us also continue to scratch our heads. We want to know more about *why* the profession seems considerably more inhospitable to women than other fields traditionally dominated by men. In "Different Voices or Perfect Storm: Why Are There So Few Women in Philosophy?" Louise Antony has suggested that people worried about the dearth of women in philosophy essentially have two choices of explanatory models. The first is what she calls, borrowing Carol Gilligan's classic nomenclature, the "different voices" model.[40] This is the model that Wesley Buckwalter and Stephen Stich start to sketch out in a 2010 paper called "Gender and Philosophical Intuition." Analyzing results from other people's surveys of nonphilosophers' responses to popular philosophical thought experiments, Buckwalter and Stich report that "when women and men with little or no philosophical training are presented with standard philosophical thought experiments, in many cases their intuitions about these cases are significantly different."[41] And Buckwalter and Stitch "suspect that these differences could be playing an important role in shaping the demography of the profession."[42] Antony argues that Buckwalter and Stich's hypothesis is not adequately supported by the evidence they present, and she worries that the very suggestion that women's philosophical voices are different from men's will be construed to mean that women are naturally prone to have the *wrong* philosophical intuitions.

In place of the "different voices" model, Antony proposes what she calls a "perfect storm" explanation for the gross lack of parity in professional philosophy between men and women. This model is essentially an extension of Haslanger's explanation. Philosophical culture, it could be argued, *intensifies* the effects of implicit bias, stereotype threat, and gender schemas: it is more stereotypically male than, say, the culture in literature departments, and its norms of behavior—including the "great man's" (my term) disdain for doing academic service work as well as our profession's unusually antagonistic way of grappling with other people's ideas, notably in colloquia and conferences—are more sharply at odds with the norms of feminine comportment than norms in other disciplines.[43]

I agree with Antony that the data Buckwalter and Stich adduce in their paper do not fully justify their claim that women's intuitions about standard philosophical thought experiments are systematically different from men's; I also agree with her that proposing a "different voices" theory without really robust evidence is a politically dicey thing to do, since, historically, women's "different" voices have almost always been deemed inferior to men's. But I am also skeptical about the "perfect storm" model. For one thing, it doesn't explain why other academic disciplines that are associated with intellectual precision and a macho work style do not invariably suffer from the extreme gender-lopsidedness that we find in philosophy. Antony's model also relies heavily on a hypothesis that strikes me as potentially just as politically dicey as the "different voices" worry when she implies that the "pugilistic style," as she puts it, that characterizes interaction among philosophers may ultimately drive women away from the field. After noting that "questions after a philosophy lecture are very apt to be challenges to some aspect of the speaker's argument," Antony writes,

> The personal characteristics that make one good at this sort of intellectual activity are qualities like assertiveness, persistence, ingenuity, tenacity, and—well, let's call it "insensitivity" to various norms governing conversation in other domains. Personal qualities that are gender-normal for women, however, are at odds with these. Women are generally expected to be deferential, pleasant, and supportive. Women who are contentious, who interrupt, or who talk for (what is perceived to be) a long time are heavily sanctioned. A woman in philosophy thus confronts another double bind. If she respects the gender norms, she is apt to be dismissed intellectually; whereas if she acts the way philosophers generally act, in violation of the gender norms, she risks being perceived as especially rude or domineering.[44]

It's important that Antony does *not* say that women leave philosophy because they are beholden to norms of femininity. Rather, following Marilyn Frye, she claims that these norms so clash with the norms of being a philosopher that women find themselves caught between a rock and a hard place: they either shut up and thus seem philosophically weak, or they talk and seem more aggressive or shrill than a man would.[45] I don't disagree that things are tough for women in the way that Antony suggests here. But to suggest that women don't enter, or don't stay in, philosophy because they are caught in this double bind can seem to suggest that *women can't take it*: that they don't have thick enough skin to hang in there. And I don't see how this claim is any less dangerous than the claim that women's intuitions with respect to philosophical thought experiments are sometimes different from men's.

In fact, I think that *both* Stich and Buckwalter *and* Antony are on to something, only in my opinion neither explanation comprehensively identifies the source of the problem. Let's take Antony first. In her description of the double bind women face, Antony does not question the *source* of the macho contentiousness that characterizes much philosophical discussion; she simply assumes that this contentiousness is a fact of life in philosophy. But it's not clear to me that the sort of combativeness that characterizes contemporary philosophical discussion is an inevitable part of philosophizing well. I suspect it is a function of a conception of philosophy on which the philosopher's job is to take up or pose a well-formed question and then to defend, via a perspicuous and sound argument, a solution to the problem it poses. Jason Stanley, in an article written in 2010 for *Inside Higher Education*, sees this process as an essentially creative one, intensely original in the way that, for example, an act of criticism by an English professor or an art historian of something made by someone else is not. Stanley writes, "Like the fiction writer or the artist, and unlike her fellow humanists, the philosopher is focusing on creating her own body of work, ideally a novel attempt at a solution to the on-going philosophical problems."[46] This is a nice romantic picture, but it ignores the realities of life in contemporary academic philosophy, including the relentless pressure to produce philosophical writing, preferably journal-article-length, for double- or triple-blind peer review; to couch one's work in terms of arguments that must be not only original but also transparently valid and plausibly sound; to explicitly acknowledge a large number of other people who have also weighed in on the problems you're considering; and to keep up with the -isms and the other jargon in your area of specialization. Stanley in this article also romanticizes philosophy by characterizing the philosopher as a childlike figure who asks big questions about the world that are charming when an actual child poses them but come off to the nonphilosopher as merely "infantile" in the philosopher's mouth, especially given that the philosopher thinks that using his technical chops is going to yield answers. He writes, "The great philosophical works have always been difficult technical tomes, pursuing arcane arguments in the service of grand metaphysical and epistemological conclusions." But of course, unless you are willing to claim that the likes of, say, Plato and Descartes and Rousseau and Hume and Mill and James (and Simone de Beauvoir) did not leave us with great philosophical works, then you will have to demur, at least when it comes to the claims about "technical tomes" and "arcane arguments." All of this is to say that the source of the combativeness that Antony thinks leaves women at a disadvantage may say more about scientism in contemporary philosophy than she is willing to admit.

Now for what Buckwalter and Stich do not consider in their speculation about the source of the gender gap in philosophy. When they suggest that women might speak philosophically in a "different voice," they frame their hypothesis as an empirical one that requires empirical evidence for confirmation. (Indeed, one of Antony's most powerful criticisms of them is that the statistics and anecdotes they adduce in their paper do not amount to robust evidence.) But Buckwalter and Stich never stop to wonder whether the responses of women not trained in philosophy to a very specific sort of philosophical thought experiment really tell us anything about women's interest in and capacity for studying philosophy. Whether or not any student will be inclined to reconsider her views or to worry about her capacity to think or to stop studying philosophy when her response to a thought experiment differs from that of her teacher depends on any number of factors other than the difference: what kind of temperament and tastes the student has; whether the teacher takes views other than his own seriously; whether the student thinks that the experiment is tracking something interesting or trivial; whether the student is offended by the casual suggestion that one might push a fat man onto a trolley track in an emergency—and on and on, ad infinitum.[47] It's not clear what kind of empirical work, if any, is going to license the conclusion that women may be inclined to speak philosophically in a different voice.

Still, there has got to be something to the idea, at least the kernel of which can be seen in the Buckwalter/Stich view, that there may be a problem with women's getting their voices heard, even if the relevant voice is not responding to the question of what Mary knew. This brings us back, finally, to the magisterial or "Great Man" model of philosophizing. Schliesser uses this nomenclature, of course, to imply that the model it names is by its nature exclusionary. If you replace the model with the scientistic one, then in principle you can be a woman, or a not-so-Great Man philosopher, which in effect means a man who couldn't have been a Great Man, that is, a man who is not a white man of a certain class (and, historically, at least, a man at least trying to pass as heterosexual). You, too, can be a member of the community of philosophers.

But I'm not sure that this is such a good deal for those of us who fall into this category. We've never had a chance to even *try* to be great, to struggle to say, without censoring ourselves, how the world looks from our point of view. Some of us have concerns—for example, about what it is to be a woman or not to be white—about which the Great Men had only really dogmatic, dumb-headed, and preposterous things—or nothing at all—to say. With respect to these concerns, we ourselves have barely begun to have a say. Some of us are happy to work on these concerns and others within the confines of Williamson's preferred list of disciplinary standards. But others of us struggle constantly with how to make what we want to say—what for all the world seems to be a *philosophical* thing to say— fit into the discipline of philosophy. At times, it seems as though there's no way to say anything without being bold in the way that the artist is bold—perhaps, à la Stanley, using the tools that main-stream (philosophical) artists use but also perhaps trying out new tools, so that one risks sounding, or even *being*, as benighted as one of Socrates's interlocutors. If the profession of philosophy and the universities in which it lives are serious about demographic diver-sity, then we need to think about how to create a space in our profes-sion for this big, bold say—and to live with the threat that it might reconfigure or even radically transform our nice, safe list of disci-plinary standards and the cottage industries they govern.[48]

9

Reel Girls and Real Girls: What Becomes of Women on Film?

$\mathcal{J}$ HAVE ARGUED in Chapters 5 and 6 of this book that J. L. Austin's careful attention to the specific ways in which our words do the things they do is the foundation of the technical structure that he lays out in *How to Do Things with Words*—that is, the story about "constatives" and "performatives," "illocutionary" and "perlocutionary" force, and so on. The theory one finds in *How to Do Things with Words* and in Austin's other writings is not top-down: it emerges from his careful attention to instances of human speech and the circumstances in which our words are able to do what they do. This priority of Austin's is shared by both Ludwig Wittgenstein and Stanley Cavell. Indeed, Austin, Wittgenstein, and Cavell are often considered principal figures in a philosophical "school" called Ordinary Language Philosophy (OLP), and this school is invariably thought to include at least several other figures. Here, for example, is a description of OLP from Wikipedia:

> This approach typically involves eschewing philosophical "theories" in favor of close attention to the details of the use of everyday, "ordinary" language. Sometimes called "Oxford philosophy," it is generally associated with the work of a number of mid-20th century Oxford professors: mainly J. L. Austin, but

also Gilbert Ryle, H. L. A. Hart, and Peter Strawson. The later Ludwig Wittgenstein is ordinary language philosophy's most celebrated proponent outside the Oxford circle. Second generation figures include Stanley Cavell and John Searle.[1]

As Avner Baz has demonstrated, what counts as "close attention to the details of the use of everyday, 'ordinary' language" varies dramatically among philosophers lumped into the OLP category.[2] This fact may account for what I have argued is the thin interpretation of Austin that we find in the rendering of his views by philosophers interested in defending the coherence of Catharine MacKinnon's claims about pornography's powers to subordinate and silence women: these philosophers may be reading Austin through the lens of a very general and influential view of what counts as OLP. This reading relies on the idea that if Austin was doing anything credible at all, he was—à la, for instance, Searle—respecting well-established boundary lines between the *literal meanings* of words and their *use* (on which any decent theory of literal meaning is closely connected to a theory of reference and a theory of truth) and thereby leaving undisturbed the general picture of language that continues to govern the current incarnation of "analytic philosophy."[3] This is to say that they see Austin as far less radical (and therefore far less crazy) than the later Wittgenstein. But those of us who learned to read Austin via the writings and teaching of Cavell interpret Austin, like Wittgenstein, despite his marked differences from Austin, as *upending* this picture.[4] What Austin shares with Wittgenstein is his commitment to keeping an eye *at all times* on our experience of the world and, therefore, on how our words gain purchase. We might call this a "look and see" approach to philosophy, after section 66 of the *Philosophical Investigations*:

> Consider for example the proceedings that we call "games." I mean board-games, card-games, ball-games, Olympic games, and so on. What is common to them all?—Don't say: "There must be something common, or they would not be called 'games'"—but look and see whether there is anything common to all.—For if you look at them you will not see something that

is common to all, but similarities, relationships, and a whole series of them at that. To repeat: don't think, but look!—

This "look and see" approach shows up everywhere in Cavell's own work but is perhaps most striking in the idiosyncratic way he attends to film. For Cavell, following the procedures of Wittgenstein and Austin, film criticism is logically prior to film theory, which by definition will always be provisional, open to the discoveries that specific acts of criticism might reveal about the general nature of the medium. More specifically, for Cavell to do "film criticism" is to make claims about, as he puts it, "the appearance and significance of just those objects and people that are to be in the succession of films, or passages of films, that matter to us."[5] This is a quotation from the last paragraph of an essay of Cavell's called "What Becomes of Things on Film," to which, of course, I'm paying homage in the title of this chapter.[6]

The key words in the quotation are the last ones: for Cavell, the only way to gauge the significance of what we see in a film is to take the measure of what matters to us. By using the first-person plural here, Cavell is suggesting that the film critic, in speaking for herself, necessarily is claiming to speak for *us*: by naming what a particular film or group of films shows and articulating its significance, the film critic is claiming—which is to say *proposing*—that what matters to her matters full stop, and she is doing so on the strength of nothing other than this very act of claiming. It follows that, on Cavell's understanding, film criticism constitutes an invitation to its audience to engage in a kind of conversation. And this conversation is bound to precede the enterprise of film *theory*, according to Cavell, insofar as that enterprise consists in exploring how the specific things that appear in film, what they signify, and how they matter are, as he puts it, "made possible by the general photogenesis of film altogether."[7] Cavell here is alluding to the fact that filmmaking requires the placement of objects and people in front of a camera—and, therefore, their *dis*placement from the outside world, as it were—in anticipation of viewers' displacing themselves from the world in order to view them.

This way of approaching the study of film is sharply different from other ways of understanding film criticism and film theory. A classic contrasting example is Laura Mulvey's "Visual Pleasure and Narrative Cinema" (1975).[8] In this foundational film theoretic essay, Mulvey adopts a Freudian framework, inflected à la Lacan, in arguing that, by definition, what becomes of women on film, at least in the case of narrative films, is that they are transformed into passive objects that encourage and absorb what she calls the male "look" or "gaze." As objects of the gaze, women play no direct or active role in advancing the plots of films. They are simply there for the purpose of spectacle. Indeed, the presence of women, their "to-be-looked-at" quality in films, threatens to stop the flow of the plot and disrupt the "diegesis," that is, the world the film narratively constructs. On Mulvey's view, a woman on film necessarily becomes a nonhuman entity that merely haunts the diegesis. Unlike her male counterparts in narrative film, who are makers of the law and masters of language, she is an object controlled and manipulated by these symbolic systems, something to be punished, devalued, ignored, or lusted after.

Of course, Mulvey concedes, the film industry does not have a monopoly on promoting the idea that women are objects there for the taking. However, what's insidious about narrative film is that it ensures that our helpless objectification of the women it depicts is reinforced by our continuously experiencing pleasure as we look at them. This pleasure is itself a function of our helplessly *identifying* ourselves with male filmic characters, that is, with the masters that men invariably become on film—and by "our" here, Mulvey means all film viewers, regardless of their gender. Because narrative film manipulates us in this way, we are morally obliged to pay attention to what becomes of women on film and thereby to destroy our pleasure in watching them, or what Mulvey calls our "scopophilia."

Can there be any doubt that there is *something* correct in what Mulvey is saying? Certainly, the idea that women on film routinely become sex objects, present simply to be looked at, regardless of what is going on in the diegesis, is confirmed by—to cite one of the most obvious examples—the sheer number of gratuitous boob shots in virtually every mainstream Hollywood film and TV show these days, even the edgiest and most respectable ones. As far as I can tell, the sole function of Morena Baccarin's character on *Homeland*—

which is, as a I write, a wildly popular television series—is to stand in the kitchen and fret while the brownies bake in the oven and then retire to the bedroom to reveal her breasts to her husband or her lover. It's as though, thanks to the volume of video now available to anyone with a smartphone, the clear pornographic possibilities that film by its nature has afforded us ever since the days of Eadweard Muybridge and his studies of naked human beings in motion have run amok, like cancer cells, strangling other potential ways that human beings, and particularly women, can appear, signify, and matter on film.[9]

But not always, and not everywhere. There are still makers of films and television programs, even those with lots of boob shots, who trust the power of the camera to surprise us when it comes to the question of what it's possible for something or someone to become on film. This trust takes different forms in the hands of different filmmakers; but, as Cavell has observed, when it comes to the filming of human beings, the best directors are attuned to the particular ways in which each transcendent actor, that is to say, each movie star, idiosyncratically and from film to film represents a standing way of being in the world for the human being. In his writing about Hollywood's golden era in the 1930s and '40s, Cavell is fond of contrasting the differences between, for example, who Cary Grant and Jimmy Stewart, or Katherine Hepburn and Claudette Colbert, become on film. But this is of course no less true in our own era; just compare Brad Pitt and Denzel Washington, or Tina Fey and Meryl Streep. In the cases of all of the actors I have just mentioned, to have seen enough of their films is to *know them on film*. So much so that it is hard for us to believe that they could be drastically different in "real life." This is because what these actors become for us on film is something that often strikes us as beyond their conscious control: Jimmy Stewart's capacity for becoming flustered or Tina Fey's capacity to give us to think that what we see in her is everything that's there.

In "What Becomes of Things on Film," Cavell claims that the great silent film stars Buster Keaton and Charlie Chaplin excelled in their transmogrification on celluloid in revealing to us different dimensions of our lives with objects. In films such as *The General*,

Keaton copes endlessly with the mechanical breakdown of various machines and other human artifacts, not in order to bring us to our knees with despair about whether we can make a home for ourselves on Earth but to allow us to laugh at what Heidegger called "the worldhood of the world." Chaplin, on the other hand, in films such as *The Gold Rush*, displays a comic resourcefulness in treating objects as what they are not: a boiled old leather shoe becomes a gourmet meal for Chaplin and an equally destitute guest; two dinner rolls impaled on forks become the legs of a can-can dancer; a dog's leash becomes a makeshift belt to prevent a man's pants from falling down while he's whirling his partner around the dance floor—even as the leash is still attached to the dog. Cavell writes that "Keaton and Chaplin make a comedy of the fact that such a creature as a human being is fated to pursue happiness, and . . . they undertake to demonstrate that such a creature is after all, and to a certain extent, under very exacting conditions, capable of happiness."[10] In what follows, I want to suggest that we find a third way of coping with one's life circumstances by making a comedy of the fact that we human creatures are fated to pursue happiness and, under certain conditions, capable of it, in the film *Lars and The Real Girl*, released in 2007.

 THE STORY THE FILM TELLS takes place in a small, iconically American middle-class town way up north in the Midwest, perhaps on the Minnesota–Canada border, mostly during a gray winter. It's the kind of town in which people work hard to make a decent living, everyone knows everyone else, and even nonbelievers go to church. We are introduced to Lars Lindstrom, played by Ryan Gosling (roughly thirty pounds heavier than usual and sporting an unfortunate mustache).[11] Lars is a twenty-seven-year-old man who works in a cubicle in a generic company and lives in the modestly comfortable refurbished stand-alone garage of his childhood home, which has recently come to be occupied by his older brother, Gus (Paul Schneider), and Gus's wife, Karin (Emily Mortimer), who is several months pregnant with their first child. We learn in due course that the brothers' mother died while giving birth to Lars, after which their father became stuck in his own grief. Gus left home as soon as he could, leaving Lars emotionally on his own. In the opening moments of the film, we learn that Emily is worried that there is something wrong with Lars, who continually rebuffs her attempts to bring him into the house—and the family.

At Lars's workplace, we are introduced to Margo (Kelli Garner), a gawky young woman whose clear interest in Lars is met by Lars's incapacity squarely to acknowledge the meaning of her interest to himself. Lars shares his work cubicle with Kurt, who sexlessly takes pleasure in smirking at what he regards as Lars's humiliation of Margo; Kurt treats Margo's mild attempts to get back at him (by stealing the action figures he keeps at his desk) as a provocation to torture her in kind. When not sneering at Margo, Kurt is wont to listen to loud music and surf the web for porn. An attempt to get Lars interested in one of his porn finds, an Internet site—one that actually exists at www.realdolls.com—which sells life-size, lifelike, anatomically correct sex toys, clearly leaves Lars cold. Nonetheless, after what we are given to understand is an intervening six weeks, we see a UPS truck pull up to Lars's garage to deliver a coffin-sized box. That evening, Lars eagerly appears at the door of the house to tell Gus and Karin that he has a visitor in the garage whom he'd like to bring for dinner, a woman from far away whom he has met through the Internet. Karin, especially, is thrilled to hear that Lars has a date and delightedly reassures Lars that it's fine for her to stay in the "pink room" in the big house (which, we soon learn, used to belong to Lars's mother) and that she and Gus will happily accommodate her being in a wheelchair. But Karin and Gus are stunned when Lars's new friend turns out to be a life-size sex doll, dressed head to toe in fishnet and gold and silver lamé, her voluptuous mouth perpetually in an open pout. They are even more taken aback by the fact that Lars seems to believe, effortlessly and genuinely, that Bianca is real; and we have extra evidence of that belief when we are shown Lars whispering with—or, rather, at—Bianca when Karin and Gus are out of earshot. At the dinner table, Lars explains to his brother and sister-in-law that Bianca, who is "half-Brazilian, half-Danish" and from "the tropics," was raised by nuns and became a missionary but is currently on sabbatical "so that she can experience the world." He asks Karin, who is partial to roomy corduroy jumpers and patterned jersey turtlenecks, if she is willing to lend Bianca some clothes, since somebody stole her luggage and her wheelchair while she was en route.

After an awkward (and from our point of view hilarious) dinner and after Bianca is installed in the Pink Room, Lars goes back to the garage and Karin sneaks a peak under Bianca's skirt. She is repulsed and fascinated (though not, presumably, for the reasons that Mulvey suggests in her discussion of the way that women on film are characteristically marked as castrated). Afraid that Lars is seriously mentally ill, Gus and Karin cook up a plan to get him to see a doctor in town who is also a psychologist. This is Dagmar, played brilliantly by Patricia Clarkson. The pretext here is that because, according to the backstory that Lars himself has provided, Bianca has come all the way from the tropics and has various health problems, it's important for her to get a checkup. Dagmar tells Gus and Karin that Lars's thinking that Bianca is real is a "delusion," which they should interpret not just as a sign that he may be mentally ill but as a form of communication, potentially "a way of working something out." She advises Gus and Karin to play along with the delusion—to treat Bianca as though she were as Lars sees her, that is, a real girl. To this Gus demurs, on the grounds that he is unable to pretend that Bianca is real; but he is reduced to silence by Dagmar's pointing out that Bianca *is* real, that indeed "she's right out there"—that is, in the waiting room. Dagmar's plan is to give "intravenous" treatments on a regular basis for what she has told Lars is Bianca's very low blood pressure; and she privately assures Gus and Karin that she will work with Lars during the treatment times to try to create some space in which he feels safe confronting whatever is driving his delusion. So Gus and Karin meet with the pastor and assorted members of Lars's church and ask them to play along as well. All agree, more or less incredulously and reluctantly, and Bianca the Real Doll soon makes her public debut, albeit dressed in Karin's frumpy clothes, at Lars's church.

The film then alternates between scenes in which Lars and Dagmar "pass the time" while Bianca receives her treatments for low blood pressure and those in which everyone in town "plays along" with the idea that Bianca is real. These descriptions of what's happening are the way Lars and the townspeople, respectively, construe what's going on, but both of them are cover stories for the actual truth. In fact, of course, it is Lars, not Bianca, who is being treated in Dagmar's office. It turns out that a main physical symptom for which he needs treatment is his inability to be touched by another person without feeling searing pain, "like when you go outside and your feet freeze and then you come back in and they thaw." His fear of being touched reads as a fear of reckoning with the loss of his mother, and thus the loss of her touch (and, as it sadly happened, that of his bereft father), as though the only way for him to survive is to deny that he is a creature made for being touched, that is, a human being. Here "being touched" has got to be both literal and figurative: Lars is clearly afraid of getting burned emotionally as well—for one thing, by the possibility that Karin, like his mother, will perish during childbirth. Of course, this is why Bianca is made for Lars, his perfect counterpart: not only is she his exact opposite, manufactured for the sole purpose of being touched by a human being; she also is incapable of touching Lars back. This means that, like all dolls, she is entirely a creation of his own projections.

But not for long. For the townspeople, in warming up to the idea of "helping" the sweet, gentle, mentally skewed Lars, begin to project a certain fantasy of their own onto Bianca. This is the fantasy that it's possible for a person to reach the morally pristine state of being utterly devoted to serving others without loss to one's own needs or sense of self. Of course, the projection onto Bianca of a missionary's moral rectitude and capacity for service—Lars has told Gus and Karin that she has "nurse's training" and that "God made her to help people"—pairs perfectly with the townspeople's own delusion, as they steadfastly repress what they cannot avoid seeing every time they look at her: namely, the particular kind of function in service of which she was in fact manufactured. This refusal to see what's right in front of their eyes is of course a form of avoiding something that they don't want to look at, both literally and figuratively: their own desires for touching and being touched, for sexual connection with others. The project of avoiding looking at Bianca involves both dressing her in the dowdiest clothes they can find and seeing to it that she is kept constantly busy—participating in church activities, reading books to "bald children" at the local hospital, working part-time in a mall clothing shop—so busy that Lars comes to resent that she has what the townspeople call "a life of her own" and starts to rebuke Bianca for it. What has happened is that in supporting Lars's delusion with their own, the townspeople have in effect stolen Bianca away from him. In making her into their own real girl, they unknowingly act as vampires, draining her of what nourishes Lars, namely, her availability to him to become nothing other than what he needs her to be. Over time, then, Bianca's blood pressure drops ever more precipitously and starts to become perilously low.

Meanwhile, at Lars's workplace, Margo, who has recently ended a half-hearted romance with a dull coworker named Erik, finds that Lars's childish, sexless cubicle-mate Kurt has escalated their tit-for-tat pranking beyond what she can manage: he has hung her teddy bear by a noose. Genuinely upset and with Lars watching, Margo confronts Kurt and demands that he remove the noose. Kurt refuses: "Face it, Margo; the bear is dead. Burn on you." Breaking into tears, Margo rushes into the break room, and a concerned Lars follows. Margo is quick to tell Lars, as he pulls up a chair at her table, that "it's not just the bear": she has ended things with Erik, not because anything happened but because "he just wasn't very interesting." She tells Lars that the only reason she went out with Erik in the first place was that she was lonely. In her confusion and tearfulness, she doesn't immediately notice that while she has been talking, Lars has quietly and gingerly removed the noose and begun to tend to the bear. I find this sequence extraordinary. Here we see Lars performing CPR on the teddy bear in an unbelievably sweet and gentle and yet at the same time emotionally masterful way—an achievement that, I submit, is a function of Ryan Gosling's particular powers on film.[12] Of course, Margo does not believe that her teddy is a Real Bear, and Lars does not believe that it's a Real Bear, but Lars's resuscitative efforts have the effect of creating something real between these two people, despite the very different topologies of their individual experiences with loneliness.

So Margo finds herself asking Lars what he is doing on Friday night, and it turns out that since Bianca has been newly elected by the good people of the town as a member of the School Board and has a meeting at that time, he is free. The two of them end up in a bowling alley and are unexpectedly joined by some acquaintances. As the camera watches her from Lars's point of view, we see that and how and why Margo—until now, no less frumpy than anyone else in the town—is transfigured for Lars into an object of desire and in this way, through her capacity to rouse and arouse him, becomes for him a real girl, someone he is able, for the first time, fully to see, to appreciate, to want. Margo's desirability is a function for Lars of her becoming animate, that is to say, of her self-animation, her embodied spontaneity, which Kelli Garner, playing Margo, is able bring out via her joy in bowling badly. It is Lars's desire for Margo that of course will sound the death knell for Bianca, since what used to seem to Lars to be Bianca's powers of auto-animation have been revealed to him as a function of his own fear and his neighbors' fears of the power of their own desire. The dropping away of this fear reveals to Lars his own loneliness. His expanded capacity for desire is equivalent for Lars, as it is for any human being in similar circumstances, to discovering in himself a bottomless capacity for, and well of, pain. The townspeople, having more experience in this neck of the emotional woods than Lars does, do what good neighbors do: they come and sit with him and feed him casseroles.

So as the grim northern winter turns to spring, Bianca falls gravely ill. After a short stint in the emergency room, she recovers enough to accompany Lars, Gus, and Karin (now very close to becoming a mother) to the local lake. Gus and Karin decide to go for a walk while Lars and Bianca remain behind. The camera is trained on them sitting closely together, Lars clearly both fighting off tears and thinking. He slowly turns toward Bianca, grabs her chin, and gives her a slow kiss, for what reads like the first time. Pulling back, he looks into her eyes and dissolves into tears, eventually weeping into her shoulder. You could read Lars here, I suppose, as not being quite aware that the reason that Bianca will die, in the very next scene, is that he will walk her into the frigid lake and figuratively drown her, as though he were still mostly delusive and sorrowful about her illness. But I submit that what we're witnessing here is Lars's painful realization that he is a human being, that is to say, someone who is capable of being overcome, drowned, by real feelings of pain, but also, it is turning out, capable of surviving these feelings. Which means that it is time for the sex toy to go back into its box—a true casket, this time—now that it has performed the unexpected function of humanizing the people who came into contact with it.

Let me conclude with the suggestion that we think of this sex toy, Bianca, as standing in for *Lars and the Real Girl*—that is, the film—itself. Like Lars, we are drawn to allow ourselves to be animated by the experience of watching movies. The ordinary things we see on the screen are transmogrified for us into objects of what Heidegger might have been willing to call our solicitude, objects that make demands upon our capacity for responsiveness and engagement. As Cavell points out often in his writings on film, the very best instances of the medium not only display but also explicitly foreground and reflect upon its expressive and evocative powers. I submit that *Lars*, which asks us to think about the real and the unreal, and specifically about what a real girl is and whether the experience of staring at such a girl in the dark in a movie theater is invariably best understood in terms of the concept of voyeurism or objectification, has much to show us about the searing pain of acknowledging our most human desires, even as we try to pretend that it's all just make-believe.[13]

Notes
Acknowledgments
Index

Notes

Preface

1. See Nancy Bauer, "Is Feminist Philosophy a Contradiction in Terms?," in *Simone de Beauvoir, Philosophy, and Feminism* (New York: Columbia University Press, 2001).

2. I was of course familiar at the time—who couldn't have been?—with Judith Butler's *Gender Trouble: Feminism and the Subversion of Identity* (New York: Routledge, 1990) and her famous claim, inspired in part by Austin's *How to Do Things with Words*, that gender should be understood as a function of "performativity." But Butler's interest in Austin struck me as pretty much limited to this riff on his terminology; and so, though I have written here and there about Butler (e.g., in "Is Feminist Philosophy a Contradiction in Terms?"), her writing did not move me to think more deeply about what Austin was doing with his words.

3. For example, Langton claims that when pornography is authoritative in a culture, which she believes it plausibly is at least in certain milieus these days, then it subordinates and silences women, while Hornsby rejects the subordination claim. For references to their relevant papers, and to other papers in the relevant literature, see the notes to Chapter 5.

4. The standard definition of pornography used by MacKinnon and Andrea Dworkin is this:

We define pornography as the graphic sexually explicit subordination of women through pictures and words that also includes (i) women are presented dehumanized as sexual objects, things, or commodities; or (ii) women are presented as sexual objects who enjoy humiliation or pain; or (iii) women are presented as sexual objects experiencing sexual pleasure in rape, incest or other sexual assault; or (iv) women are presented as sexual objects tied up, cut up or mutilated or bruised or physically hurt; or (v) women are presented in postures or positions of sexual submission, servility, or display; or (vi) women's body parts—including but not limited to vaginas, breasts, or buttocks—are exhibited such that women are reduced to those parts; or (vii) women are presented being penetrated by objects or animals; or (viii) women are presented in scenarios of degradation, humiliation, injury, torture, shown as filthy or inferior, bleeding, bruised, or hurt in a context that makes these conditions sexual. (Dworkin and MacKinnon, *Pornography and Civil Rights: A New Day for Women's Equality* (Minneapolis: Organizing Against Pornography, 1988), 138.)

For an example of work that questions the value of Austin's "speech-act theory" in understanding what pornography does, see Ishani Maitra's "Silencing Speech" (*Canadian Journal of Philosophy* 39, no. 2 (June 2009): 324f), in which Maitra argues that feminist philosophers interested in defending the silencing claim—mentioned in note 3 above and discussed in more depth in Chapter 5—should be turning to H. P. Grice, not Austin, for help.

5. For example, in *Only Words* (Cambridge, MA: Harvard University Press, 1996), 121, n. 3.

6. She is, for example, deeply suspicious of what she regards as the stronghold that she believes Cartesian epistemology holds in philosophy and the law. See, e.g., *Toward a Feminist Theory of the State* (Cambridge, MA: Harvard University Press, 1989), chapter 6, "Method and Politics," especially the first full paragraph on p. 123.

7. MacKinnon, "Foreword," in *Speech and Harm: Controversies over Free Speech*, ed. Maitra and Mary Kate McGowan (Oxford: Oxford University Press, 2012), xv. Lorna Finlayson makes a similar point about the tone of MacKinnon's remarks in this foreword. I share Finlayson's concern about the value of cannibalizing Austin to buttress the views of MacKinnon and Dworkin, though we are reaching this conclusion in importantly different ways. See Finlayson, "How to Screw Things with Words," *Hypatia*, first published online June 30, 2014.

8. As philosophical defenders of MacKinnon are wont to observe, it's true that MacKinnon has been accused of mounting philosophically indefensible arguments. The locus classicus here is W. A. Parent, "A Second Look at Pornography and the Subordination of Women," *The Journal of Philosophy* 87, no. 4 (April 1990): 205–11. However, the vast majority of MacKinnon naysayers disagree with her not because they think she makes bad arguments but because they think she is *wrong*.

9. "Pornutopia" is reprinted from *n+1* magazine, no. 5 (Winter 2007): 63–73. "Lady Power" and the follow-up article "Authority and Arrogance: A Response" are reprinted from the *New York Times Opinionator* blog (*The Stone*). The first post was published on June 20, 2010, and is available at http://opinionator.blogs.nytimes.com/2010/06/20/lady-power/; the second post was published on June 30, 2010, and is available at http://opinionator.blogs

.nytimes.com/2010/06/30/authority-and-arrogance-a-response. I thank the *New York Times* for permission to reprint these pieces.

10. Charlotte Witt, ed., *Feminist Metaphysics: Explorations in the Ontology of Sex, Gender and the Self* (New York: Springer, 2010). I thank Springer for permission to reprint this essay.

11. *Reading Cavell* (New York: Routledge, 2006), 68–97. I thank Routledge for permission to include this new version of the essay in the present volume.

12. Langton, "Speech Acts and Unspeakable Acts," *Philosophy and Public Affairs* 22, no. 4 (1993): 293–330.

Chapter 1

1. Carl Elliott, a philosopher at the University of Minnesota who a few years ago in an article in the *Atlantic Monthly* brought wide attention to the phenomenon of voluntary amputation, has raised the question of whether perversions are contagious: whether you can catch one simply from becoming aware of it. It may well be the case that certain sexual preferences are largely a function of learning what's out there. But this does not change the fact that there's a whole lot out there.

2. Some of the material in this section is expressed in similar form in "Beauvoir on the Allure of Self-Objectification" (Chapter 4 of this book). See the preface for my rationale for allowing this overlap to stand.

Chapter 2

1. This piece was published in the *New York Times* blog *The Stone* on June 20, 2010.

2. The video interview from which this quotation is taken is no longer available on the Internet. Any number of news outlets have commented on it, however; you can find them by entering the quotation into a search engine.

3. The Powers interview is available at http://articles.latimes.com/2009 /dec/13/entertainment/la-ca-lady-gaga13-2009dec13.

4. The interview in which she is quoted is available at http://www.rolling stone.com/music/news/the-broken-heart-and-violent-fantasies-of-lady-gaga -20100708.

5. Laurie Fendrich, "Lady Gaga: Hope for the Homely," available at http: //chronicle.com/blogs/brainstorm/lady-gaga-hope-for-the-homely/24961.

Chapter 3

1. See *Jacobellis v. Ohio*, 378 U.S. 184 (1964).

2. *Miller v. California*, 413 U.S. 15 (1973).

3. For an argument that it's reasonable to categorize all of these thinkers as, broadly speaking, part of what I am calling the phenomenological tradition, see Simon Glendinning, *In the Name of Phenomenology* (London: Routledge, 2007). For a capsule summary of the view expressed in this book, see

Glendinning, "What Is Phenomenology?" *Philosophy Compass* 3, no. 1 (January 2008): 30–50.

4. For the record, I take this mutual informing to be under study in Hegel's *Phenomenology of Spirit*.

5. See, for example, Martha C. Nussbaum, "Objectification," *Philosophy & Public Affairs* 24, no. 4 (1995): 249–91, and "Feminism, Virtue, and Objectification" in *Sex and Ethics: Essays on Sexuality, Virtue and the Good Life*, ed. Raja Halwani (Basingstoke: Palgrave Macmillan, 2007); Sally Haslanger, "On Being Objective and Being Objectified," in *A Mind of One's Own*, ed. Louise M. Antony and Charlotte Witt, 2nd ed., 209–53 (Boulder: Westview Press, 2002); Catharine A. MacKinnon, *Only Words* (Cambridge, MA: Harvard University Press, 1993); Rae Langton, "Speech Acts and Unspeakable Acts," *Philosophy and Public Affairs* 22, no. 4 (1993): 293–330; Barbara Herman, "Could It Be Worth Thinking about Kant on Sex and Marriage?," in *A Mind of One's Own*, ed. Antony and Witt, 53–72; Evangelia Papadaki, "Sexual Objectification: From Kant to Contemporary Feminism," *Contemporary Political Theory* 6 (2007): 330–48, "Women's Objectification and the Norm of Assumed Objectivity," *Episteme: A Journal of Social Epistemology* 5, no. 2 (2008): 239–50; "What Is Objectification?," *Journal of Moral Philosophy* 7 (2010): 16–36, and "Feminist Perspectives on Objectification," *Stanford Encyclopedia of Philosophy* (available at http://plato.stanford.edu/archives/spr2010/entries/feminism-objectification/, March 10, 2010; substantial revision June 6, 2014); M. C. Dillon, "Sex Objects and Sexual Objectification: Erotic versus Pornographic Depiction," *Journal of Phenomenological Psychology* 29, no. 1 (1998): 92–115; Raja Halwani, *Philosophy of Love, Sex, and Marriage: An Introduction* (New York: Routledge, 2010); Patricia Marino, "The Ethics of Sexual Objectification: Autonomy and Consent," *Inquiry* 51, no. 4 (2008): 345–64; Mary Kate McGowan, "Debate: On Silencing and Sexual Refusal," *Journal of Political Philosophy* 17, no. 4 (2009): 487–94; and Carolyn McLeod, "Mere and Partial Means: The Full Range of the Objectification of Women," in *Feminist Moral Philosophy*, ed. Samantha Brennan (Calgary: University of Calgary Press, 2003). For an interesting and subtle challenge to this literature, see Jennifer M. Saul, "On Treating Things as People: Objectification, Pornography, and the History of the Vibrator," *Hypatia* 21, no. 2 (April 1, 2006): 45–61.

6. See Saul, "Stop Thinking So Much about 'Sexual Harassment,'" *Journal of Applied Philosophy* 31, no. 3 (August 1, 2014): 307–21, for an argument about sexual harassment that, in its deflationary aspects, seems to me to bear a family resemblance to my project in this chapter. Saul argues that people who are trying to fight sexual harassment by laying out a set of criteria for what counts as the phenomenon are not using their time wisely. My argument shares features with Saul's but goes further in suggesting that it is a waste of time for philosophers to try to specify the marks and features of (in my case) sexual objectification. One difference between sexual harassment and sexual objectification is that the former is also a legal notion; Saul may well agree with what I'm saying when it comes to sexual objectification.

7. I am deeply grateful to Chris Strauber, Humanities Research Librarian at Tufts, for researching the origin of the term *sexual objectification* for me. Neither of us could pinpoint a founding instance of the term. We did discover

that it was used to mean "dehumanization" (though not in the context of a discussion of gender) in some mid-20th-century psychoanalytic literature; see, e.g., Thomas Hora, "Ontic Perspectives in Psychoanalysis," *The American Journal of Psychoanalysis* 19 (1959): 134–142. It's also clear that the feminist use of the term "objectification" to name a dimension of sexism spiked after the publication of Laura Mulvey's iconic essay in feminist film studies, "Visual Pleasure and Narrative Cinema," originally published in 1975 in the journal *Screen* (Vol. 3, no. 16 (Sept. 21, 1975), 6–18).

8. See Marx, "Estranged Labour," in Karl Marx, Friedrich Engels, and Robert C Tucker, *The Marx-Engels Reader*, ed. Robert C Tucker (New York: Norton, 1978).

9. See, e.g., Wilhelm Dilthey, *Selected Works*, vol. 4, ed. R. A. Makkreel and F. Rodi (Princeton, NJ: Princeton University Press, 1996), 236–37.

10. Here there may be resonances between my view and that of Sally Haslanger and her work on social kinds. See especially Part Three of Haslanger, *Resisting Reality: Social Construction and Social Critique* (New York: Oxford University Press, 2012).

11. Of course, instances of sexual objectification are not always purely visual. Consider the ditty Seth McFarlane composed and performed at the 2013 Academy Awards ceremony:

We saw your boobs
We saw your boobs
In the movie that we saw, we saw your boobs.
Meryl Streep, we saw your boobs in *Silkwood*
Naomi Watts' in *Mulholland Drive*
Angelina Jolie, we saw your boobs in *Gia*
They made us feel excited and alive.
Anne Hathaway, we saw your boobs in *Brokeback Mountain*
Halle Berry, we saw them in *Monster's Ball*
Nicole Kidman in *Eyes Wide Shut*
Marisa Tomei in *The Wrestler*, but
We haven't seen Jennifer Lawrence's boobs at all. . . .
And whatever you're shooting right now.
We saw your boobs
We saw your boobs . . .

(Source: http://knowyourmeme.com/memes/we-saw-your-boobs)

12. See https://facadeweekly.files.wordpress.com/2013/05/lynx-ad-wash-me.jpg.

13. See http://symbolicslyness.files.wordpress.com/2011/09/bkseveninch.jpg.

14. See http://thesocietypages.org/socimages/2009/09/24/power-sex-and-shoelaces/#comments (the first three images),

15. See http://infofascination.blogspot.com/2010_06_01_archive.html.

16. See https://www.flickr.com/photos/cyclecrank/4681474609/.

17. See http://www.campaignlive.co.uk/news/943769/.

18. http://mancunion.com/wp-content/uploads/2013/11/TomFord.jpeg.

19. Herman, "Could It Be Worth Thinking about Kant on Sex and Marriage?"

20. Immanuel Kant, *Lectures on Ethics* (Indianapolis: Hackett Publishing Company, 1980), 164.

21. For a history of coverture law in England, see Tim Stretton and Krista J. Kesselring, *Married Women and the Law Coverture in England and the Common Law World* (Montreal: McGill Queens University Press, 2013); and in the United States, Nancy F. Cott, *Public Vows: A History of Marriage and the Nation* (Cambridge, MA: Harvard University Press, 2002).

22. Some philosophers, however, have made heroic efforts to redeem Kant on this front; for what I regard as the best attempt, see Mari Mikkola, "Kant on Moral Agency and Women's Nature," *Kantian Review* 16, no. 1 (March 2011): 89–111.

23. Nussbaum, "Objectification."

24. Ibid., 257.

25. Ibid.

26. Langton, *Sexual Solipsism: Philosophical Essays on Pornography and Objectification* (New York: Oxford University Press, 2009), 228–29.

27. Nussbaum, "Objectification," 256–57.

28. Ibid., 265.

29. Ibid., 290.

30. See especially Martha Nussbaum, *Women and Human Development: The Capabilities Approach* (Cambridge: Cambridge University Press, 2000). See also Amartya Sen, "Gender Inequality and Theories of Justice," in *Women, Culture, and Development: A Study of Human Capabilities*, ed. Martha C. Nussbaum and Jonathan Glover (Oxford: Clarendon Press, 1995). Both Nussbaum and Sen have written extensively, and in a similar vein, about women and adaptive preferences.

31. See, e.g., "Speaker's Freedom and Maker's Knowledge" in Langton, *Sexual Solipsism*, 289–310.

Chapter 4

1. Sally Haslanger seems to harbor this hope: "A consequence of my view is that when justice is achieved, there will no longer be white women (there will no longer be men or women, whites or members of any other race). At that point we—or more realistically, our descendants—won't need the concepts of race and gender to describe our current situation" (Haslanger, "What Are We Talking About? The Semantics and Politics of Social Kinds," *Hypatia* 20, no. 4 (2005): 11. This article is reprinted in Haslanger, *Resisting Reality: Social Construction and Social Critique* (Oxford: Oxford University Press, 2012), 365–80.). Since I won't have the opportunity to do so later, let me say here that it is not clear to me that the cases of gender and race are parallel in the way that Haslanger implies they are. To put the point in Haslanger's terms: I doubt that there will ever come a time in which there will no longer be men or women, but the reasons for this doubt, which will become clearer later in this chapter, appear to me not to have analogues in the case of race.

2. See Judith Butler, *Gender Trouble: Feminism and the Subversion of Identity* (New York: Routledge, 1990), especially chapter 1. For a similar argument about the dicey political effects of deploying the concept *lesbian*, see Butler, "Imitation and Gender Insubordination," in *The Second Wave: A Reader in Feminist Theory*, ed. Linda J. Nicholson, 300–321 (New York: Routledge, 1997).

3. I do not mean to imply that these issues are not important. My concern is with the long-term stasis in the terms of the debate and the assumptions that guide it.

4. The key concept here is *fetish*: my point is that what I am calling gender eliminativism and gender reificationism do not take the phenomenology of womanhood seriously. They treat women's experience mainly as something to be analyzed away. As my characterization of Catharine MacKinnon's position suggests, however, the two -isms are not mutually exclusive. You can coherently believe both the gender-reificationist view that what it is to be a woman is consistent across beings properly called "women" (namely, to be treated as an object for men's sexual exploitation and consumption) and the gender-eliminativist claim that the world would and could be a better place without "women," so construed, in it. Furthermore, both gender-eliminativists and gender-reificationists can endorse social constructionism. In coining the term *gender reificationism* instead of using the old term *gender essentialism*, I mean to underscore, as MacKinnon does, that you can have a definite view about what gender is and still think that gender is socially constructed. For a decisive argument against the view that gender essentialism and social constructionism are mutually exclusive, see Charlotte Witt, *The Metaphysics of Gender* (Oxford: Oxford University Press, 2011).

5. Simone de Beauvoir, *The Second Sex*, trans. H. M. Parshley (New York: Vintage, 1949/1989), xix. The original French reads: *On ne sait plus bien s'il existe encore des femmes, s'il en existera toujours, s'il faut ou non le souhaiter, quelle place elles occupent en ce monde, quelle place elles devraient y occuper* (Beauvoir, *Le deuxième sexe* I (Paris: Gallimard, 1949/1999), 11).

6. Beauvoir, *The Second Sex*, xx–xi. Translation modified. The original French reads: *Et en vérité il suffit de se promener les yeux ouverts pour constater que l'humanité se partage en deux catégories d'individus dont les vêtements, le visage, le corps, les sourires, la démarche, les intérêts, les occupations sont manifestement différents: peut-être ces différences sont-elles superficielles, peut-être sont-elles destines à disparaître. Ce qui est certain c'est que pour l'instant elles existent avec une éclatante évidence* (Beauvoir, *Le deuxième sexe* I, 13).

7. "If I wish to define myself, I am obliged first off to declare: 'I am a woman'; this truth is the background against which all further assertions will stand out" (Beauvoir, *The Second Sex*, xxi; translation modified). The original French reads: *Si je veux me définir je suis oblige d'abord de déclarer: « Je suis une femme »; cette vérité constitue le fond sur lequel s'enlèvera toute autre affirmation* (Beauvoir, *Le deuxième sexe*, 14). For my interpretation of this move of Beauvoir's, see Nancy Bauer, *Simone de Beauvoir, Philosophy, and Feminism* (New York: Columbia University Press, 2001), especially chapters 1 and 2.

8. Beauvoir, *The Second Sex*, 732. The French reads: *les hommes et femmes affirment sans équivoque leur fraternité* (Beauvoir, *Le deuxième sexe* II, 663).

9. Beauvoir, *The Second Sex*, 729. The French reads: *Il semble à peu près certain qu'elles accéderont d'ici un temps plus ou moins long à la parfaite égalité économique et sociale* (Beauvoir, *Le deuxième sexe* II, 659).

10. My translation. The French reads: *entraînera une métamorphose intérieure* (Beauvoir, *Le deuxième sexe* II, 659).

11. Butler is actually an exception here. In her very early work in feminist philosophy she explicitly and frequently expresses her debt to Beauvoir. However, Butler's view is that Beauvoir did not understand the implications of her views when taken to their logical limits. See, e.g., Butler, "Sex and Gender in Simone de Beauvoir's Second Sex," *Yale French Studies* no. 72 (1986): 35–49.

12. I say "in the West" rather than "at my university" or even "in the United States" because of responses I've gotten to this chapter from young European women.

13. Dan Kindlon, *Alpha Girls: Understanding the New American Girl and How She Is Changing the World* (New York: Rodale, 2006), 7.

14. Ibid., xiv.

15. Ibid., xv.

16. Ibid., 12.

17. Ibid., 15.

18. Ibid., 31.

19. Ibid., xv.

20. Ibid., 233, 234.

21. For an interesting discussion of *Girls Gone Wild* and related phenomena, see Ariel Levy, *Female Chauvinist Pigs: Women and the Rise of Raunch Culture* (New York: Free Press, 2006).

22. You could make the case, I think, that Descartes's understanding of this split is fundamentally phenomenological as well, at least in its origins. Descartes of course postulates that the mind is radically different from the body and in fact has priority over the body when it comes to explaining how we have any experience of the world. But this postulate is a conclusion he reaches from the experience of being able to doubt the existence of his body but not his mind. In the introduction to *The Second Sex*, I have suggested, Beauvoir proceeds as though she is rewriting the *Meditations* from the point of view of someone who is investigating what a woman is and therefore cannot doubt the existence of her own body without sabotaging the project from the start. See chapter 2 of Bauer, *Simone de Beauvoir, Philosophy, and Feminism*.

23. Beauvoir, *The Second Sex*, xxx.

24. Ibid., xxiv. See also Beauvoir, *Le deuxième sexe* I, 18.

25. Beauvoir, *The Second Sex*, xxvii, translation modified. The French reads: *Refuser d'être l'Autre, refuser la complicité avec l'homme, ce serait pour elles renoncer à tout les avantages que l'alliance avec la caste supérieure peut leur conférer. L'homme suzerain protègera matériellement la femme-lige et il se chargera de justifier so existence: avec le risque économique elle esquive le risque métaphysique d'une liberté qui doit inventer ses fins sans secours. . . . C'est un chemin facile: on évite ainsi l'angoisse et la tension de l'existence authentiquement assumée* (Beauvoir, *Le deuxième sexe* I, 21).

26. Beauvoir, *The Second Sex*, 728. The French reads: *au lieu de vivre l'ambiguïté de sa condition* (Beauvoir, *Le deuxième sexe* II, 658).

27. Beauvoir, *The Second Sex*, 402. The French reads: *l'expérience érotique est une de celles qui découvrent aux êtres humains de la façon la plus poignante l'ambiguïté de leur condition; ils s'y éprouvent comme chair et comme esprit, comme l'autre et comme sujet* (Beauvoir, *Le deuxième sexe* II, 190).

28. Beauvoir, *The Second Sex*, 402.

29. These last few thoughts are expressed in similar form in "Pornutopia" (Chapter 1 of this book). See the preface for my rationale for allowing this overlap to stand.

Chapter 5

1. See Stanley Cavell's account of Austin's delight in this particular instance of wordplay in "Austin at Criticism," in *Must We Mean What We Say?*, 2nd ed. (Cambridge: Cambridge University Press, 2002), 97–114.

2. Here I have in mind work in pragmatics by some of its most influential practitioners: John Searle, Kent Bach, François Récanati, and Charles Travis. See, for example, Searle, "Austin on Locutionary and Illocutionary Acts," *The Philosophical Review* 77, no. 4 (October 1, 1968): 405–24; Bach, "Speech Acts and Pragmatics," in *Blackwell Guide to the Philosophy of Language*, ed. Michael Devitt and Richard Hanley (Malden, MA: Blackwell, 2003), 147–67; Récanati, *Literal Meaning: The Very Idea* (Cambridge: Cambridge University Press, 2003); Charles Travis, "Pragmatics," in *A Companion to the Philosophy of Language*, ed. C. Wright and B. Hale (Oxford: Blackwell, 1997), 87–107.

3. See Ludwig Wittgenstein, *Philosophical Investigations/Philosophische Untersuchungen*, trans. G. E. M. Anscombe (Oxford: Blackwell, 2003), §66.

4. I borrow the metaphor from Austin's discussion of his philosophical method in "A Plea for Excuses," in which he notes that

> we should prefer a field which is not too much trodden into bogs or tracks by traditional philosophy, for in that case even "ordinary" language will often have become infected with the jargon of extinct theories, and our own prejudices too, as the upholders or imbibers of theoretical views, will be too readily, and often insensibly, engaged. . . . Granted that our subject is . . . neighbouring, analogous or germane in some way to some notorious centre of philosophical trouble, then . . . we should be certain of what we are after: a good site for *field work* in philosophy. Here at last we should be able to unfreeze, to loosen up and get going on agreeing about discoveries, however small, and on agreeing about how to reach agreement. (J. L. Austin, *Philosophical Papers*, ed. J. O. Urmson and G. J. Warnock (New York: Oxford University Press, 1979), 182–83.)

5. Austin, *How to Do Things with Words*, 2nd ed., ed. J. O. Urmson and Marina Sbisá (Cambridge, MA: Harvard University Press, 1975), 2.

6. Ibid., 2–3. Let me note that it is not at all clear that Austin is here *endorsing* a form of ethical non-cognitivism. To the contrary, it seems that he is dubious about the doctrine. Consider two pieces of indirect evidence for this judgment. First, the paragraph in which the sentence I've just quoted is embedded takes digs at various fashions in the philosophy of Austin's day no

fewer than five times. The context of the remark about "ethical propositions" is this: Austin first notes the development of the view that certain statements— those that are not "verifiable" (his scare quotes)—are in fact pseudo-statements and then notes a "second stage" in this development, in which pseudo-statements are reconceived as utterances that were never intended to be stating things in the first place. "Ethical propositions" exemplify—"perhaps"—such (non-)pseudo-statements. Second, on 19–20, when Austin is in the middle of his discussion of the "infelicities" to which all attempts to act, via words or otherwise, are subject, he says this: "A great many of the acts which fall within the province of Ethics are *not*, as philosophers are too prone to assume, simply in the last resort *physical movements*: very many of them have the general character, in whole or part, of conventional or ritual acts, and are therefore, among other things, exposed to infelicity." If you put this together with what Austin says in the sentence to which this note is attached, you see how much of a stretch it is to imagine that he is agreeing with non-cognitivists that "ethical propositions" are intended as prescriptivists say they are. His view, rather, seems to be that ethics is about acts, verbal or otherwise; and therefore the question of whether "ethical propositions" are genuine propositions does not arise. See also this passage, in the paragraph after the "province of Ethics" sentence: "The more we consider a statement not as a sentence (or proposition) but as an act of speech (out of which the others are logical constructions) the more we are studying the whole thing as an act" (20).

7. Cavell suggests that Austin's characterization of the perlocution leaves much to be desired. He puts pressure both on Austin's lack of interest in the expressive powers of speech and on his insinuation that the relationship between a given stretch of speech and the perlocution it achieves is essentially arbitrary. See "Passionate and Performative Utterances: Morals of Encounter," in *Contending With Stanley Cavell*, edited by Russell B. Goodman (Oxford: Oxford University Press, 2005), 197-198. This essay appears in slightly different form as "Performative and Passionate Utterance" in Cavell, *Philosophy the Day after Tomorrow* (Cambridge, MA; Belknap Press of Harvard University Press, 2006). I discuss Austin on perfomative force later in the present chapter and at greater length in Chapter 6.

8. For the record: there are important distinctions between the sorts of infelicity that we find in these two cases. In the christening case, Austin observes, we will say that the ship was not in fact christened—that, because I am not authorized to christen your ship, the procedure does not come off, that it "misfires." But my insincerity in swearing that I'll be there at five does not likewise nullify my promise, though what I've done constitutes an "abuse" of the procedure and renders my act of promising "hollow" or "void."

9. Austin, *How to Do Things with Words*, 148.

10. Ibid.

11. Ibid., 21. Jennifer Hornsby, in a series of papers (cited in note 24 below) on the role of illocution in a theory of language, especially a theory sensitive to the moral and political dimensions of linguistic communication, argues that Austin's characterization of illocution suffers from his failure to distinguish carefully between the concept of an *action* and that of an *act*. In particular, she

thinks, Austin's sloppiness here made it impossible for him to draw a principled line between illocution and perlocution.

12. Austin, *How to Do Things with Words*, 38.

13. Ibid., 163–64.

14. This from conversations with Cavell, who participated in some of these sessions.

15. Elizabeth Barnes adopts a version of this view in a recent paper:

> When we are making claims about genders, races, social types, and social structures, we're not speaking "Ontologese"—we're not trying to limn the fundamental structure of the universe. But neither are we doing ordinary language philosophy. We're not asking how ordinary speakers use gender and race terms, or whether ordinary speakers quantify over social kinds. . . . Trans women are women, whether or not ordinary speakers are happy to apply the term "woman" to them. Genders are not biological, whether or not the folk theory of gender assumes that genders are co-extensive with (and perhaps identical to) biological sex categories. And so on.

("Going Beyond the Fundamental: Feminism in Contemporary Metaphysics," unpublished paper (August 13, 2014, version), 11.) Sally Haslanger remarks that "the complexity of our use of words in different contexts is something ordinary language philosophers were well attuned to, and some of their methods and ideas are tremendously valuable for this project," where "this project" is an attempt to justify social constructionist accounts of gender (Haslanger, "What Good Are Our Intuitions?," *Aristotelian Society Supplementary Volume* 80, no. 1 (June 1, 2006): n. 16, 107). However, she seems to understand OLP as fundamentally committed to the idea that the "ordinary" usages are the ones that get the most votes. On her view, ordinary usage fixes the *reference* of terms like *woman* but not their content, which we can discover only by using social theory.

16. See Austin, "A Plea for Excuses," 185, n. 1.

17. This claim of course needs fleshing out. What I have in mind is the way that Searle and certain other "speech-act theorists" (e.g., Bach and Récanati) embrace the standard division of labor in contemporary philosophy of language according to the categories of syntax, semantics, and pragmatics. On my view, Austin's work constitutes a radical challenge to the enterprise of making sweeping claims about how our use of words works and thus to the very idea of "philosophy of language," at least as it is currently construed. For a start on a defense of this claim, see Chapter 7.

18. Austin, "Performative Utterances," *Philosophical Papers*, 239.

19. Langton's many writings on this topic include the following: "Whose Right? Ronald Dworkin, Women, and Pornographers," *Philosophy and Public Affairs* 19, no. 4 (1990): 311–59; "Speech Acts and Unspeakable Acts," *Philosophy and Public Affairs* 22, no. 4 (Autumn 1993): 293–330; "Sexual Solipsism," *Philosophical Topics* 23, no. 2 (Fall 1995): 49–87; "Pornography, Speech Acts, and Silence," in *Ethics in Practice*, ed. Hugh LaFollette (Basil Blackwell, 1997), 338–49; "Free Speech and Illocution" (with Jennifer Hornsby), *Legal Theory* 4

(1998): 21–37; "Subordination, Silence, and Pornography's Authority," *Censorship and Silencing: Practices of Cultural Regulation*, ed. Robert Post (Los Angeles: Getty Museum Publishing, 1998); "Scorekeeping in a Pornographic Language Game" (with Caroline West), *Australasian Journal of Philosophy* 77, no. 3 (September 1999): 303–19; "Pornography and Free Speech," *The Philosophers' Magazine* 11 (2000): 41–42; "Projection and Objectification," in *The Future for Philosophy*, ed. Brian Leiter (Oxford: Oxford University Press, 2004), 285–303; "Disenfranchised Silence," in *Common Minds*, ed. Geoffrey Brennan et al. (Oxford: Oxford University Press, 2007), 199–214; and "Beyond Belief: Pragmatics in Hate Speech and Pornography," in *Speech and Harm: Controversies over Free Speech*, ed. Mary Kate McGowan and Ishani Maitra (Oxford: Oxford University Press, 2012). Many of Langton's papers on sexuality, pornography, and related topics have been collected in Langton, *Sexual Solipsism: Philosophical Essays on Pornography and Objectification* (Oxford: Oxford University Press, 2009).

20. As Jennifer Hornsby notes, the right to "free speech" is notably more sacrosanct in the United States—where it is constitutionally protected—than it is in other democracies (where it is not). See, e.g., Hornsby's "Free and Equal Speech," *Imprints* 1, no. 2 (1996): 59–60.

21. Readers familiar with Austin's views may balk at my elision here of *illocutionary* and *performative*. See Chapter 7 for an explanation.

22. See Langton, "Speech Acts and Unspeakable Acts," 307–8. A number of philosophers have written on the subject of pornography's authority, including Lester Green (see: "Pornographies," *The Journal of Political Philosophy* 7, no. 3 (1999): 1–26; and "Pornographizing, Subordinating, and Silencing," in *Censorship and Silencing: Practices of Cultural Regulation*, ed. Robert C. Post (Los Angeles: Getty Museum, 1998), 285–311); Mary Kate McGowan (see "On Pornography: MacKinnon, Speech Acts, and 'False' Construction," *Hypatia* 20, no. 3 (July 1, 2005): 22–49; and "Conversational Exercitives: Something Else We Do with Our Words," *Linguistics and Philosophy* 27, no. 1 (February 1, 2004): 93–111); Nellie Wieland (see "Linguistic Authority and Convention in a Speech Act Analysis of Pornography," *Australasian Journal of Philosophy* 85, no. 3 (2007): 435–56); and Ishani Maitra (see "Subordinating Speech," in *Speech and Harm*, ed. Maitra and McGowan (Oxford: Oxford University Press, 2012), 94–120). In Chapter 6, I look at the question of pornography's authority in more depth and in the context of asking questions about the basis of the *philosopher's* authority.

23. See Austin, *How to Do Things with Words*, 153–55. I discuss verdictives in more depth below.

24. Not all philosophers who apply analyses fueled by philosophy of language and, in particular, by Austin agree that pornography is a kind of speech. Most notably, perhaps, Jennifer Hornsby rejects this view. Relevant papers of hers include "Things Done with Words," in *Human Agency: Language, Duty, and Value*, ed. Jonathan Dancy, J. M. E. Moravcski, and C. Taylor (Stanford: Stanford University Press, 1988); "Philosophers and Feminists on Language Use," *Cogito* 2, no. 3 (Autumn 1988): 13–16; "Speech Acts and Pornography," *Women's Philosophical Review*, November 1993, reprinted in an amended version

in *The Problem of Pornography*, ed. Susan Dwyer (Florence, KY: Wadsworth, 1995); "Illocution and Its Significance," *Foundations of Speech Act Theory*, ed. Savas L. Tsohatzidis (New York: Routledge, 1994); "Free and Equal Speech," *Imprints* 1, no. 2 (1996): 59–76; "Disempowered Speech," *Philosophical Topics* 23, no. 2 (Fall 1995): 127–47; and "Feminism in Philosophy of Language: Communicative Speech Acts," in *The Cambridge Companion to Feminism in Philosophy*, ed. Miranda Fricker and Hornsby (Cambridge: Cambridge University Press, 2000), 87–106.

25. Langton, "Speech Acts and Unspeakable Acts," 293.

26. A number of philosophers and legal theorists have argued that pornography is not speech in *either* sense of the term. See, e.g., Frederick Schauer, *Free Speech: A Philosophical Enquiry* (Cambridge: Cambridge University Press, 1982); Jennifer Hornsby, "Speech Acts and Pornography," in *The Problem of Pornography*, ed. Susan Dwyer (Independence, KY: Cengage, 1995); and Andrew Koppelman, "Is Pornography 'Speech'?," SSRN Scholarly Paper (Rochester, NY: Social Science Research Network, March 1, 2007).

27. See Cavell's *The World Viewed* (Cambridge, MA: Harvard University Press, 1979), chapter 2; and Bazin's "The Ontology of the Photographic Image," in *What Is Cinema?*, vol. 1 (Berkeley: University of California Press, 1967), 9–16.

28. Austin, *How to Do Things with Words*, 119.

29. In the context of arguing that we need the techniques of analytic philosophy of language if we are to understand properly what the word *speech* means in the concept *free speech*, Hornsby acknowledges that "most pornographic material is not linguistic" and that some people "move, without any argument, between 'speech' in a narrow sense (confined to the linguistic) and 'speech' in the broadest sense (including all 'expression')." But, as an analytic philosopher of language, she is not interested in thinking about how nonlinguistic pornography does whatever it does. See Hornsby, "Free and Equal Speech," 62.

30 Austin, *How to Do Things With Words*, 119.

31. On Hornsby's view, Austin's claim about the important role convention plays in illocution was rash; it stemmed, she thinks, from his paying too much attention to highly ritualized illocutions, such as marrying, christening ships, baptizing, and so on. Hornsby argues that in many cases a sufficient condition for the success of a person's illocution is simply that her utterer grasps that she is attempting to perform it. For example, if you understand me to be trying to tell you something, then I will have successfully performed the illocution of *telling*. See Hornsby, "Illocution and Its Significance."

32. Catharine A. MacKinnon and Andrea Dworkin, *In Harm's Way: The Pornography Civil Rights Hearings* (Cambridge, MA: Harvard University Press, 1998), 439. In an antipornography ordinance that they helped the city of Minneapolis draft in the early 1980s, Dworkin and MacKinnon stipulate that the word "pornography" should be understood to denote:

the sexually explicit subordination of women, graphically depicted whether in pictures or in words, that also includes one or more of the following: (i) women are presented dehumanized as sexual objects, things or commodities; or (ii) women are presented as sexual objects who enjoy pain or humiliation; or (iii) women are presented as sexual objects who experience sexual pleasure in being raped; or (iv) women are presented as sexual objects tied up or cut up or mutilated or bruised or physically hurt; or (v) women are presented in postures of sexual submission or sexual servility, including by inviting penetration; or (vi) women's body parts—including but not limited to vaginas, breasts, or buttocks—are exhibited, such that women are reduced to those parts; or (vii) women are presented as whores by nature; or (viii) women are presented being penetrated by objects or animals; or (ix) women are presented in scenarios of degradation, injury, or torture, shown as filthy or inferior, bleeding, bruised, or hurt in a context that makes these conditions sexual. (*In Harm's Way*, 325)

This is the definition of pornography with which Langton and many others are working. See, e.g., "Speech Acts and Unspeakable Acts," 293–294.

33. United States Court of Appeals, Seventh Circuit, *American Booksellers v. Hudnut*, 771 F.2d 323 (1985), section I.

34. This accusation, from *American Booksellers v. Hudnut*, 598 F. Su 1316, 1334 (S.D. Ind. 1984), is quoted in Langton, "Speech Acts and Unspeakable Acts," 294.

35. MacKinnon and Dworkin, *In Harm's Way*, 439.

36. See, e.g., Nagel, "Personal Rights and Public Space," *Philosophy and Public Affairs* 24, no. 2 (Spring 1995): 83–107; Dworkin, "Do We Have a Right to Pornography?," in *A Matter of Principle* (Cambridge, MA: Harvard University Press, 1985), 335–72; Dworkin, "Liberty and Pornography," *New York Review of Books* 38, no. 14 (August 15, 1991); Dworkin, "Women and Pornography" (a review of Catharine MacKinnon's *Only Words*), *New York Review of Books* 40, no. 17 (October 21, 1993); and Dworkin (in an exchange with MacKinnon in the wake of his review of her book), "Women and Pornography," *New York Review of Books* 41, no. 5 (March 3, 1994).

37. Hornsby and Langton see a certain irony in liberals' understanding their view to be grounded in Mill's, for they read Mill in his famous chapter on the liberty of thought and expression to be championing not just the freedom to think and say what one wishes but, more essentially, the freedom to *do* things with one's words—what they call "freedom of illocution." For reasons that will, I hope, become clearer in the present chapter, as well as in Chapters 6 and 7, I have doubts about whether this notion is coherent.

38. Dworkin, "Do We Have a Right to Pornography?," 353.

39. See Dworkin, "Do We Have a Right to Pornography?," 356; and Nagel, "Personal Rights and Public Space," 106.

40. A landmark obscenity case, which defines "obscenity" in terms of what would offend "the average person" with respect to "community standards," is *Miller v. California*, 413 U.S. 15, 24 (1973). I discuss this case in a different context in Chapter 3.

41. See, e.g., MacKinnon, "Equality and Speech," in *Only Words* (Cambridge, MA: Harvard University Press, 1993), 69–112. See also her essay "Not a Moral Issue," in *Feminism Unmodified* (Cambridge, MA: Harvard University Press,

1988), 162–64; and her letter to the editor of *The New York Review of Books* in response to Ronald Dworkin's review of *Only Words*, in "Pornography: An Exchange," *New York Review of Books* 41, no. 5 (March 3, 1994).

42. See, e.g., Edward I. Donnerstein, Daniel Linz, and Steven Penrod, *The Question of Pornography: Research Findings and Policy* (New York: Free Press, 1987).

43. Langton, "Speech Acts and Unspeakable Acts," 313.

44. Ibid., 307–8. Austin introduces the category of "verdictives" on 153–55 of *Words*. Until further notice, all of the quotations from Austin are from this section of the book.

45. Austin calls preference-based opinions about how things should be "exercitives"; I discuss them in more depth later in this chapter. The material I cite below on verdictives is from *How to Do Things With Words*, 153–155.

46. See Langton, "Subordination, Silence, and Pornography's Authority," 267–70.

47. Langton, "Speech Acts and Unspeakable Acts," 307–8; my emphasis.

48. Austin, *How to Do Things with Words*, 155.

49. See Langton, "Speech Acts and Unspeakable Acts," 315f.

50. Recent changes in marriage laws in a number of US states and elsewhere in the world give us reason to hope that this example will become archaic in the foreseeable future.

51. Langton considers all of these examples in some depth in "Speech Acts and Unspeakable Acts." See 316–17 for her discussion of the first two examples and 320–22 for her treatment of the second two.

52. For various reasons that are not relevant here, Hornsby, in her somewhat different treatment of illocutionary silencing, prefers to think of illocutionary silencing as involving not a failure of "uptake," per se, but of what she calls "receptivity." Hornsby discusses the reasons for her way of understanding what's at the crux of illocutionary success in all of her writings on this subject; see note 24 for a list of these writings, and note especially her treatment of this subject in "Illocution and Its Significance."

53. Hornsby, "Illocution and Its Significance," 206, n. 28.

54. Ibid., 199.

55. For the idea that pornography "works by a process of psychological conditioning," see Langton and West, "Scorekeeping in a Pornographic Language Game," 303.

56. The *Hustler* spread is discussed in "Scorekeeping in a Pornographic Language Game," 311. Langton and West thank Catherine Itzin for drawing their attention to this example, which appears on p. 30 of *Pornography: Women, Violence, and Civil Liberties*, ed. Itzin (Oxford: Oxford University Press, 1993). The *Hustler* spread apparently is from the January 1983 issue; I have been unable to obtain a copy of it.

57. See Langton and West, "Scorekeeping in a Pornographic Language Game," 311.

58. David Lewis, "Scorekeeping in a Language Game," *Journal of Philosophical Logic* 8 (1979): 339–59, reprinted in Lewis's *Philosophical Papers*, vol. I (Oxford: Oxford University Press, 1983), 233–49.

59. The Jane example is from Langton and West, "Scorekeeping in a Pornographic Language Game," 308–10.

60. Langton and West, "Scorekeeping," 309. I note here a certain irony in Langton and West's relying on Lewis's notion of a language game, rather than that of Wittgenstein, from whom Lewis appropriates the term. Lewis's goal is to unearth a certain deep structure he presumes governs human conversation, one, specifically, that allows the presuppositions with which interlocutors are operating to be introduced in a tacit but conventional way. The idea that in our talk we rely on a species of attunement with one another is also important to Wittgenstein. But his work contests the notion that this attunement is a kind of *convention*. Unlike Wittgenstein, Lewis is not inclined to wonder whether our linguistic attunement with one another is deeper or more complicated than the notion of "convention" implies. I have come to appreciate the idea that we ought to wonder about this and that developing the notion of attunement requires a kind of Gestalt shift for those who describe human conversation as resting on "agreement" or convention, from Stanley Cavell. See, for example, Cavell's sustained discussion of Kripke's (mis)characterization of Wittgenstein's views on conversational attunement in "The Argument of the Ordinary," in *Conditions Handsome and Unhandsome* (Chicago: University of Chicago Press, 1990), 64–100.

61. See Langton and West, "Scorekeeping in a Pornographic Language Game," 310.

62. Langton and West do not have much to say about exactly what constitutes a "language game of sex." One gets the sense that by this concept they intend to include all attempts at illocutionary acts that have to do with sexual matters. This would mean that a woman's unspoken attempt at a refusal of sex—her look of horror or revulsion, say—would count as part of such a language game, albeit one in which the woman's attempt to pull off the illocutionary act of refusal does not count as a correct move in the game, given the presuppositions that pornographic materials have introduced into it without challenge. See Chapters 6 and 7 for more discussion of these matters, and see note 60 above for an indication of the direction in which my worries run.

63. Langton, "Speech Acts and Unspeakable Acts," 326.

64. Ibid.

65. Ibid., 312.

66. I am not including URLs here because they tend to change frequently, but examples of all of these fetishes are easily found online. See also my mentioning of such fetishes in a slightly different context in Chapter 1.

67. The Lewisian locus classicus here is *Convention: A Philosophical Study* (Cambridge, MA: Harvard University Press, 1969).

68. See Maitra, "Subordinating Speech," 117.

69. See Chapter 7 for a more extended discussion of the question of pornography's authority.

70. See, e.g., Marx's *Economic and Philosophical Manuscripts of 1844–1845*, *The Marx -Engels Reader*, ed. Robert C. Tucker, 2nd ed. (New York: Norton, 1978), 66–125.

71. See Sigmund Freud, *Civilization and its Discontents*, trans. and ed. By James Strachey (New York: W. W. Norton, 1961), 35-38.

72. See Linda Williams, *Hard Core: Power, Pleasure, and the "Frenzy of the Visible,"* expanded ed. (Berkeley: University of California Press, 1999), especially chapter 2.

73. Cavell, *The World Viewed*, enlarged ed. (Cambridge, MA: Harvard University Press, 1979), 44.

74. Unlike certain film theorists, Cavell is not suggesting that film-watchers (contemporary human beings, that is) are inherently voyeuristic, though that may be so. Rather, he is fleshing out a set of claims about film's power as a medium to transfigure the human body.

75. Cavell, *The World Viewed*, 45.

76. See note 32.

77. See *Brandenburg v. Ohio*, 395 U.S. 444 (1969).

78. In effect, I argue that, at the end of the day, Austin strategically undermines the work he has done in attempting to categorize utterances using various distinctions—that is, between *constative* and *performative*, and later in *How to Do Things With Words*, among *locutionary*, *illocutionary*, and *perlocutionary* forces and effects.

79. This is of course a key insight of critical race theory. See especially the essays in the groundbreaking volume *Words That Wound: Critical Race Theory, Assaultive Speech, And The First Amendment*, by Mari J. Matsuda, Charles R. Lawrence III, Richard Delgado, and Kimberlé Crenshaw. (Boulder, CO: Westview Press, 1993).

80. See "Passionate and Performative Utterances: Morals of Encounter," *op. cit.*, 191.

81. Cavell, *The World Viewed*, 21.

82. Ibid., 23.

83. Williams, *Hard Core*, Chapter 2.

84. Cavell, *The World Viewed*, 17.

85. Linda Williams, *Hard Core: Power, Pleasure, and the "Frenzy of the Visible,"* expanded ed. (Berkeley: University of California Press, 1999), 49.

86. A reader who reviewed the draft manuscript of this book for Harvard University Press wrote in her comments, "The author's apparent recommendation to go and watch more pornography is surprising given the background feminist argument that pornography is a kind of hate speech: it is like recommending to a member of a target race that they immerse themselves in racist propaganda." I hope that it is clear that I am not recommending that all women, let alone all people, go and watch more pornography; I am suggesting that people who choose to write about what pornography does need to familiarize themselves with it. This suggestion is at the heart of Chapter 1.

Chapter 6

1. J. L. Austin, *How to Do Things with Words*, 2nd ed., ed. J. O. Urmson and Marina Sbisà (Cambridge, MA: Harvard University Press, 1975), 13.

2. J. L. Austin, *How to Do Things with Words*, 2nd ed., ed. J. O. Urmson and Marina Sbisà (Cambridge, MA: Harvard University Press, 1975), 13.

3. Ibid., 148. Since his witticisms are generally not idle throwaways, one might productively wonder exactly what Austin had in mind in appropriating Einstein's terms to identify his two "theories." I thank James Shelley for this point.

4. Jennifer Hornsby takes Austin to hold the view—a view she herself explicitly endorses—that Austin has no bone to pick with semantic theory: "Locutionary acts he thought of as belonging in the territory of those concerned with 'sense and reference'—of semantic theorists, that is" (Hornsby, "Feminism in the Philosophy of Language," in *The Cambridge Companion to Feminism in Philosophy*, ed. Miranda Fricker and Hornsby (Cambridge: Cambridge University Press, 2000), 89). In footnote 17 on p. 102 of this essay, Hornsby says that she relies here on the following remark in *How to Do Things with Words*: "A locutionary act [. . .] is roughly equivalent to uttering a certain sentence with a certain sense and reference, which again is roughly equivalent to 'meaning' in the traditional sense" (109). But Austin says nothing here that would indicate that he approves of semantic theory-making. Indeed, his relentless interest in redirecting philosophers' attention away from standard-fare theory-making seems to caution against eliding his definition of a "locutionary act" with the idea that any "territory of those concerned with 'sense and reference'" belongs to semantic theorists.

5. Austin introduces the notion of "uptake" on p. 117 of *How to Do Things With Words*.

6. Both papers are anthologized in J. L Austin, *Philosophical Papers*, ed. J. O. Urmson and G. J. Warnock (Oxford: Oxford University Press, 1979).

7. Austin, *How to Do Things with Words*, 150. Austin mentions some of these classes earlier in the book but gives them extended extension only in this end section.

8. Ibid., 151.

9. Among others, Rae Langton and Mary Kate McGowan have argued, though in different ways, that pornography possesses both exercitive and verdictive powers. See especially Langton, "Speech Acts and Unspeakable Acts," *Philosophy and Public Affairs* 22, no. 4 (1993): 293–330; McGowan, "Conversational Exercitives and the Force of Pornography," *Philosophy & Public Affairs* 31, no. 2 (April 1, 2003): 155–89; and McGowan, "On Pornography: MacKinnon, Speech Acts, and 'False' Construction," *Hypatia* 20, no. 3 (July 1, 2005): 22–49.

10. Austin, *How to Do Things with Words*, 157.

11. Ibid., 163.

12. Ibid., 162.

13. In the essay "Pretending" in Austin, *Philosophical Papers*, 260.

14. Austin, *How to Do Things With Words*, 148.

15. Here is Hornsby on this point: "Where an illocutionary act is in question, there is, as it were, no distance between doing it and doing it intentionally." See Hornsby, "Illocution and Its Significance," in *Foundations of Speech Act Theory: Philosophical and Linguistic Perspectives*, ed. Savas L Tsohatzidis (New York: Routledge, 1994), 194.

16. The example is Scott Soames's; see Soames, *Beyond Rigidity: The Unfinished Semantic Agenda of Naming and Necessity* (Oxford: Oxford University

Press, 2002), 78. This example is also discussed in François Récanati, *Literal Meaning: The Very Idea* (Cambridge: Cambridge University Press, 2003), 60f.

17. Hornsby writes that "it is sufficient for an action's being of some sort which is an illocutionary sort that it have as an effect an audience's taking it some way" (Hornsby, "Illocution and Its Significance," 194). Alexander Bird (in "Illocutionary Silencing," *Pacific Philosophical Quarterly* 83, no. 1 (2002): 1–15) mounts what I think is a compelling argument against this view in a discussion of the Langton–Hornsby story about how pornography might be seen to perform the illocutionary act of silencing women. On this story, women who attempt to refuse sex from certain men, namely, those who have been taught by pornography that "no" does not constitute a refusal in the language game of sex, cannot convey their intentions to refuse and therefore cannot, indeed, refuse. (Daniel Jacobson and, even more compellingly, Nellie Wieland have argued convincingly that this story has the unfortunate consequence of getting rapists off the ethical hook. See Jacobson, "Freedom of Speech Acts?: A Response to Langton," *Philosophy and Public Affairs* 24, no. 1 (1995): 64–79; and Wieland, "Linguistic Authority and Convention in a Speech Act Analysis of Pornography," *Australasian Journal of Philosophy* 85, no. 3 (2007): 435–56.) Bird shows that grasping a woman's intentions in this scenario is beside the point: when you don't want sex, saying "no!" amounts to a refusal; and someone who does not hear it as a refusal has, to say the least, failed to grasp the nature of the speech act. (Notice that in insisting that we understand the illocutionary act of refusal in this way, Bird is making a *political* point, not just a "linguistic" one.)

An unfortunate part of Bird's argument is that he takes Austin to agree with Langton and Hornsby about the vital role that uptake of a speaker's intentions plays in the production of all happy speech acts. But Austin does not agree. Bird relies on the following passage in *How to Do Things with Words*: "Unless a certain effect is achieved, the illocutionary act will not have been happily, successfully performed. . . . I cannot be said to have warned an audience unless it hears what I say and takes what I say in a certain sense. An effect must be achieved on the audience if the illocutionary act is to be carried out. . . . Generally the effect amounts to bringing about the understanding of the meaning and of the force of the locution. So the performance of an illocutionary act involves the securing of *uptake*" (Austin, *How to Do Things with Words*, 116–17). I take it that Austin here commits himself only to the idea that an illocutionary act is—"*generally*" speaking—happily performed only if the audience grasps what the act is—which is not necessarily the same as grasping the *intentions* of the speaker. Of course, an audience's not grasping a speaker's intention might also result in an act's coming off unhappily.

18. See Jacques Derrida, *Limited Inc* (Evanston, IL: Northwestern University Press, 1988); and Searle, "Reiterating the Differences: A Reply to Derrida" in *Glyph: Johns Hopkins Textual Studies*, ed. Samuel Weber et al. (Baltimore: Johns Hopkins University Press, 1977).

19. See Austin, *How to Do Things with Words*, 31.

20. Perhaps I can gesture at what I mean by *style* by naming some philosophers who clearly thought that their way of writing was integral to their philosophizing: Plato, Descartes, Kierkegaard, Nietzsche, Carnap (yes, Carnap), Frantz Fanon, Simone de Beauvoir, Marilyn Frye.

21. See also Chapter 8, which in effect treats the material in this postscript from a slightly different vantage point.

22. It has been suggested to me that counterexamples include Grice's theory of implicature and Fodor's theory of the modularity of the mind. It seems to me that (1) neither "implicature" nor "modularity of the mind" constitutes a *theory* of anything and (2) that people disagree in important ways about the details of theories, including, respectively, those of Grice and Fodor, in which these concepts play a major role.

23. Timothy A. Williamson, "Past the Linguistic Turn," in *The Future for Philosophy*, ed. Brian Leiter (Oxford: Oxford University Press, 2006), 128.

24. Ibid., 112–13.

25. Ibid., 126.

26. Ibid., 127.

27. Ibid., 112.

28. Mark Richard has suggested to me that a better motivation for the vagueness problem might go as follows. We are very interested in arguing validly, where *valid* is defined by classical logic. But vagueness casts doubt on classical logic (specifically, the claim that *p or not-p* is a logical truth. And there is just no alternative logic that commands assent and has much hope of telling us what to say about vague claims. Richard may in fact be correct here. But I am arguing that the vagueness of words like *child* and *adult* is of no *philosophical* matter whatsoever. We draw sharp lines between *p* and *not-p* when we need to, recognizing that the exact place we draw them is more or less arbitrary. When we need to argue validly (e.g., in a philosophical context) we can stipulate our way to the point at which we can do so. In other words, "vagueness" in ordinary contexts doesn't threaten the enterprise of classical logic. Indeed, vagueness in ordinary contexts doesn't pose a puzzle as to how we manage to argue validly. (See the discussion of Russell to follow later in this chapter.)

29. For the record: I am not at all here endorsing the practice of trying a minor "as an adult."

30. This, by the way, is Williamson's own preferred solution to the problem. He thinks that concepts are (or can be made to be) precise; the problem is that it's hard for us to *know* where the line in fact is. So what was a problem for philosophy of language becomes, in Williamson's hands, a problem for epistemology.

31. Bertrand Russell, "Vagueness," *Australasian Journal of Philosophy and Psychology* no. 1 (1923): 84–92.

Chapter 7

1. J. L. Austin, *How to Do Things with Words*, 2nd ed., ed. J. O. Urmson and Marina Sbisà, (Cambridge, MA: Harvard University Press, 1975), 91.

2. Austin might be said to have thought that the study of what he called the "perlocutionary force" of our utterances, the effects they *happen* to have on various individuals, is roughly equivalent to what now gets called pragmatics. But (a) by definition *illocutionary* force, nonetheless, is not incidental to the meaning of our sentences and (b) it could be argued that Austin was not as

sanguine as he might appear about (1) the independence of perlocutionary force from illocution and meaning and (2) the unpredictable, unconventional nature of perlocution. (Stanley Cavell, for one, suggests that the domain of the perlocutionary is all too mappable; see "Passionate and Performative Utterance," in *Philosophy the Day after Tomorrow* (Cambridge, MA: Harvard University Press, 2006).) See also my brief discussions of Cavell's thoughts on this subject in Chapter 5 and my reading of Austin in Chapter 6.

3. For a sense of what "pragmatics" is, as articulated by philosophers who accept the tripartite division of labor in philosophy of language but also are convinced that not enough heed is paid to pragmatics, see, e.g., John R. Searle, *Speech Acts: An Essay in the Philosophy of Language* (Cambridge: Cambridge University Press, 1970); Kent Bach, "Speech Acts and Pragmatics," in *Blackwell Guide to the Philosophy of Language*, ed. Michael Devitt and Richard Hanley (Malden, MA: Blackwell, 2003), 147–67; Récanati, *Meaning and Force: The Pragmatics of Performative Utterances* (Cambridge: Cambridge University Press, 1987); Charles Travis, "Pragmatics," in *A Companion to the Philosophy of Language*, ed. C. Wright and B. Hale, 87–107 (Oxford: Blackwell, 1997); Robyn Carston, *Thoughts and Utterances: The Pragmatics of Explicit Communication* (Malden, MA: Blackwell, 2002); Dan Sperber and Deirdre Wilson, *Relevance: Communication and Cognition* (Cambridge, MA: Blackwell, 1995); and Jennifer Hornsby, "Illocution and Its Significance," in *Foundations of Speech Act Theory: Philosophical and Linguistic Perspectives*, ed. Savas L. Tsohatzidis (London: Routledge, 1994). The Tsohatzidis volume provides a good sense of how, in the main, Austin has been taken up by his admirers. For an understanding of pragmatics on which the standard view of the nature and importance of literal meaning is questioned, see François Récanati, *Literal Meaning: The Very Idea* (Cambridge: Cambridge University Press, 2003).

4. MacKinnon makes this claim in a number of places, including "Pornography: On Morality and Politics," chapter 11 of *Toward a Feminist Theory of the State* (Cambridge, MA: Harvard University Press, 1989); and "Not a Moral Issue," chapter 13 of *Feminism Unmodified: Discourses on Life and Law* (Cambridge, MA: Harvard University Press, 1987). See also MacKinnon's attempts, co-orchestrated by the feminist activist Andrea Dworkin, to make pornography legally actionable as recorded in MacKinnon and Dworkin, *In Harm's Way: The Pornography Civil Rights Hearings* (Cambridge, MA: Harvard University Press, 1997).

5. Of course, at this very moment I take myself to be engaged in that last activity. But, for the record, I do not believe that bringing worrisome premises to the fore is a *hallmark* of specifically philosophical activity. Later on in this chapter, I will indicate why.

6. See Nancy Bauer, *Simone de Beauvoir, Philosophy, and Feminism* (New York: Columbia University Press, 2001), especially chapter 1.

7. I have much more to say on this subject in Chapter 8.

8. Plato, *Republic*, 518b–d. Quoted from G. M. A Grube and C. D. C Reeve, *Republic* (Indianapolis: Hackett Pub. Co., 1992). I am indebted to Stanley Cavell for teaching me the bearing of this passage on what tends to get called "philosophical method."

9. We find here a resonance with Austin, who believed that nothing could ground, in a once-and-for-all way, the meaning and force of our words.

10. See Chapter 5 for a more extended discussion of Langton's views.

11. See Thomas Nagel, "Personal Rights and Public Space," *Philosophy & Public Affairs* 24, no. 2 (April 1, 1995): 83–107; Ronald Dworkin, "Do We Have a Right to Pornography?," in *A Matter of Principle* (Cambridge, MA: Harvard University Press, 1985), 335–72; and Dworkin, "Two Concepts of Liberty," in *Isaiah Berlin: A Celebration*, ed. Edna Ullmann-Margalit and Avishai Margalit (Chicago: University of Chicago Press, 1991), 100–9. Dworkin is especially sneering in his attitude toward MacKinnon in a series of pieces he wrote for *The New York Review of Books*, including Dworkin, "Liberty and Pornography," *New York Review of Books* 21, no. 15 (August 15, 1991): 12–15; "Women and Pornography," *New York Review of Books* 21, no. 16 (October 21, 1993): 36–42, a review of MacKinnon's *Only Words*; and, in reply to MacKinnon in the wake of this review, "Pornography: An Exchange," *New York Review of Books* 41, no. 5 (March 3, 1994).

12. For this and the following quotation, see MacKinnon, *Feminism Unmodified*, 176; both quoted in Rae Langton, "Speech Acts and Unspeakable Acts," *Philosophy and Public Affairs* 22, no. 4 (1993): 294.

13. MacKinnon, "Not a Moral Issue, "*Feminism Unmodified*, 186 (quoted in Langton, "Speech Acts and Unspeakable Acts," 297).

14. "In this article I exploit the work of [Austin] to illuminate and defend [MacKinnon]" (Langton, "Speech Acts and Unspeakable Acts," 297). For the second quotation, see the same paper, 299.

15. I do not intend *reactions* here to be a technical term. But for clarity's sake, let me explain that in using this word I have in mind responses beyond what Austin called "uptake," that is the registering by an audience member of what someone producing a stretch of speech takes herself to be doing (i.e., the intended illocution).

16. Langton, "Speech Acts and Unspeakable Acts," 300.

17. See Richard Rorty, "Feminism and Pragmatism," *Michigan Quarterly Review* 30 (April 15, 1991): 231–58.

18. All quotations in this paragraph: Langton, "Speech Acts and Unspeakable Acts," 312.

19. Langton not surprisingly disagrees. She believes that the experiments run by Donnerstein and others give us good empirical evidence, as do first-person accounts by pornography users. For discussion of Donnerstein, see., e.g., Langton, "Speech Acts and Unspeakable Acts," as well as my comments on Donnerstein in Chapter 5. For Langton's discussion of first-person accounts by pornography users, see Langton, "Comments on A. W. Eaton's 'A Sensible Antiporn Feminism,'" *Symposia on Race, Gender, and Philosophy* 4 (Spring 2008).

20. What I'm claiming here is in effect a placeholder for a way of understanding the nature of empirical judgment. I discuss this subject in a different context in Chapter 3.

21. Langton, "Speech Acts and Unspeakable Acts," 311.

22. Throughout her writings, MacKinnon herself provides a story about why men regard pornography as authoritative, which has to do with the way

that, on her view, pornography eroticizes men's subordination of women. One way to put the question I am raising here is this: does the power of this story to depict the world accurately stand or fall on "empirical evidence"? For other expressions of concern about Langton's depiction of the pornographer's authority, see Lester Green, "Pornographizing, Subordinating, and Silencing," in *Censorship and Silencing* (Los Angeles: Getty Museum, 1998), 285–311; and Nellie Wieland, "Linguistic Authority and Convention in a Speech Act Analysis of Pornography," *Australasian Journal of Philosophy* 85, no. 3 (2007): 435–56. For Langton's response to Green, see Langton, *Sexual Solipsism: Philosophical Essays on Pornography and Objectification* (Oxford: Oxford University Press, 2009), 89–102. Ishani Maitra has claimed that, in the paper that spawned Chapter 5 of the present book (which in this respect is identical to the new version) I argued that "pornography is not authoritative" and that "speech that fails to provide an excuse to those who do as it instructs is not authoritative" (Maitra, "Subordinating Speech," in *Speech and Harm: Controversies over Free Speech*, ed. Maitra and Mary Kate McGowan (Oxford: Oxford University Press, 2012).) I certainly have not meant to make either of these claims.

23. Langton, "Speech Acts and Unspeakable Acts," 313.

24. For an illuminating discussion of Carnap's views on the relationship between philosophy and politics, see Michael Friedman's excellent *A Parting of the Ways: Carnap, Cassirer, and Heidegger* (Chicago: Open Court, 2000), especially 16–22, which includes a brief discussion of the political remarks Carnap makes in the preface to the *Aufbau*. I discuss Carnap again in a somewhat different context in Chapter 8.

Chapter 8

1. Here is the official description of the guiding concerns of the conference: "Can there be progress in philosophy? It is often said that philosophical problems are perennials for which it is pointless to expect a solution. On the other hand, professional philosophy seems to have organised itself, perhaps unconsciously, around the opposite view: how else to explain the panoply of conferences, graduate programs, journals, websites etc? Who is right? What might philosophical progress be? Is it rational to think that there is (has been, will be) any?" (http://cass.anu.edu.au/story/harvard-anu-symposium-progress-philosophy, accessed July 12, 2013).

2. This is my example, not Stanley's.

3. This claim has also been articulated and defended by Timothy Williamson, whose views I criticized briefly in the postscript to Chapter 6 and will discuss again momentarily.

4. I haven't been able to find the source for this quotation.

5. Feynman was more ecumenical than Romano; he thought that all philosophers, not just contemporary professors working in the analytic tradition, were useless. In *The Pleasure of Finding Things Out*, for example, he writes, "My son is taking a course in philosophy, and last night we were looking at something by Spinoza and there was the most childish reasoning! There were all these attributes, and Substances, and all this meaningless chewing around, and

we started to laugh. Now how could we do that? Here's this great Dutch philosopher, and we're laughing at him. It's because there's no excuse for it! In the
same period there was Newton, there was Harvey studying the circulation of
the blood, there were people with methods of analysis by which progress was
being made! You can take every one of Spinoza's propositions, and take the
contrary propositions, and look at the world and you can't tell which is right"
(Feynman, *The Pleasure of Finding Things Out: The Best Short Works of Richard
P. Feynman*, ed. Jeffrey Robbins (New York: Basic Books, 2005), 195).

6. In case you are curious about the details of this exchange: Romano
quoted the following sentence from Stanley's book: "If x asserts 'it is possible
that p', then x implicates, via this maxim, 'I do not know that p.'" Romano took
Stanley to mean that to say, "It is possible that p" is to *imply* that you don't
know that p; and it seemed obvious to Romano that one might have occasion to
say that p is possible without implying that one didn't know that p, so that what
Stanley was arguing was patently wrong. *Imply* and *implicate* are both technical
terms in philosophy. When we say that p implies q, we are talking about *semantical* properties of language: to commit oneself to p is, when p implies q, to
commit oneself to q. But *implicate* is a Gricean term of art (see, e.g., Paul Grice,
Studies in the Way of Words (Cambridge, MA: Harvard University Press, 1991).
It's used with reference to the (so-called) *pragmatic* properties of speakers'
utterances. If x asserts that p is possible and if saying p conversationally implicates a commitment to q, then x implicates that q. Furthermore, Romano
ignored the Gricean "conversational maxim" to which the quotation he
adduced refers. According to that maxim, we generally converse with one
another according to a number of tacit principles, including the principle that
interlocutors ought to assert the most informative propositions they can. So
when x says that it is possible that p, her words do not (semantically) *imply* that
she does not know that p; rather, the maxim (pragmatically) instructs x's interlocutors to *assume* that x does not know that p. The context of this material in
Stanley's book is his arguing that if one has a prodigal tendency to provide
pragmatic explanations of apparently semantic intuitions, one will end up
undermining the whole enterprise of giving semantical explanations. In the
stretch of text from which Romano was quoting, Stanley concedes that in some
special cases—such as the case in which it's clear that x knows that p—the oddness of x's asserting "it's possible that p" does call for a pragmatic explanation
(as when—and this is my example—the train pulls in to the station and my
neighbor on the platform says, "It's possible that a train is here"). See Stanley,
Knowledge and Practical Interests (New York: Oxford University Press, 2008),
14–15.

7. A cell-phone video of the Stanley–Romano encounter, taken by an audience member, includes a number of audience-reaction shots. The video had
garnered 4,297 hits on Vimeo as of the early summer of 2013—at least five times
more than any other conference video posted on the site; see http://vimeo
.com/29390796, which, for better or worse, cuts off some of the more impas-
sioned back and forth between Romano and the audience.

8. This email to one of the organizers was sent on April 17, 2011.

9. Though at that time Romano's book *America the Philosophical* had yet to be published, his polemical style and philosophical point of view were abundantly clear from his earlier writings. See, e.g., "Hail Heidegger!," *The Chronicle of Higher Education*, October 18, 2009; and "Between the Motion and the Act, *The Nation* 257, no. 16 (November 15, 1993): 563–70, the latter of which is a shockingly clueless and callous review of Catharine MacKinnon's book *Only Words* (Cambridge, MA: Harvard University Press, 1993). It begins with the sentence "Suppose I decide to rape Catharine MacKinnon before reviewing her book."

10. The idea that in weighing in on what often get called the fundamental questions we philosophers arrogate the authority of reason and therefore are constantly at risk of being merely arrogant is one I learned from Stanley Cavell. This theme runs through out his writing; see, e.g., "Philosophy and the Arrogation of Voice," in *A Pitch of Philosophy: Autobiographical Exercises* (Cambridge, MA: Harvard University Press, 1996). See also Chapter 7 of the present book.

11. Yale graduate students, mentored by Tamar Gendler, would soon turn this group into a "Minorities and Philosophy" (MAP) movement, which now has chapters in many graduate programs in Philosophy.

12. See, e.g., Williamson, "Must Do Better," in *Truth and Realism*, ed. Michael P. Lynch and Patrick Greenough (Oxford: Oxford University Press, 2006), 177–87; "Past the Linguistic Turn?," in *The Future for Philosophy*, ed. Brian Leiter (Oxford: Oxford University Press, 2006), 106–28; and *The Philosophy of Philosophy* (Oxford: Wiley-Blackwell, 2007).

13. Williamson, "Must Do Better," 279.

14. Ibid., see 285 and forward.

15. Ibid., 285.

16. Ernest Sosa, "Can There Be a Discipline of Philosophy? And Can It Be Founded on Intuitions?," *Mind and Language* 26, no. 4 (September 2011): 461. I thank Avner Baz for drawing this article to my attention.

17. Poor Williamson plays a similar role in the postscript to Chapter 6. This is a function of his having expressed better than anyone else I know the understanding of the philosophy and its value that troubles me.

18. Williamson, "Must Do Better," 278.

19. All quotations in this paragraph are from Williamson, "Past the Linguistic Turn?," 126–28.

20. Except where otherwise noted, all quotations in this paragraph are from Williamson, "Must Do Better," 286–89.

21. Williamson, "Must Do Better," 292. I was in attendance at this conference. At the time, it struck me that Williamson's remarks had been composed—fittingly enough, given his task of commenting on the entire event—during the conference itself; they seemed to me to be an expression of his frustration with what he perceived to be the uneven quality of the papers. My sentiments about the papers is well expressed by Tim Maudlin's review of *Truth and Realism*, edited by conference organizers Michael Lynch and Patrick Greenough, which collects a number of the conference contributions: "One

gets the sense that there is not even any clear agreement about what the issues are, especially with respect to the topic of realism. Everyone seems to be talking past one another, and often in individually obscure ways." See Maudlin, "Review of Truth and Realism," *Notre Dame Philosophical Reviews*, June 2007. Available at http://ndpr.nd.edu/news/22996-truth-and-realism/.

Because the following facts are examples of a claim about the nature of philosophical progress that I will elaborate later in this chapter, let me note that all fifteen contributors to the volume of papers that emerged from the conference (Greenough and Lynch, *Truth and Realism*) are men, as are both editors. Thirty philosophers were invited to give papers, comment on individual papers or on the whole conference, or chair one of its eight sessions; of these, twenty-six were men and two of the participating women simply chaired sessions. No woman presented a "main" session paper. The four people who offered comments on the whole conference were men; "Must Do Better" (revised and expanded in published form) is a version of Williamson's contribution to this über-commentary. Nine men and zero women were engaged to sit in the audience as "invited discussants." A "postgraduate preconference" consisted of presentations by nine men and no women. Twenty-one graduate students are thanked in the introduction to the conference volume for being "stalwart helpers" and "paragons of efficiency"; of these, half are women.

22. "Past the Linguistic Turn," 126.

23. Available at http://www.newappsblog.com/2011/08/on-wasted-philosophic -livesparfits-fanaticism.html. The square brackets are Schliesser's.

24. Schliesser used the phrase *founding myth* not in his post but in private correspondence with me. The phrase makes clear that Schliesser does not mean to be flatly endorsing "analytic philosophy" in the material I've quoted from his blog post.

25. Derek Parfit, *On What Matters*, vol. 2 (Oxford: Oxford University Press, 2011), 10; Mark Schroeder, "Review of *On What Matters*, Vols. 1 and 2," *Notre Dame Philosophical Reviews*, August 1, 2011; available at https://ndpr.nd.edu /news/25393-on-what-matters-volumes-1-and-2/.

26. See Parfit, *On What Matters*, vol. 1, 12; vol. 2, 303, 304, 367.

27. *Moral progress*, as a phrase, is Schroeder's. But Parfit speaks often of the progress to be made in moral philosophy and in his hopes for convergence among human beings in their understanding of moral truths.

28. See, e.g., *On What Matters*, vol. 2, 563, where Parfit claims that over the centuries "there has been slow but accelerating progress" with respect to human beings' acceptance of the substantive moral claim "that everyone's well-being matters equally, and that everyone has equal moral claims" and that, therefore, it is immoral to enslave people or otherwise treat them as though they had "lesser status."

29. See, e.g., section 121, pp. 549–64 of Parfit, *On What Matters*, which is titled "The Convergence Claim." The main goal of this section is to argue that the three major normative views in Western ethics (consequentialism, Kantianism, and contractualism) ultimately converge on the same moral principles. From *On What Matters*, vol. 1, 418–19: "It has been widely believed that there are . . . deep disagreements between Kantians, Contractualists, and

Consequentialists. That, I have argued, is not true. These people are climbing the mountain on different sides."

30. See Larissa McFarquhar's profile of Parfit, "How to Be Good," in *The New Yorker*, September 5, 2011: 42–53. Available at http://www.newyorker .com/magazine/2011/09/05/how-to-be-good.

31. For an extended discussion of these matters in the context of a defense of ordinary language philosophy, see Avner Baz, *When Words Are Called For: A Defense of Ordinary Language Philosophy* (Cambridge, MA: Harvard University Press, 2012).

32. Perhaps the most famous articulation of this view is that of Judith Butler who argues that "sex . . . [has] been gender all along." See Butler, *Gender Trouble: Feminism and the Subversion of Identity* (New York: Routledge, 1990), 8.

33. My own views on this subject are deeply informed by those of Simone de Beauvoir; see my *Simone de Beauvoir, Philosophy, and Feminism* (New York: Columbia University Press, 2001). For a like-minded critical analysis of Butler's position, see Toril Moi, *What Is a Woman? And Other Essays* (New York: Oxford University Press, 2001), especially the title essay. For a series of thought-provoking essays arguing that the "social construction" of gender (and race) ought to take place within the context of a realist social ontology, see Sally Haslanger, *Resisting Reality: Social Construction and Social Critique* (Oxford: Oxford University Press, 2012), especially "Social Construction: Myth and Reality," 183–218. For an outside-the-box argument that gender essentialism (properly understood) is not incompatible with the idea that gender norma-tivity is socially constructed and imposed, see Charlotte Witt, *The Metaphysics of Gender* (Oxford: Oxford University Press, 2011).

34. Williamson has had a lot to say about the proper role of "intuitions"—or, more precisely, the effective lack thereof—in philosophy; see Williamson, "Evidence in Philosophy," in *The Philosophy of Philosophy*, 208–46. On Williamson's view, *intuition* does not name some special philosophical capacity; rather, it's just another name for *judgment*, and its use in philosophy is continuous with the kind of judgment that we employ in everyday cases. (For a different defla-tionary account of the role of intuition in philosophy, see Herman Cappelen, *Philosophy without Intuitions* (Oxford: Oxford University Press, 2012). For a critical review of Williamson's and Cappelen's arguments, see Avner Baz, "Must Philosophers Rely on Intuitions?," *Journal of Philosophy* 109, no. 4 (April 2012): 316–37.

35. For these demographical statistics I am relying on Louise Antony, "Different Voices or Perfect Storm: Why Are There So Few Women in Philosophy," *Journal of Social Philosophy* 43, no. 3 (2012): 252, n. 6; and Kathryn T. Gines, "Being a Black Woman Philosopher: Reflections on Founding the Collegium of Black Women Philosophers," *Hypatia* 26, no. 2 (2011): 429–37.

36. Sally Haslanger, "Changing the Ideology and Culture of Philosophy: Not by Reason Alone," *Hypatia* 23, no. 2 (2008): 210.

37. See Virginia Valian, *Why So Slow?: The Advancement of Women* (Cambridge, MA: MIT Press, 1999).

38. Evidence for these claims can be found at http://kieranhealy.org/blog /archives/2011/02/04/gender-divides-in-philosophy-and-other-disciplines/.

39. Haslanger, "Changing the Ideology and Culture of Philosophy," 211–12.

40. See Carol Gilligan, *In a Different Voice: Psychological Theory and Women's Development* (Cambridge, MA: Harvard University Press, 1982).

41. Buckwalter and Stitch, "Gender and Philosophical Intuition" (Version 3.0, September 26, 2010), 1. Available at http://papers.ssrn.com/sol3/papers.cfm?abstract_id=1683066.

42. Ibid.

43. See Antony, "Different Voices or Perfect Storm," especially 235–36.

44. Ibid., 238.

45. See Marilyn Frye's brilliant essay "Oppression," in *The Politics of Reality: Essays in Feminist Theory* (Trumansburg, NY: Crossing Press, 1983).

46. Stanley, "The Crisis in Philosophy," *Inside Higher Education*, April 5, 2010. Available at http://www.insidehighered.com/views/2010/04/05/stanley.

47. Antony makes a number of similar claims in her objections to Buckwalter and Stitch; see, e.g., "Different Voices or Perfect Storm," 235–36, for an interesting discussion of the ways that a professor's reaction to student views can cause problems for women.

48. For more of my musings on this topic, see also my "On Making Progress in Philosophy (All Other Things Not Equal)" (unpublished).

Chapter 9

1. http://en.wikipedia.org/wiki/Ordinary_language_philosophy, accessed August 25, 2013. The *Internet Encyclopedia of Philosophy* (accessed on the same date) mentions Austin, Ryle, Hart, Strawson, Cavell, and Searle (but not Hart) as well as John Wisdom, Norman Malcolm, Alice Ambrose, Morris Lazerowitz, and several others. As of the same date, there is no entry on "Ordinary Language Philosophy" in *The Stanford Encyclopedia of Philosophy* (plato.stanford.edu).

2. See Avner Baz, *When Words Are Called For* (Cambridge, MA: Harvard University Press, 2012), especially chapter 2, "The Main Arguments against Ordinary Language Philosophy." Unlike me, Baz regards the "OLP" moniker as serviceable; his reasons for thinking so are articulated on p. xiii of *When Words Are Called For*. My view is that given the history of the moniker, including its prodigal application to a range of philosophers with very different views, its use will forever threaten to distort what philosophers who share our orientation are trying to do.

3. Although Searle, for instance, is often thought to count as an improvement on Austin, it is not hard to make the case that the two philosophers are on a very different page. See, e.g., Alice Crary, "Austin and the Ethics of Discourse," in *Reading Cavell*, ed. Crary and Sanford Shieh, 42–67 (London: Routledge, 2006); and Cavell, "Counter-Philosophy and the Pawn of Voice," in *A Pitch of Philosophy: Autobiographical Exercises* (Cambridge, MA: Harvard University Press, 1996), 53–128.

4. See Parts One and Two of Cavell, *The Claim of Reason* (New York: Oxford University Press, 1979), for a very careful parsing of the differences

between Austin and Wittgenstein as well as an extended argument for understanding their views as similarly radical.

5. Cavell, "What Becomes of Things on Film?," in *Themes out of School: Effects and Causes* (Chicago: University of Chicago Press, 1988), 182–83.

6. Ibid., 173–83. Here is the passage from which I've pulled the quoted words:

> The moral I draw is this: the question of what becomes of objects when they are filmed and screened—like the question what becomes of particular people, and specific locales, and subjects and motifs when they are filmed by individual makers of film—has only one source of data for its answer, namely the appearance and significance of just those objects and people that are in fact to be found in the succession of films, or passages of films, that matter to us. To express their appearances, and define those significances, and articulate the nature of this mattering, are acts that help to constitute what we might call film criticism. Then to explain how these appearances, significances, and matterings—these specific events of photogenesis—are made possible by the general photogenesis of film altogther, by the fact, as I more or less put it in *The World Viewed*, that objects on film are always already displaced, *trouvé* (i.e., that we as viewers are always already displaced before them), would be an undertaking of what we might call film theory.

7. Ibid., 183.

8. Laura Mulvey, "Visual Pleasure and Narrative Cinema," *Screen* 16, no. 3 (September 1, 1975): 6–18. This essay has been reprinted numerous times.

9. Cavell discusses the pornographic possibilities of film in his first book on the subject, *The World Viewed*. He writes,

> A nude is a fine enough thing in itself, and no reason is required to explain nakedness: we were born that way and besides "the human body is the best picture of the human soul" [quoting here Wittgenstein's *Philosophical Investigations* (2003), II, iv, p. 152]. But to be undressed is something else, and it does require a reason; in seeing a film of a desirable woman we are looking for a reason. When to this we join our ontological status— invisibility [to the "desirable woman" in the film]—it is inevitable that we should expect to find a reason, to be around when a reason and an occasion present themselves, no matter how consistently our expectancy is frustrated. The ontological conditions of the motion picture reveal it as inherently pornographic (though not of course inveterately so). (45)

The World Viewed was first published in 1971. Whether or how one might transpose these remarks to a gender-neutral register is not obvious. (See also my brief discussion of part of this passage at the end of Chapter 5.)

10. Cavell, "What Becomes of Things on Film?."

11. I find the fact that this film got made, and by the individuals who made it, amazing. The director, Craig Gillespie, has spent most of his career making commercials; his other two films thus far are *Fright Night* (2011) and *Mr. Woodcock* (also, astonishingly, 2007). The screenwriter, Nancy Oliver, has forever

been best friends with and head writer for Alan Ball, who created both *Six Feet Under* and *True Blood*; as far as I can gather, she simply pulled the astonishing script for *Lars and the Real Girl* out of a hat.

12. And, as far as I can tell, only on film: in my experience, Gosling is horribly disappointing in interviews.

13. This chapter is based on the keynote address I gave at the Hamilton College inaugural Undergraduate Philosophy Conference, "Philosophy of Film and Television," in May 2013. I am grateful to Martin Shuster for extending to me the invitation to speak at this wonderful event and to members of the audience, especially Anneliese Cooper, for their helpful comments and questions.

Acknowledgments

My work on the chapters that constitute this book was made possible by generous support from Tufts University and by angelic support from the Radcliffe Institute for Advanced Study at Harvard University, which granted me a residential fellowship during the 2002–2003 academic year to get the project under way and allowed me to spend another month in residence in June 2013 so that I could complete the manuscript for submission to Harvard University Press. In April 2013, the Institute also funded an Exploratory Seminar on Feminism and Ordinary Language Philosophy, led by Sarah Beckwith, Alice Crary, Sandra Laugier, Toril Moi, Linda Zerilli, and me, at which I received excellent feedback on what is now Chapter 3 of this book.

I thank Mitch Kellaway, who served as my research assistant during my second stint at the Institute and for the few months following. I am also grateful to the three readers engaged by Harvard University Press to review the original manuscript. Many thanks especially to the most critical reviewer, who took the time to point out various errors in my exposition and thereby may have saved me from altogether alienating those readers who were already primed to find some of what I say—for example, my criticism of certain appropriations of Austin in understanding how pornography works—difficult to stomach.

I would never have started this project, let alone finished it, without the endless encouragement and moral and material support of Sally Haslanger. My interest in writing about pornography, and about the dominant discourse on pornography within analytic philosophy, began with Sally's inviting me to speak on Rae Langton's "Speech Acts and Unspeakable Acts" at one of the January intersession programs organized annually by the MIT philosophy faculty. Shortly thereafter, Sally founded the now-famous Workshop on Gender and Philosophy (WOGAP), at which I presented early drafts of much of this book. In addition to being an outstanding philosopher and champion of human rights in every conceivable form, Sally is the Platonic Form of a friend. This book would not have existed without her.

WOGAP began as a reading group of four: Sally (then new at MIT), me (just starting at Tufts), and Ásta Sveinsdottir and Ishani Maitra, then graduate students at MIT and now distinguished senior philosophers. Though our philosophical orientations do not always align, I have learned an enormous amount from both Ásta and Ishani and from many other WOGAP participants over the years. A stroke of luck brought Rae Langton to MIT in 2004. Though, as is clear from this book, Rae and I are often on rather different philosophical pages, she has been an unfailingly generous interlocutor and friend. Ditto for Mary Kate McGowan, whose comments on my writings on J. L. Austin were especially trenchant and challenging. I also want to thank the many other feminist philosophers and colleagues who have written about pornography, sexual objectification, and related topics, all of whom have been very tolerant of my various public screeds, including, notably, Lina Papadaki and Mari Mikkola.

Anyone who in this day and age continues to think that "feminist philosophy" is not a serious or coherent enterprise should read the papers in the volume *A Mind of One's Own*, edited by Louise Antony and Charlotte Witt (2nd ed., Westview Press, 2002), still, in my view, the single best collection of papers in feminist philosophy. From the very beginning of my work in the field as a graduate student, I have deeply admired both Louise and Charlotte and for many years now have had the pleasure of calling both of them my friends. Their faith in what I'm doing has been critical to the completion of this project.

The first piece of writing I published on the material in this book was "How to Do Things with Pornography," which began as a talk at a 2002 conference at Wesleyan honoring Stanley Cavell and was published in a volume called *Reading Cavell* (2006), edited by Sanford Shieh (the conference organizer) and Alice Crary. Sanford made it the case that I could see myself, in 1991, having a career as a feminist philosopher. And dating from that same time, Alice has understood where I'm coming from philosophically better than anyone on the planet: she gets the weird combination of feminism and phenomenology, ordinary-language-style, that drives my work. It is a pleasure once again to thank both of these wonderful friends.

Aficionados of the work of Cora Diamond will recognize in these pages the extent to which her sui generis philosophizing has inspired me. While our philosophical preoccupations are somewhat different, we very much share a sense that professional philosophers ought to be thinking more carefully than we are wont to do about what we are doing with our words.

I am very lucky to work with splendid colleagues in the Philosophy Department at Tufts University. I am especially grateful to my oldest friend in professional philosophy, Erin Kelly, who first suggested to her then-new colleagues in the department to consider hiring me, and to George Smith, a philosopher and historian of science who for decades has taken it as a matter of obvious fact that no decent philosophy department should fail to offer its students courses in feminist philosophy and philosophy of race. I also owe a great debt to Avner Baz, a friend and philosopher more ethically attuned to other people than anyone else I know; he repeatedly reminds me what really matters, in philosophy and otherwise. Finally, what got me through the many moments of self-doubt that I suffered in writing these chapters was the encouragement of the wonderful undergraduates, graduate students, and teaching assistants I have had the honor and pleasure to work with.

Since the summer of 2012, I have served at Tufts as Dean of Academic Affairs for Arts and Sciences, a gig that, among other things, has given me a new perspective on my own academic field. My thanks (I think) to Joanne Berger-Sweeney, now President of Trinity College, for persuading me to put down my plough and come join her team in the A&S deans' office. This book would never have made it to the finish line without the exemplary collegiality and good sense of Jim Glaser and Margery Davies.

Because I have been working on the project so long, many people have had the opportunity to raise their eyebrows at me—and it. Many thanks to my hosts and audiences at MIT, Wesleyan University, various meetings of the Society for Women in Philosophy and of the American Philosophical Association, The College of the Holy Cross, Dartmouth College, University of Sheffield, University of Iowa, University of New Mexico, Brandeis University, University of Chicago, Auburn University, Bates College, University of Oregon, University of Maine, Universidad Nacional Autónoma de México, Yale University, Calvin College, Duke University, Hamilton College, Northwestern University, Université Paris I, Humboldt Universität zu Berlin, University of Bergen, Harvard University, Bard College, and the New School University.

Many people have discussed the topics of this book with me over the years, often both encouraging me and challenging me. An incomplete list of interlocutors to whom I'm indebted includes Amy Allen, Anne Barnhill, Sarah Beckwith, Susan Brison, Mika Cooper, Anne Eaton, Juliet Floyd, Michael Glanzberg, Keren Gordeisky, Mark Greif, Ruth Groenhout, John Gunnell, Matt Halteman, Arata Hamawaki, Christine Hamm, Cressida Heyes, Jennifer Hornsby, Andrew Janiak, Kathrin Koslicki, Sandra Laugier, Kate Manne, Sarah McGrath, Shannon Mussett, Magdalena Ostas, Salla Peltonen, Jennifer Purvis, Fred Schauer, Naomi Scheman, Eric Schliesser, Martin Shuster, Susanna Siegel, Peg Simons, Corina Stan, Christina Van Dyke, Shelby Weitzl, and Linda Zerilli.

In the moments when I am most convinced that, after all, I have nothing worthwhile to say, the only person who can convince me otherwise is Toril Moi. A more giving friend, intellectually and otherwise, is simply not imaginable. She is Simone de Beauvoir's rightful heir: an independent woman with a dazzlingly brilliant mind who fights tirelessly to improve the odds that all women will live meaningful lives.

As will be obvious to most of my readers, lurking behind everything I say and do philosophically is a deep debt to my teacher and friend, Stanley Cavell. Those of us who have been transformed by his thought uniformly struggle to figure out how to go on with it; even though of course Stanley has not said everything there is to say philosophically, our own thoughts and expressions are deeply rooted in what we have learned from him, as a teacher and a friend. Succeeding in the profession of philosophy would have been easier for us, or at least for me, had I been mentored by someone with a less original mind. But I wouldn't have stayed in the profession without his example.

I thank my dear parents, Art Bauer and Danita Bauer, who have (mostly) refrained for all these years from asking me when this book was going to be done. I am extremely lucky as well to have the world's best kids, Anneliese Cooper and Max Cooper, and best stepkids, Eleanor Richard and Michael Richard, all of whom are fearsomely sharp and tenacious philosophical inter-locutors. They have taught me whatever it is I get right and are embarrassed for me and for themselves with respect to all that I get wrong in my character-izations of popular cultural and contemporary sexual mores. This book is dedicated to Max: I have done what I can in it to pay homage to the virtues of wit, bravery, candor, empathy, joie de vivre, and compassion that he manifests every waking moment.

What great luck to have spent the years I have been laboring over this project with Mark Richard. It's true that his philosophical views are often pro-foundly wrong and that he doesn't hear much of what I say. But what a won-derful mind and huge heart he has and how fortunate I am to be his partner, in life and (more or less) in philosophy.

Credits

Chapter 1 was originally published as "Pornutopia" in *n+1*, Issue 5 (Winter 2007): 63–73, and is reprinted by permission of the editors.

Chapter 2 was originally published as two New York Times blog posts: "Lady Power" on June 20, 2010, http://opinionator.blogs.nytimes.com/2010/06/20/lady-power/; and "Authority and Arrogance: A Response" on June 30, 2010, http://opinionator.blogs.nytimes.com/2010/06/30/authority-and-arrogance-a-response. Both are reprinted by permission of the *New York Times*.

Chapter 4 is reprinted, with minor edits, from Charlotte Witt, ed., *Feminist Metaphysics: Explorations in the Ontology of Sex, Gender and the Self* (New York: Springer, 2010), pp. 117–130, by permission of Springer Science+Business Media LLC.

Chapter 5 is reprinted, with substantive edits, from Alice Crary and Sanford Shieh, eds., *Reading Cavell* (New York: Routledge, 2006), pp. 68–97, by permission of Routledge, an imprint of the Taylor & Francis Group.

Index